MW00777376

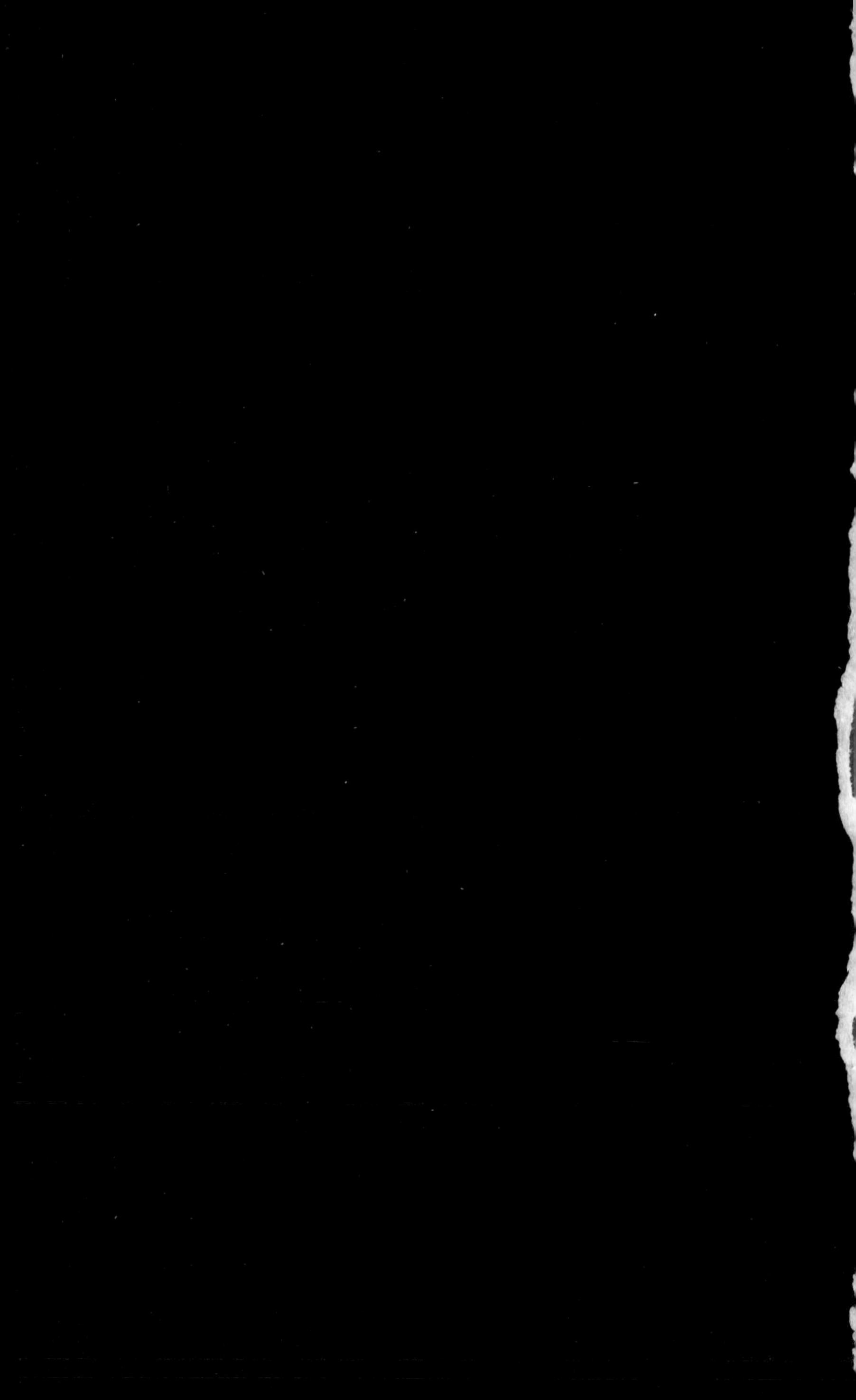

臺灣
亞洲之心
Taiwan
THE HEART OF ASIA

臺灣，是亞洲生命的脈搏，蘊藏豐富多樣獨特的自然生態、人文風貌及生活風格，時時刻刻展現澎湃生命力。

臺灣，是太平洋上美麗活力的島嶼，多元且細緻，不同角落的風情、文化蓬勃發展，處處充滿在地與動人的故事。

臺灣，是值得循著璞石紋理，細細發掘極具國際獨特價值的瑰寶島嶼。

臺灣，絕對是到訪亞太地區的重要旅遊目的地。

Taiwan is the beating heart of Asia. The beautiful island boasts a dazzling combination of natural wonders, vivid culture and eclectic lifestyles, all constantly pulsing with in energy and vigour.

Taiwan is the sparkling gem in the Pacific Ocean where customs and cultures flourish – dynamic, diverse and magnificent. No matter where you go, the epic stories you come across never fail to touch your heart.

Taiwan is the Treasure Island worth exploring in the finest detail. Like retrieving jade hidden in rocks, you need time to appreciate its distinctive beauty and its great value to the global community.

Taiwan is surely one of the most important travel destinations in the Asia-Pacific region.

旅行臺灣，就是現在！

TIME FOR TAIWAN

VISIT THE TREASURE ISLAND NOW

臺灣最精華的自然美景和觀光資源集合在9座自然景觀公園及13處風景區，融合成獨特自然景觀與多元文化，妝點出精彩的美麗景致，每一處都有讓遊客怦然心動的絕妙美景，每一角皆值得讓遊客停留下腳步慢慢欣賞，用低碳方式盡情感受獨一無二的臺灣之旅吧！

With nine natural parks and 13 scenic areas, Taiwan boasts natural beauty and countless sightseeing spots. Its unique landscapes are weaved into a tapestry of diverse cultures making these sites truly breathtaking. At every corner tourists will need to slow their pace to take it all in. Let's embark on a low-carbon journey across Taiwan...

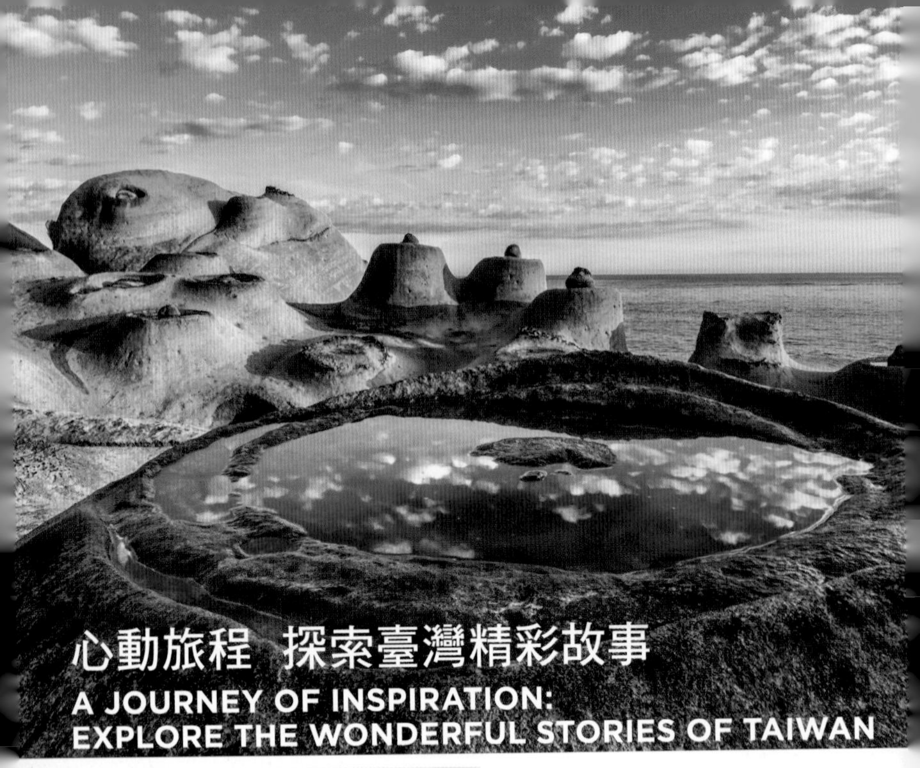

心動旅程 探索臺灣精彩故事

A JOURNEY OF INSPIRATION: EXPLORE THE WONDERFUL STORIES OF TAIWAN

臺灣四面環海，長年來經歷地層板塊不斷運動，形構出變化萬千的奇岩、海岸及高山美景。透過不同角度細細品味臺灣自然之美，欣賞東北角海岸大海雕塑海岸岩石的力量、讚嘆北海岸宛若火星地質及西拉雅草山月世界月球表面的荒漠美景、走訪巍峨矗立澎湖柱狀玄武岩，探索特殊且珍貴的大地之美，絕對讓您滿載而歸！

Taiwan is an island subject to ceaseless tectonic movement which has given rise to a plethora of fascinating rock formations, coastal features and staggering mountains. By travelling around Taiwan, you can savour its natural beauty from all different angles. Behold the power of the sea that shaped the rugged coastal rocks in the Northeast Coast Scenic Area. Contemplate the eerily Martian-like landscapes of the North Coast, or the barren beauty of Caoshan Moon World in the Siraya National Scenic Area. Get up close and personal with the towering basalt columns in Penghu. Sample the variety of precious beauties that the island has to offer and you won't regret it.

深度體驗臺灣在地風光最好的方式，便是透過單車欣賞臺三線沿途好客風景、尋訪臺灣東西南北四極點燈塔美麗身影、倘佯東部太平洋蔚藍海岸與花東縱谷巍峨壯闊山巒間、飽覽大鵬灣濕地生態與潟湖之美，以及騎遇全球最美自行車道之一的日月潭環湖公路，踏上臺灣來趟單車旅程，近距離感受各地依山傍水風光及各有姿態的文化特色，絕對是不可多得的慢旅體驗！

The best way to experience Taiwan's vast natural world is to ride a bike down Provincial Highway 3. Discover the gorgeous views, interact with the friendly people and locate the lighthouses in all four corners of the island. Take a leisurely ride along the Pacific's emerald coast in the east, or admire the skyscraping mountains from the East Rift Valley. Explore the ecology of wetlands and lagoons of Dapeng Bay, or ride a bike on the Sun Moon Lake Ring Road, one of the most scenic cycling routes in the world. A bike trip in Taiwan is a great way to see its natural highlights and delve into the unique culture of every area.

© National Kaohsiung Center for the Arts (Weiwuying)

鐵道旅行是欣賞臺灣各地自然美景最快的方式，不論是從北到南車窗外沿途的大霸尖山及雪山聖稜線之美，雲嘉南平原遼闊的壯麗，以及東部太平洋及綿延山景間的浩瀚穹蒼皆映入眼簾；此外，體驗阿里山「之」字型鐵道奇景，感受四季自然美景轉折變化以及濤濤雲海，安排一趟臺灣鐵道旅行，飽覽這片土地上獨一無二的美麗。

For those pressed for time, touring around Taiwan by train is the most efficient way to see the most within the shortest time frame. Travelling from north to south, you'd get to see Dabajian Mountain and the famous Holy Ridge of the Xueshan Range passing right by the train windows. From the sweeping views of the magnificent Southwest Plain, to the horizon dividing the Pacific Ocean and the boundless sky in the east alongside the rolling mountains, you can cover the greatest sights from the comfort of a modern train compartment. On top of that, a ride on the zigzag railway all the way up to Alishan is a must to witness the changes in scenery through the seasons and the mesmerizing beauty of the "sea of clouds".

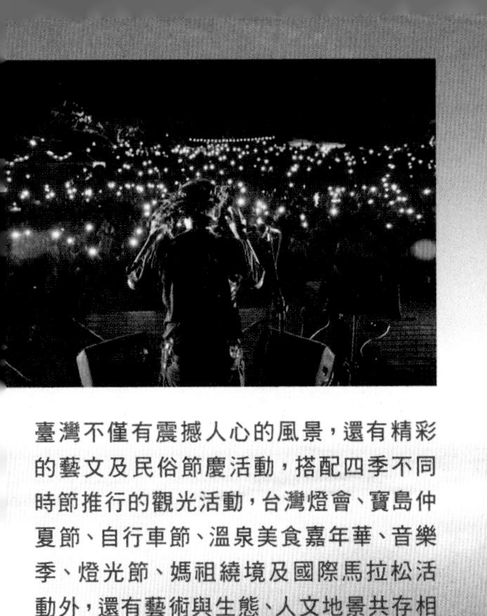

臺灣不僅有震撼人心的風景，還有精彩的藝文及民俗節慶活動，搭配四季不同時節推行的觀光活動，台灣燈會、寶島仲夏節、自行車節、溫泉美食嘉年華、音樂季、燈光節、媽祖繞境及國際馬拉松活動外，還有藝術與生態、人文地景共存相依的東海岸大地藝術節(TEC LandArt Festival)及月光・海音樂會，皆呈現在地文化內涵及獨特魅力與美學內涵，這是臺灣對各地旅人美麗的邀約，深入臺灣譜出一段精彩屬於自己的故事！

Breathtaking vistas are not the only treasure that Taiwan has in store, however; the island is also famous for its myriad of spectacular arts and folk festivals which occur throughout the year. These include the Lantern Festival, the Formosa Summer Festival, the Mazu Festival, a Cycling Festival, a Hot Spring & Fine-Cuisine Carnival, music festivals, light festivals and international marathon races, to name but a few. Last but not least, the TEC LandArt Festival and Moonlight-Sea Concert emphasize the co-existence of art and ecology; human activities and the natural landscape, truly showcasing the wisdom, charm and aesthetics of Taiwan's indigenous tribes.

2020 脊梁山脈旅遊年
YEAR OF MOUNTAIN TOURISM

臺灣是世界少有的高山島嶼，擁有複雜多變又奇特的地理景觀，3,000公尺以上的高山多達268座，其中3,952公尺的玉山更是東北亞第一高峰；因山巒層疊、溪谷縱橫，所形成以「奇、險、峻、秀」的中央山脈、雪山山脈、玉山山脈、阿里山山脈和海岸山脈5大山脈，結合周邊獨具魅力的山城小鎮、歷史古道、部落文化與生態步道，讓臺灣的山林之美驚艷國際，體驗臺灣山脈旅遊獨具魅力的經典之路，絕對讓您流連忘返。

Taiwan boasts complex and varied landscapes, with 268 mountains taller than 3,000 meters in height. Among them, the 3,952-metre Mt. Jade is the highest peak in Northeast Asia. The five mountain ranges of Taiwan, namely the Central Mountain Range, Xueshan Range, Yushan Range, Alishan Range and coastal Range, sport countless peaks in the foreground and the background, punctuated by rivers and streams, rendering a rugged beauty that is awe-inspiring. These mountains come complete with charming towns, historic trails, tribal cultures, and ecological trails that make Taiwan's wilderness truly a once-in-a-lifetime experience.

臺灣，多次獲得國際媒體推薦為亞洲最值得旅遊地之一，甚至稱讚臺灣是亞洲旅遊秘境。2020是臺灣「脊梁山脈旅遊年」，邀請大家親自前來探索臺灣山林秘境，品味動人的脊梁山脈旅程，盡享臺灣原味美食。

Taiwan is frequently recommended by international media as one of Asia's best tourism destinations. 2020 is the Year of Mountain Tourism in Taiwan. We earnestly invite travellers from all over the world to come and experience the best-kept secret of Taiwan – the beauty and charm of its mountains and the surrounding wilderness.

亞洲之心(the Heart of Asia)臺灣，
張開雙手歡迎您的到來！

Come and visit Taiwan, the Heart of Asia, where you will always be welcomed with open arms!

米其林指南

THE MICHELIN GUIDE

臺北 - 臺中

TAIPEI - TAICHUNG

從臺北到臺中的尋味之旅

IN SEARCH OF GOOD FOOD: FROM TAIPEI TO TAICHUNG

2020年是艱難的一年，當饕客們重新出門吃飯之際，米其林評審員更沿著鐵路邁力往南走，跨出臺北，到達另一流行美食指標地——臺中。

臺中或許尚未登上國際大都市之列，但卻不減繁華，同時保有樸實的傳統文化。在這裡，豐饒的物產為廚師帶來源源不絕的靈感和優質食材，相對便宜的租金更為年輕餐飲業者造就了利好的經營條件，小吃攤、異國料理店、無菜單私廚等，都在此城遍地生花。

評審員在此繼續以匿名身份尋訪優質美食，首次名單包括了逾五十家餐廳——異國料理大放異彩，在地美食亦同時發光發亮。獲選為星級餐廳或必比登美食的店家當中，除了有老招牌，也不乏本地出生、努力在崗位上默默磨礪的年輕廚師。

另一方面，雖然業界面對嚴厲挑戰，臺北的評鑑繼續擴大，新增的餐廳涵蓋了超過十種菜系，反映城市美食的多元，魅力持續增長中。

願讀者享受我們推薦的美食體驗，在能夠外出用餐的時光，細味廚師們精心準備的每一道菜。

如對本指南有任何意見，請電郵至：michelinguide.taiwan@michelin.com

2020 has been a tough year for everyone but, as we overcome the challenges and walk out of the shadows, gastronomes are beginning to resume their dining out routines. To offer them even more choice, the Michelin inspectors in Taiwan have explored beyond Taipei. They hopped on the train and travelled south, to another popular food mecca – Taichung.

Taichung may not be considered a big city with as much international buzz as its northern counterpart, but its prosperity is set nicely against a backdrop of rustic, unspoiled culture and traditions. The abundance of natural produce and food sources in Taichung has inspired countless local chefs, while the relatively affordable rents create a favourable environment for young and adventurous restaurateurs. Little wonder that a myriad of food establishments have thrived here.

Our inspectors undertook their search for the best food in Taichung in total anonymity. The first selection of 50+ Taichung restaurants includes Asian, European and local offerings. In the list of Stars and Bib Gourmands you'll find both longstanding household names and interesting new restaurants, helmed by young local chefs exploring their culinary identities.

Meanwhile in Taipei, despite severe challenges faced by the hospitality industry, the list of restaurants included in the Michelin guide continues to grow. Newly added establishments cover more than 10 different types of cuisine, testimony to the city's kaleidoscopic charisma as a food capital.

We hope our readers will enjoy the various experiences we recommend and will appreciate the pleasure of eating out, and savour each dish as it's meticulously prepared by long-missed chefs.

We wish you many wonderful meals and great stays in Taiwan. If you have any comments about our guide, please write to: michelinguide.taiwan@michelin.com.

目錄
CONTENTS

Raohe St. Night Market
歡迎光臨

金榜題名
春
神來一筆

承諾

不論身處日本、美國、中國或歐洲，我們的獨立評審員均使用一致的評選方法對餐廳和酒店作出評估。米其林指南在世界各地均享負盛名，關鍵在其秉承一貫宗旨，履行對讀者的承諾：

評審員以匿名方式定期到訪餐廳和酒店，以一般顧客的身份對餐廳和酒店的食品和服務品質作出評估。評審員自行結賬後，在需要時會介紹自己，並會詳細詢問有關餐廳或酒店的資料。

為保證本指南以讀者利益為依歸，餐廳的評選完全是我們獨立的決定。我們不會向收錄在指南內的餐廳收取任何費用，所有評選經編輯和評審員一同討論才作出決定，最高級別的評級以國際水平為標準。

本指南推介一系列優質餐廳和酒店，當中含括不同的舒適程度和價格，這全賴一眾評審員使用一致且嚴謹的評選方法。

所有實用資訊、分類及評級都會每年修訂和更新，務求為讀者提供最可靠的資料。

為確保指南的一致性，每個國家地區均採用相同的評審和分類準則，縱然各地的飲食文化不同，我們評選時的準則完全取決於食物品質和廚師的廚藝。

米其林的目標多年來貫徹始終──致力令旅程盡善盡美，讓您在旅遊和外出用膳時不但安全，且充滿樂趣。

THE MICHELIN GUIDE'S COMMITMENTS

Whether they are in Japan, the USA, China or Europe, our inspectors apply the same criteria to judge the quality of each and every restaurant and hotel that they visit. The MICHELIN guide commands a **worldwide reputation** thanks to the commitments we make to our readers – and we reiterate these below:

Our inspectors make regular and **anonymous visits** to restaurants and hotels to gauge the quality of products and services offered to an ordinary customer. They settle their own bill and may then introduce themselves and ask for more information about the establishment.

To remain totally objective for our readers, the selection is made with complete **independence**. Entry into the guide is free. All decisions are discussed with the Editor and our highest awards are considered at an international level.

The guide offers a **selection** of the best restaurants and hotels in every category of comfort and price. This is only possible because all the inspectors rigorously apply the same methods.

All the practical information, classifications and awards are revised and updated every year to give the most **reliable information** possible.

In order to guarantee the **consistency** of our selection, our classification criteria are the same in every country covered by the MICHELIN guide. Each culture may have its own unique cuisine but **quality** remains the **universal principle** behind our selection.

Michelin's mission is to **aid your mobility**. Our sole aim is to make your journeys safe and pleasurable.

米其林美食評級分類

星級美食

聞名遐邇的米其林一星✿、二星✿✿和三星✿✿✿推介，推薦的是食物品質特別出色的餐廳。我們的評級考慮到以下因素：材料的品質和搭配、烹調技巧和味道層次、菜餚所展示的創意，少不了的是食物水平的一致性。

✿✿✿ 卓越的烹調，值得專程造訪。
✿✿ 烹調出色，不容錯過！
✿ 優質烹調，不妨一試！

必比登美食推介

米其林寶寶標誌表示該餐廳提供具品質且經濟實惠的美食：費用在1,000元或以下（三道菜色但不包括飲料）。

米其林餐盤

評審員萬裡挑一的餐廳，食材新鮮、烹調用心，菜餚美味。

米其林圖標

米其林是追尋最佳餐廳的專家，邀請您共同發掘豐富多元的餐飲世界。在品評餐廳烹調素質同時，我們亦將其裝潢、服務和整體氛圍加入考慮，換言之，是包含味覺、感官和整體用餐經驗的全方位評估。

兩組關鍵詞助你挑選合適的餐廳，紅色為菜色種類；金色是環境氛圍：

臺灣菜 • *傳統*

設施及服務

只接受現金
輪椅通道
陽臺用餐
上佳景觀
代客泊車
停車場
室內停車場
私人廂房
吧檯式
建議訂位
不設訂位
非吸煙房
會議室
室內 / 室外游泳池
水療服務
健身室

供應優質餐酒

新增推介

酒店—以舒適程度分類

紅色代表上佳

豪華
高級舒適
十分舒適
舒適
頗舒適

THE MICHELIN GUIDE'S SYMBOLS

Michelin are experts at finding the best restaurants and invite you to explore the diversity of the gastronomic universe. As well as evaluating a restaurant's cooking, we also consider its décor, the service and the ambience - in other words, the all-round culinary experience.

Two keywords help you make your choice more quickly: red for the type of cuisine, gold for the atmosphere:

Taiwanese • Traditional

FACILITIES & SERVICES

- Cash only
- Wheelchair accessible
- Terrace dining
- Interesting view
- Valet parking
- Car park
- Garage
- Private room
- Counter
- Reservations recommended
- Reservations not accepted
- Non smoking rooms
- Conference rooms
- Indoor / Outdoor swimming pool
- Spa
- Exercise room
- Interesting wine list
- New entry in the guide

HOTEL CLASSIFICATION, ACCORDING TO COMFORT

Particularly pleasant if in red

- Luxury
- Top class comfort
- Very comfortable
- Comfortable
- Quite comfortable

STARS

Our famous One ✿, Two ✿✿ and Three ✿✿✿ Stars identify establishments serving the highest quality cuisine – taking into account the quality of ingredients, the mastery of techniques and flavours, the levels of creativity and, of course, consistency.

✿✿✿ Exceptional cuisine, worth a special journey!

✿✿ Excellent cuisine, worth a detour!

✿ High quality cooking, worth a stop!

BIB GOURMAND

This symbol indicates our inspectors' favourites for good value. These restaurants offer quality cooking for $1,000 or less (price of a 3-course meal excluding drinks).

PLATE

Good cooking.
Fresh ingredients, capably prepared:
simply a good meal.

永新巷
Yongxin Ln.

PLUS

臺北

TAIPEI

©fazon1/istock

ohe St. Night Market
迎
光
臨
各國名藥
媽祖廟
服務台
松鶴
國宴主廚經典美食新人氣王
台港日料
台港日料理

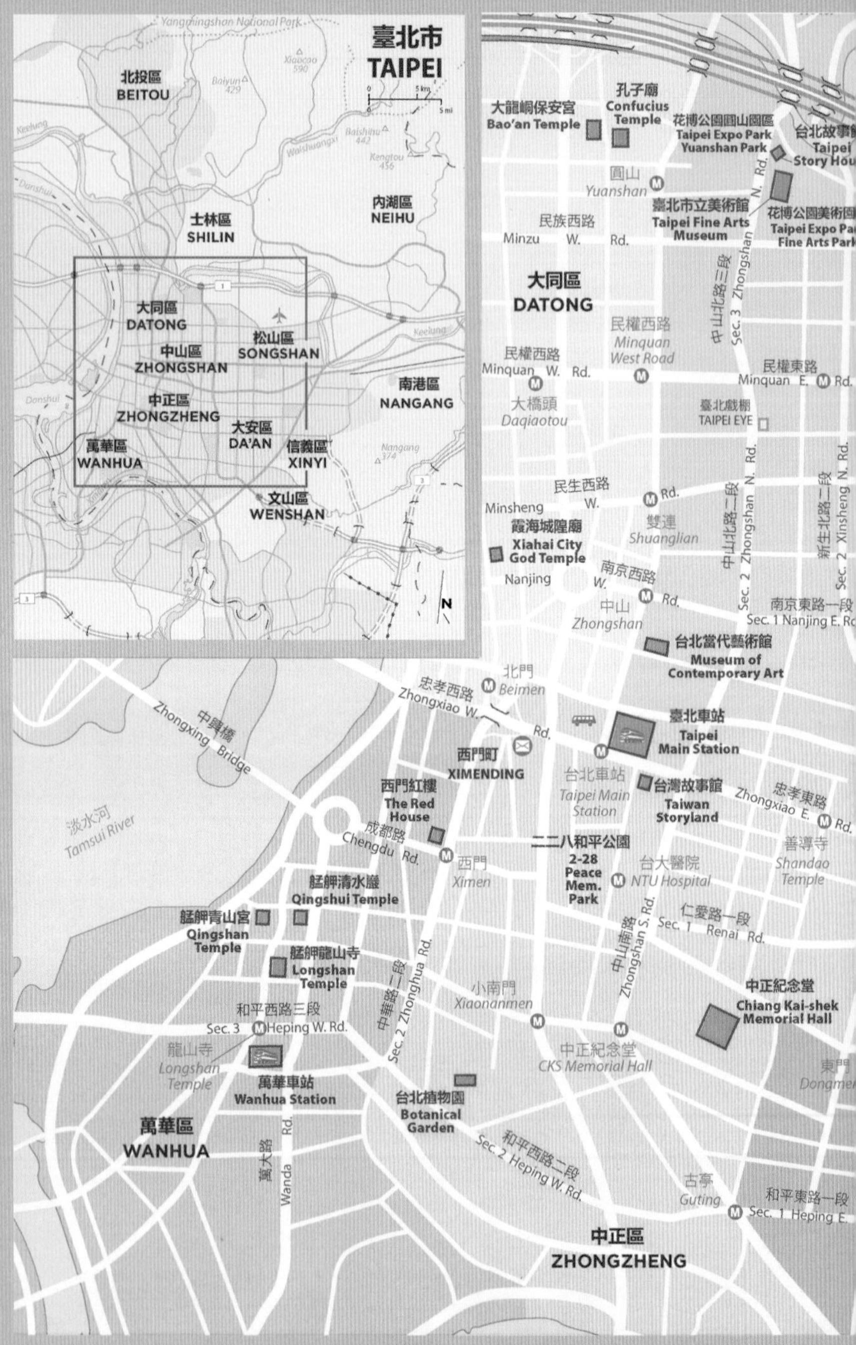

臺北市
TAIPEI
Yangmingshan National Park
北投區
BEITOU
士林區
SHILIN
內湖區
NEIHU
大同區
DATONG
松山區
SONGSHAN
中山區
ZHONGSHAN
南港區
NANGANG
中正區
ZHONGZHENG
大安區
DA'AN
萬華區
WANHUA
信義區
XINYI
文山區
WENSHAN
大龍峒保安宮
Bao'an Temple
孔子廟
Confucius Temple
花博公園圓山園區
Taipei Expo Park Yuanshan Park
台北故事館
Taipei Story House
圓山
Yuanshan
臺北市立美術館
Taipei Fine Arts Museum
花博公園美術園區
Taipei Expo Park Fine Arts Park
民族西路
Minzu W. Rd.
中山北路三段
Sec. 3 Zhongshan N. Rd.
民權西路
Minquan W. Rd.
Minquan West Road
民權東路
Minquan E. Rd.
大橋頭
Daqiaotou
臺北戲棚
TAIPEI EYE
民生西路
Minsheng W. Rd.
雙連
Shuanglian
霞海城隍廟
Xiahai City God Temple
中山北路二段
Sec. 2 Zhongshan N. Rd.
新生北路二段
Sec. 2 Xinsheng N. Rd.
南京西路
Nanjing W. Rd.
中山
Zhongshan
南京東路一段
Sec. 1 Nanjing E. Rd.
台北當代藝術館
Museum of Contemporary Art
北門
Beimen
忠孝西路
Zhongxiao W. Rd.
中興橋
Zhongxing Bridge
西門町
XIMENDING
臺北車站
Taipei Main Station
台北車站
Taipei Main Station
台灣故事館
Taiwan Storyland
忠孝東路
Zhongxiao E. Rd.
西門紅樓
The Red House
淡水河
Tamsui River
成都路
Chengdu Rd.
西門
Ximen
二二八和平公園
2-28 Peace Mem. Park
台大醫院
NTU Hospital
善導寺
Shandao Temple
艋舺清水巖
Qingshui Temple
艋舺青山宮
Qingshan Temple
仁愛路一段
Sec. 1 Renai Rd.
中山南路
Zhongshan S. Rd.
艋舺龍山寺
Longshan Temple
中華路二段
Sec. 2 Zhonghua Rd.
小南門
Xiaonanmen
中正紀念堂
Chiang Kai-shek Memorial Hall
和平西路三段
Sec. 3 Heping W. Rd.
龍山寺
Longshan Temple
中正紀念堂
CKS Memorial Hall
東門
Dongmen
萬華車站
Wanhua Station
台北植物園
Botanical Garden
萬華區
WANHUA
萬大路
Wanda Rd.
和平西路二段
Sec. 2 Heping W. Rd.
古亭
Guting
和平東路一段
Sec. 1 Heping E.
中正區
ZHONGZHENG

臺北市
TAIPEI
0 500 m
0 500 yds
N
基隆河 Keelung
中山高速公路
Sun Yat-sen Freeway
林安泰古厝
Lin An Tai Homestead
花博公園新生園區
Taipei Expo Park Xinsheng Park
民族東路
Minzu E. Rd.
臺北松山機場
TAIPEI SONGSHAN AIRPORT
行天宮
Hsing Tian Temple
行天宮
Xingtian Temple
松山機場
Songshan Airport
民權東路三段
Sec. 3 Minquan E. Rd.
交通部觀光局旅遊服務中心
TOURISM BUREAU TRAVEL SERVICE CENTER
民生東路二段
Sec. 2 Minsheng E. Rd.
民生東路三段
Sec. 3 Minsheng E. Rd.
民生東路五段
Sec. 5 Minsheng E. Rd.
松江路
Songjiang Rd.
中山區
ZHONGSHAN
松山區
SONGSHAN
南京復興
Nanjing Fuxing
南京東路三段
Sec. 3 Nanjing E. Rd.
南京東路四段
Sec. 4 Nanjing E. Rd.
南京東路五段
Sec. 5 Nanjing E. Rd.
台北小巨蛋
Taipei Arena
南京三民
Nanjing Sanmin
松江南京
Songjiang Nanjing
袖珍博物館
Miniatures Museum of Taiwan
華山1914文化創意產業園區
Huashan 1914 Creative Park
敦化北路
Dunhua N. Rd.
復興北路
Fuxing N. Rd.
光華數位新天地
Guang Hua Digital Plaza
財團法人台灣觀光協會
TAIWAN VISITORS ASSOCIATION
松山文創園區
Songshan Cultural and Creative Park
忠孝復興
Zhongxiao Fuxing
忠孝東路三段
Sec. 3 Zhongxiao E. Rd.
忠孝東路四段
Sec. 4 Zhongxiao E. Rd.
市政府
Taipei City Hall
忠孝新生
Zhongxiao Xinsheng
忠孝敦化
Zhongxiao Dunhua
交通部觀光局
TOURISM BUREAU
仁愛路三段
Sec. 3 Renai Rd.
復興南路
Fuxing S. Rd.
台北探索館
Discovery Center
大安森林公園
Da'an Park
信義路三段
Sec. 3 Xinyi Rd.
大安
Da'an
信義路四段
Sec. 4 Xinyi Rd.
信義安和
Xinyi Anhe
台北101
Taipei 101
台北101/世貿
Taipei 101/ World Trade Center
象山
Xiangshan
大安森林公園
DA'AN FOREST PARK
復興南路二段
Sec. 2 Fuxing S. Rd.
敦化南路二段
Sec. 2 Dunhua S. Rd.
大安區
DA'AN
和平東路二段
Sec. 2 Heping E. Rd.
科技大樓
Technology Building
信義區
XINYI
六張犁
Liuzhangli

Robert CHG/iStock

北投區
士林區

BEITOU & SHILIN

北投區 BEITOU
士林區 SHILIN

餐廳
RESTAURANTS

金蓬萊遵古台菜
GOLDEN FORMOSA

臺灣菜 · 傳統

Taiwanese · Traditional

家族經營的金蓬萊始於六十年代的北投，最初供應搭配酒品享用的酒家菜，調味偏向濃重。現時掌勺的第三代仍沿用家族秘方，例如招牌菜排骨酥，選用臺灣豬隻的腹斜排，以不同油溫炸兩次，以保留水分同時令外表酥脆；須預訂的肚包雞鍋以大豬肚包覆起骨小土雞及十多種食材，以秘方藥材慢火燉七小時而成，適合多人共享。

In the 1960s, the family started serving heavily seasoned food to go with alcoholic drinks. The third-generation owner still follows the same family recipes from the old days. Their signature deep-fried pork ribs are made with local pork, fried twice to seal in the juices and to crisp up the crust. The tonic soup chicken-in-tripe is a deboned free-range bird slow-cooked for seven hours inside pork tripe with various herbs and condiments.

TEL. 02 2871 1517

士林區天母東路101號

101 Tianmu East Road, Shilin

www.goldenformosa.com.tw

■ 價錢 **PRICE**

午膳 Lunch
點菜 À la carte $ 800-1,500
晚膳 Dinner
點菜 À la carte $ 800-1,500

■ 營業時間 **OPENING HOURS**

午膳 Lunch 11:30-13:30
晚膳 Dinner 17:30-20:00

■ 休息日期 **ANNUAL AND WEEKLY CLOSING**

除夕至初五及週一休息
Closed CNY eve to fifth day of CNY and Monday

TEL. 02 2874 1981

士林區天母東路97號

97 Tianmu East Road, Shilin

redlantern.eatingout.com.tw

■ 價錢 PRICE

午膳 Lunch
點菜 À la carte $ 400-800
晚膳 Dinner
點菜 À la carte $ 400-800

■ 營業時間 OPENING HOURS

午膳 Lunch 11:30-14:00
晚膳 Dinner 17:00-22:00

■ 休息日期 ANNUAL AND WEEKLY CLOSING

週二至週五午膳及週一休息
Closed Tuesday to Friday lunch and Monday

女娘的店

MOTHER'S KITCHEN

臺灣菜 · 傳統

Taiwanese · Traditional

從店外的竹籬、木門前的門聯、古老的飯桌以至四周的器物，餐廳裡裡外外皆仿照五十年代的臺灣農村而製。菜餚也充滿古早味，以溫體黑毛豬腹料理的烘肉口感滑嫩且不油膩，為必點招牌菜色；三杯田雞在鍋子中滋滋作響，香味四溢，更是使人欲罷不能；更別忘了來一碗豬油飯。欲品嚐務必提前訂位。

Décor lifted out of rustic farmhouses circa 1950s and memorabilia from the owner's hometown provide the backdrop for classic comfort food. Only black pig slaughtered on the same day is used for the meltingly soft, traditional braised pork belly. The sizzling and aromatic three-cup frog is another speciality not to be missed - round it out with lard on steamed rice and marble soda. Bookings are recommended and there's live music on Saturday nights.

番紅花印度美饌
SAFFRON FINE INDIAN CUISINE

印度菜·異國風情

Indian • Exotic Décor

裝潢展現出高級餐廳的氣派與格調，紅磚白牆亦配合其印度餐廳的風格。食客坐在棗紅色的天花吊燈下，邊用餐邊欣賞印籍廚師即場製作印度薄餅，印度氣氛情懷洋溢而出。餐廳的招牌菜色為喀拉拉雞肉咖哩及芫荽雞肉咖哩。菜色選擇眾多，若難以決擇不妨讓訓練有素的服務生為你提供意見。

The white stucco façade and columns look rustic and elegant, while the full-length windows let in plenty of natural light. The interior of terracotta floor, textured wall, burgundy lanterns and dark wood furniture all help build up an appetite for an exotic meal. Signature dishes include murgh Kerala (Kerala-style roast chicken) and murgh kothmeri (coriander chicken). There are even chefs in one corner making naan bread to order.

TEL. 02 2871 4842

士林區天母東路38之6號

38-6 Tianmu East Road, Shilin

■ 價錢 PRICE

午膳 Lunch
點菜 À la carte $ 700-800
晚膳 Dinner
點菜 À la carte $ 800-1,000

■ 營業時間 OPENING HOURS

午膳 Lunch 11:30-14:00
晚膳 Dinner 17:30-21:30

■ 休息日期 ANNUAL AND WEEKLY CLOSING

除夕至初一休息
Closed CNY eve to first day of CNY

蓬萊
PENG LAI

臺灣菜・簡樸

Taiwanese • Simple

TEL. 02 2891 2778

北投區中和街238號

238 Zhonghe Street, Beitou

www.ponlai.com.tw

■ 價錢 PRICE

午膳 Lunch
點菜 À la carte $ 200-400
晚膳 Dinner
點菜 À la carte $ 200-400

■ 營業時間 OPENING HOURS

午膳 Lunch 11:00-13:30
晚膳 Dinner 17:00-20:30

■ 休息日期 ANNUAL AND WEEKLY CLOSING

除夕至初五及週一休息
Closed CNY eve to fifth day of CNY and Monday

由陳良枝開創的蓬萊以酒家菜起家，現由第三代接手經營。快將失傳的老臺菜如蟳肉蚵仔羹、螺肉魷魚蒜鍋等，仍然保留在菜單上。很多食客專程來品嚐軟玉豆腐，有別於包入香蕉的傳統版本，餐廳改以豆腐包著火腿、蝦仁和香菜。別忘了來一客招牌排骨酥，連著骨頭的小排經二十小時醃製，令人吮指回味。

This simple shop is famous for its pork ribs that are marinated for 20 hours before being deep-fried until crispy on the outside and tender on the inside. Another favourite is 'Jadeite tofu' – shrimp, ham, coriander and tofu wrapped up in fried tofu skin. Crabmeat and baby oyster thick soup, and whelk and squid soup with leeks are the other recipes from a bygone era that are now seldom found elsewhere.

松園禪林 - 原心
PINE GARDEN

創新菜・簡約

Innovative • Minimalist

松園禪林位處靜謐的陽明山公園內，只有十六張餐桌的餐廳以日本風格裝潢，各位置均可眺望如畫的園林景色，叫人悠然神往。顧客可品嚐包含八道菜的無菜單套餐，廚師按季節變換菜色，烹調風格兼收日本、廣東和老臺灣特色。飽餐一頓後別忘了遊覽公園和細賞壯麗的風景。

Located in the hills above the city, this Zen-inspired restaurant is ensconced in the somewhat neglected Song Yuan Gardens. It is known for its distinctly Japanese interior, with its 16 tables overlooking the garden. The 8-course menu pays homage to Japanese, Cantonese and Taiwanese cuisines using fresh seasonal ingredients. After dining, take a stroll and soak up the gorgeous views in the garden.

TEL. 02 2861 3578

士林區菁山路101巷160號

160, Lane 101, Jingshan Road, Shilin

www.pinegarden.url.tw

■ 價錢 **PRICE**

午膳 Lunch
套餐 Set Menu $ 1,650
晚膳 Dinner
套餐 Set Menu $ 1,650

■ 營業時間 **OPENING HOURS**

午膳 Lunch 12:00-13:30
晚膳 Dinner 18:00-19:30

■ 休息日期 **ANNUAL AND WEEKLY CLOSING**

除夕、農曆除夕及週一休息
Closed New Year's eve, CNY eve and Monday

TEL. 02 2877 1168

士林區中山北路七段55號

55, Section 7, Zhongshan North Road, Shilin

www.splr.com.tw

■ 價錢 **PRICE**

午膳 Lunch
點菜 À la carte $ 500-600
晚膳 Dinner
點菜 À la carte $ 500-700

■ 營業時間 **OPENING HOURS**

午膳 Lunch 11:00-13:30
晚膳 Dinner 17:00-20:30

■ 休息日期 **ANNUAL AND WEEKLY CLOSING**

除夕至初五休息
Closed CNY eve to fifth day of CNY

興蓬萊台菜
SHING-PENG-LAI

臺灣菜・溫馨

Taiwanese • Family

於1987年開業的餐廳現已交棒至第二代，雖曾兩次遷址，老顧客依舊接踵而至。老闆承襲了父輩好手藝和招牌菜，其中排骨酥選用溫體黑毛豬肋排，以秘方醃製後炸至金黃，厚實酥香，不愧為鎮店招牌。羊奶埔土雞盅以採自拉拉山的羊奶埔根莖與土雞燉煮數小時，多少饕客慕名而至。白斬放山雞膠質豐厚，吃罷香氣於口腔縈繞，也不容錯過。

Celebrities and socialites have been coming here since 1987 for its famous "goat nipple" chicken soup (by pre-order only). Don't be alarmed – goat nipple is actually stems and roots of the Taiwanese fig tree that the owner digs up in Lala Mountain every week. Simmered for hours with free-range chicken she raises herself, the soup is as tasty as it is healing. Also try their steamed free-range chicken and crispy blistered pork ribs.

THE RESTAURANT

時尚歐陸菜 • 時尚

European Contemporary •
Contemporary Décor

坐落於溫泉酒店內，偌大的空間設開放式廚房，也可選擇於陽臺用餐。中午時段，陽光灑落在落地窗邊，看著戶外充滿綠意的景色，讓人感到無限放鬆。主廚善用在地食材，糅合亞洲風味和歐陸料理手法，設計出每季更換的菜單，廣受好評。除了來此品嚐美食，許多旅客也會在該酒店泡湯，不妨安排半日的湯屋美食之旅。

Inside a villa-style hotel away from the city is this airy, sun-drenched restaurant. The full-length windows also bring the lush outside in. From the on-view kitchen, the chefs prepare modern European cuisine with an Asian twist. The head chef's passion for travel shines through in a menu which changes every season. Book your private hot spring bath session with the hotel and make it a day to remember.

TEL. 02 6611 8888

北投區中山路32號 (三二行館)

Villa 32, 32 Zhongshan Road, Beitou

www.villa32.com

■ 價錢 **PRICE**

午膳 Lunch
套餐 Set Menu $ 1,380-5,280
點菜 À la carte $ 2,200-7,600
晚膳 Dinner
套餐 Set Menu $ 2,380-6,680
點菜 À la carte $ 2,200-7,600

■ 營業時間 **OPENING HOURS**

午膳 Lunch 12:00-13:30
晚膳 Dinner 18:00-20:30

讚 N
ZAN

鐵板燒 · 典雅

Teppanyaki • Elegant

TEL. 02 2880 1880

士林區承德路四段192之1號B1

B1, 192-1, Section 4, Chengde Road, Shilin

www.zan-matsutou.com.tw

■ 價錢 PRICE

午膳 Lunch
套餐 Set Menu $ 1,580-6,900
晚膳 Dinner
套餐 Set Menu $ 3,080-6,900

■ 營業時間 OPENING HOURS

午膳 Lunch 11:30-13:30
晚膳 Dinner 17:30-21:00

■ 休息日期 ANNUAL AND WEEKLY CLOSING

除夕至初五休息
Closed CNY eve to fifth day of CNY

用餐環境雅致，融合義大利彩色玻璃窗、中式古典桌椅及名貴餐具，彰顯對細節的講究。資深主廚曾於日本鐵板燒名店受訓，堅持採用有機蔬菜、現撈與野生漁獲。特別推薦美國原種極黑牛、昆布鹽燜鮑魚，以及澎湖野生明蝦佐法式醬。同時提供日本各等級之和牛，其中飛驒牛的風味尤其出色，須提前預訂。

A mishmash of different styles seems to work miraculously here – Italian stained glass window and a marble counter are juxtaposed with Chinese wooden furniture and silver cutlery. The chef was trained in one of most prestigious teppanyaki restaurants in Japan and has over 40 years of experience under his belt. Signatures include U. S. SRF Wagyu, braised abalone in kombu salt, and prawns with French sauce. Hida beef is also available for pre-ordering.

Shaiith/iStock

北投區 **BEITOU**
士林區 **SHILIN**

夜市 NIGHT MARKETS

士林夜市 Shilin

市內規模最大，也是最知名的夜市。由1900年代媽祖廟前攤販聚集演變而成，充斥著價格相宜的小吃和零售店鋪，不論何時皆人山人海。

By far the biggest and the most well-known night market in Taipei has come a long way since its beginnings in the 1900s when a few vendors gathered in front of the Matsu temple. It is now jam-packed with shoppers and diners day and night.

鍾家原上海生煎包
CHUNG CHIA SHENG JIAN BAO

夜市內的老字號，每個生煎包都煎得底部酥脆，外皮鬆軟。有高麗菜和鮮肉口味。

This stall sells pan-fried buns with crispy bottoms and fluffy tops. Choose between cabbage and pork fillings.

士林區小東街38號
38 Xiaodong Street, Shilin
價錢 **PRICE:** $ 14
營業時間 **OPENING HOURS:** 15:00-21:00
週三休息 **Closed Wednesday**

好朋友涼麵
GOOD FRIEND COLD NOODLES

麻醬涼麵除了麻醬香，更滲出檸檬清香，與別不同；也可加上特製辣醬。別忘了配上一碗臺式味噌湯加蛋。

Noodles dressed in sesame sauce impart a hint of lemony fragrance, a perfect match for egg drop miso soup.

士林區大南路31號
31 Danan Road, Shilin
價錢 **PRICE:** $ 45-95
營業時間 **OPENING HOURS:** 17:30-23:30
週四休息 **Closed Thursday**

士林夜市
Shilin

海友十全排骨
HAI YU PORK RIBS

開店逾四十年，其湯品以秘方燉製，每種使用十五種以上中藥材，香醇味美且具保健功效。

For over 40 years, a secret recipe has been used to make the tasty and healthy pork rib soup with over 15 herbs.

士林區大東路49號

49 Dadong Road, Shilin

價錢 **PRICE:** $ 90-200

營業時間 **OPENING HOURS:** 14:30-01:00

阿輝麵線
A HUI VERMICELLI

攤子臨近廟口，不設座位。麵線帶蔬菜甜味，實而不華，設兩種份量，也可加配花枝或大腸。

This stall by the temple with no seating serves no-frills vermicelli soup with pork chitterlings or cuttlefish.

士林區大南路52之1號

52-1 Danan Road, Shilin

價錢 **PRICE:** $ 30-140

營業時間 **OPENING HOURS:** 14:00-23:45

bonchan/iStock

北投區 BEITOU
士林區 SHILIN

酒店
HOTELS

三二行館
VILLA 32

溫泉・時尚

Thermal Spa • Contemporary

三二行館遠離市中心，於飽含地熱能的山峽中自成一角。遠離囂塵，整所酒店只提供五間套房，讓入住的旅客感覺更為不凡。清幽環境、天然溫泉與出眾服務配合出格外和煦的氣氛。房間類型分為歐陸風格與和室設計，均附溫泉浸池，後者的為露天。酒店亦提供男女分區、多樣化的芳療療程以及大眾或私人溫泉浴池。

Nestled in a geothermal valley out of the city centre, this five-room villa is feted for its serenity, natural hot spring and outstanding service. Three European suites feature modern décor and hot spring tubs, while the two Japanese suites come with mat flooring and an open-air tub. The spa, with separate male and female areas, offers a range of pools and treatments.

TEL. 02 6611 8888
www.villa32.com

北投區中山路32號
32 Zhongshan Road, Beitou

5 套房/**Suites** $ 16,800-30,000

餐廳推薦/**Recommended restaurants:**
The Restaurant

J. Fuste Raga/Premium/age fotostock

WHAT IS NATURAL MINERAL WATER?

Natural mineral water originates from an underground aquifer, is protected from all risks of pollution, and emerges from a unique source. It is characterized by a **constant level of minerals and purity at the source.**

This makes the water UNIQUE

PLAIN WATERS	EVIAN NATURAL MINERAL WATER	NATURAL MINERAL WATER	DRINKING WATER	FILTERED WATER
UNIQUE SOURCE	●	●	Variable	Variable
STABLE NATURAL MINERAL COMPOSITION	●	●	●	○
NATURAL FILTRATION PROCESS	●	●	○	○
CHEMICAL TREATMENT	○	○	●	●

March 2018 Danone internal source

SPARKLING WATERS	FERRARELLE SPARKLING NATURAL MINERAL WATER	FILTERED SPARKLING WATER
UNIQUE SOURCE	●	Variable
NATURAL GAS FROM SOURCE	●*	○
BICARBONATED (Meaning > 600 mg/L according to law)	●	○

March 2018 Danone internal source
**Reinforced*

大同區

DATONG

餐廳 RESTAURANTS

✿✿✿

頤宮

LE PALAIS

粵菜・典雅

Cantonese • Elegant

各式各樣的瓷器和仿古書畫令環境於傳統中不失格調。細看餐墊，印上了本年度的天干地支、對應時令的食材墨寶和詩詞，足見餐廳的用心和細緻。自2000年由澳門來臺發展的陳師傅一直專注廣東菜色，且堅持事事親力親為，需預訂的先知鴨和火焰片皮鴨是其巧手之作，豆腐菜色更展現其出神入化的技巧，點菜時不妨預留一份原味蛋塔。

Chef Chan moved to Taiwan from Macau nearly 20 years ago and specialises in Cantonese cuisine of the highest quality. The lavishly furnished dining room feels modern and chic, but with nice traditional touches such as ceramic art, calligraphy and paintings. The cooking is truly outstanding, with the Cantonese-style crispy roast duck, the tofu dishes and the baked egg custard tarts especially impressive; consider pre-ordering the roast baby duck. Service is thoughtful and friendly.

TEL. 02 2181 9985

大同區承德路一段3號17樓
(君品酒店)

17F, Palais de Chine Hotel, 3, Section 1, Chengde Road, Datong

www.palaisdechinehotel.com

■ 價錢 **PRICE**

午膳 Lunch
點菜 À la carte $ 2,000-5,000
晚膳 Dinner
點菜 À la carte $ 2,000-5,000

■ 營業時間 **OPENING HOURS**

午膳 Lunch 11:30-14:30
晚膳 Dinner 17:30-21:30

TEL. 02 2557 7087
大同區安西街106號
106 Anxi Street, Datong

■ 價錢 **PRICE**
點菜 À la carte $ 70-200

■ 營業時間 **OPENING HOURS**
08:00-15:00

■ 休息日期 **ANNUAL AND WEEKLY CLOSING**
除夕至初五、端午節、中元節及中秋節休息
Closed CNY eve to fifth day of CNY, Dragon Boat Festival, Zhongyuan Festival and Mid-Autumn Festival

賣麵炎仔
MAI MIEN YEN TSAI

麵食 · 簡樸

Noodles · Simple

這小麵攤開業逾八十年，為老臺北人所熟悉，位於樸實陳舊的公寓並不減其魅力，門前仍是人潮不絕。提供油麵、米粉與黑白切；湯頭以全雞、豬肉與內臟熬煮而成，十分清甜。燒肉、白斬雞和花枝都是必點配菜，而皮酥肉嫩的燒肉僅在十點後供應。麵攤不設菜單及價目表，貼心的老闆會按用餐人數配菜。

This shop on the ground floor of a somewhat dilapidated apartment has over 80 years of history. There is always a queue lining up for their egg or rice noodles, either served in a flavoursome stock made with pork bones, offal and chicken, or dressed in a sweet sauce. Side dishes such as pork offal, boiled chicken and blanched squid are also not to be missed. The signature fried braised pork, crispy and succulent, is only available after 10am.

GneshYeh/iStock

夜市 NIGHT MARKETS

寧夏夜市
Ningxia

知名度不亞於士林夜市，曾獲多項「夜市之最」殊榮，是最多雜誌報導的。以傳統小吃為主，也有不少老店。

As famous as its Shilin counterpart, it gets the most press coverage of all night markets in Taipei. Most stalls sell Taiwanese snacks and many have been in business for decades.

方家雞肉飯
FANG CHIA SHREDDED CHICKEN ON THE RICE

淋上雞汁與油蔥的雞絲飯香味四溢。招牌滷豆腐軟嫩得超乎想像。

The chicken rice is irresistibly aromatic while the tofu in a spiced marinade is velvety beyond imagination.

大同區寧夏路44之2號60號攤
Stall 60, 44-2 Ningxia Road, Datong
價錢 **PRICE:** $ 70-170
營業時間 **OPENING HOURS:** 17:30-23:30
週一休息 **Closed Monday**

劉芋仔
LIU YU ZI

香酥芋丸外殼香脆、裹著細香的芋蓉；蛋黃芋餅滋味鹹香，客人絡繹不絕。

Plain taro balls boast creamy mashed taro; those with salted egg yolk and pork floss have extra flavour.

大同區寧夏路91號攤
Stall 91, Ningxia Road, Datong
價錢 **PRICE:** $ 50-120
營業時間 **OPENING HOURS:** 17:00-00:00

寧夏夜市 Ningxia

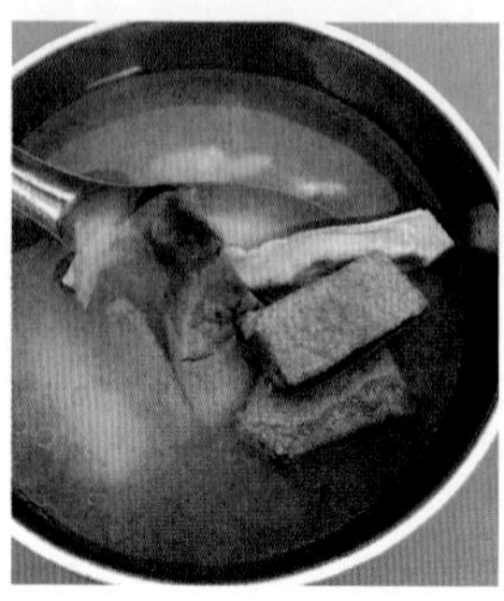

豬肝榮仔
RONG'S PORK LIVER

豬肝湯清甜醇厚，帶厚度的豬肝脆口而無粉感；肉粽質感軟嫩，蘸上店家特調的甜辣醬更是滋味。

Crunchy liver slices in a rich broth are never grainy. Don't miss the pork zongzi with sweet hot sauce.

大同區寧夏路68號前008及010號攤

Stall 008 & 010, 68 Ningxia Road, Datong

價錢 **PRICE:** $ 55-115

營業時間 **OPENING HOURS:** 18:30-01:00

週一休息 **Closed Monday**

圓環邊蚵仔煎
YUAN HUAN PIEN OYSTER EGG OMELETTE

創立於1965年，蚵仔煎選用每天從臺南直送的蚵仔，特調醬汁別有風味。蒸米糕也值得一試。

Has been making its tasty omelettes, with oysters from Tainan drizzled in homemade sweet hot sauce, since 1965.

大同區寧夏路46號

46 Ningxia Road, Datong

價錢 **PRICE:** $ 70-240

營業時間 **OPENING HOURS:** 12:00-14:30; 16:30-01:00

延三夜市
Yansan

舊稱「大橋頭夜市」或「臺北橋夜市」，沿路兩旁店家林立，有不少經營了超過三十年的傳統小吃攤販，也有飯麵等美食選擇。

It is also called "Ta-chiao-tou Night Market" because of the Taipei Bridge nearby. Many traditional snack stalls have been here for over 30 years.

高麗菜飯 原汁排骨湯
CABBAGE RICE AND PORK RIB SOUP

高麗菜飯配上清澈的蘿蔔排骨湯，簡單卻令人回味無窮。

Simple but addictive, cabbage rice and clear pork rib radish soup are the comfort food everyone craves.

大同區延平北路三段17巷2號

2, Lane 17, Section 3, Yanping North Road, Datong

價錢 **PRICE:** $ 20-90

營業時間 **OPENING HOURS:** 11:00-20:30

週一休息 **Closed Monday**

大橋頭老牌筒仔米糕
DA-QIAO-TOU TUBE RICE PUDDING

以圓糯米製成的米糕軟嫩而不爛；可選配肥或瘦肉，再佐以自製醬料，美味非常。

The steamed sticky rice is chewy but never mushy. Choose lean or fatty pork and drizzle with homemade sauce.

大同區延平北路三段41號

41, Section 3, Yanping North Road, Datong

價錢 **PRICE:** $ 70-150

營業時間 **OPENING HOURS:** 06:00-18:00

除夕至初六、端午節5天及週二休息 **Closed CNY eve to sixth day of CNY, 5 days Dragon Boat Festival and Tuesday**

延三夜市
Yansan

施家鮮肉湯圓
SHIH CHIA BIG RICE BALL

創立於六十年代，鮮肉湯圓最受歡迎，外皮軟嫩，肉餡飽滿，咬下時肉汁隨之流出，讓人欲罷不能。

Its gooey glutinous rice balls with juicy pork filling have been hugely popular with locals since the 1960s.

大同區延平北路三段58號

58, Section 3, Yanping North Road, Datong

價錢 **PRICE:** $ 80-250

營業時間 **OPENING HOURS:** 11:00-23:00

NatashaBreen/iStock

酒店
HOTELS

君品

PALAIS DE CHINE

豪華・個人化

Luxury • Personalised

酒店位處客運轉運站旁的繁忙交通要道，位置便捷。旅客莫因擔心街道的繁囂會打擾休息而卻步，因為此處的獨特魅力值得體會，當走進於六樓的大堂時，其高雅而神秘的氣氛率先展現出酒店特色。中西氣息於典雅的房間設計中配合得天衣無縫，如果想享用更寧靜的私人時間，不妨選擇入住較後方的房間。

Its convenient location at a busy junction next to the airport MRT station may not appeal to all and don't be put off by the full-sized horse statue at its ground floor entrance. It's the lobby on the 6th floor that reveals the charisma of this atmospheric and sophisticated hotel. The elegant rooms seamlessly blend Eastern and Western influences. Do ask for a quieter one at the back.

TEL. 02 2181 9999
www.palaisdechinehotel.com

大同區承德路一段3號
3, Section 1, Chengde Road, Datong

272 客房/**Rooms** $ 6,500-19,550
14 套房/**Suites** $ 12,000-32,200

餐廳推薦/**Recommended restaurants:**
頤宮 Le Palais ✿✿✿

tmprtmpr/iStock

中山區

ZHONGSHAN

餐廳 RESTAURANTS

✿✿

RAW

創新菜・型格

Innovative • Design

廚師江振誠憑著新加坡André打響名堂，其後回歸出生地開設了這家餐廳。其內部由兩個巨形流線型木製雕刻貫穿，叫人難以將目光從中轉移，然而食物應獲得同等的注目——九道菜的套餐展示一系列具創意的菜餚，擺盤精緻現代，呈現豐富的味道與質感，部分菜色更滲入了臺灣小吃元素。唯要從網上系統成功訂位，讀者還真需要多一點耐性。

The owner-chef of the world-famous Restaurant André in Singapore opened Raw in his home town in 2014. The strikingly futuristic Weijenberg-designed interior features two gigantic pine wood organic forms that lend the faux industrial space a back-to-nature feel. The 9-course prix-fixe menu showcases the chef's creative take on Taiwanese cuisine with the occasional street food influence - expect modern presentation and a stimulating blend of flavours, textures and temperatures.

TEL. N/A

中山區樂群三路301號

301, Lequn 3rd Road, Zhongshan

www.raw.com.tw

■ 價錢 **PRICE**

午膳 Lunch
套餐 Set Menu $ 1,850-3,500
晚膳 Dinner
套餐 Set Menu $ 1,850-3,500

■ 營業時間 **OPENING HOURS**

午膳 Lunch 11:30-14:30
晚膳 Dinner 18:00-22:00

■ 休息日期 **ANNUAL AND WEEKLY CLOSING**

除夕至初六、週一及週二休息
Closed CNY eve to sixth day of CNY, Monday and Tuesday

ZHONGSHAN 中山區

祥雲龍吟
SHOUN RYUGIN

時尚日本菜 · 經典

Japanese Contemporary · Classic Décor

TEL. 02 8501 5808

中山區樂群三路301號5樓

5F, 301 Lequn 3rd Road, Zhongshan

www.nihonryori-ryugin.com.tw

■ 價錢 **PRICE**

晚膳 Dinner
套餐 Set Menu $ 4,200-6,500

■ 營業時間 **OPENING HOURS**

晚膳 Dinner 18:00-21:30

■ 休息日期 **ANNUAL AND WEEKLY CLOSING**

除夕至初二及週一休息
Closed CNY eve to second day of CNY and Monday

與東京的龍吟同出一脈，此店主廚常常走訪在地農場，以上乘食材、糅合傳統與現代的烹調技巧，造就令人回味的日本料理。踏入餐廳，會先獲邀到等候區品茶，為饗宴打開序幕。其中，招牌菜乳鴿採用一個月大的屏東乳鴿，以稻草和備長炭燒烤而成，肉質細嫩滋味。鰻魚則會根據季節決定烹調方式，同樣大受歡迎。

Sister to Ryugin in Tokyo, Shoun Ryugin delivers similarly creative cuisine using local produce. The head chef visits local farms regularly and prepares the food using traditional Japanese techniques. The 7- and 10-course menus are expertly rendered, with a map showing the ingredients' origin. Squab from Pingtung is grilled over Bincho charcoal and straw to accentuate its delicate texture, while eel is cooked in various ways according to the season.

態芮
TAÏRROIR

創新菜・型格

Innovative • Design

電梯門徐徐開啟，一千多片恍似懸浮於天花的銅片叫人目眩神馳，就座後仍目不暇給。主廚兼具中西菜背景，將時令在地食材，融合西式手法，重新詮釋臺灣料理的精神與文化意涵。晚餐手路菜套餐中，九道菜都取材臺灣經典好菜，並帶有極具趣味的名稱。透過團隊親切的解說，可細味寶島各地的飲食特色。

The 1,876 copper tiles hanging from the ceiling are quite a spectacle, but they don't outshine the Taiwanese cuisine on the table – reinvented with local produce, French techniques and artful plating. Well versed in Western and Chinese cooking, Chef Kai relives his food memories with acumen and witty word play, as manifested by the 9-course menu. A portmanteau of Taiwan and terroir, Taïrroir pays tribute to his Taiwanese roots.

TEL. 02 8501 5500

中山區樂群三路299號6樓

6F, 299 Lequn 3rd Road, Zhongshan

www.tairroir.com

■ 價錢 **PRICE**

午膳 Lunch
套餐 Set Menu $ 1,880-2,880
晚膳 Dinner
套餐 Set Menu $ 4,280

■ 營業時間 **OPENING HOURS**

午膳 Lunch 12:00-13:00
晚膳 Dinner 18:30-20:00

■ 休息日期 **ANNUAL AND WEEKLY CLOSING**

元旦、除夕至初三及週二休息
Closed New Year's Day, CNY eve to third day of CNY and Tuesday

A CUT

牛排屋・時髦

Steakhouse • Fashionable

位處經典飯店地下一樓，名字上的A字寓意優質的食品與服務，也貼切地道出真實用餐體驗。鋪上藍綠色眩彩地氈的大廳舒適優雅，餐廳選用美國與澳洲為主的上等牛肉，其中推薦屬肋眼芯部位的A Cut牛排，在富有經驗的主廚處理下，軟嫩且肉香淋漓，令人口齒留香。前菜與甜點每季更換，讓常客每次光臨都有不同享受。

Not only does this steakhouse deliver on the top-quality beef its name promises, it also offers an all-round Grade A experience. As opposed to the hotel's classic furnishings, A Cut greets diners with an open kitchen and a hip, glitzy bar encased by walls of wine cabinets. The menu features premium cuts from the U.S. and Australia, including the bestselling A Cut steak, a U.S. Idaho SRF Wagyu ribeye cap with a robust flavour and fantastic marbling.

TEL. 02 2571 0389

中山區中山北路二段63號B1

B1, Ambassador Hotel, 63, Section 2, Zhongshan North Road, Zhongshan

www.ambassador-hotels.com

■ 價錢 **PRICE**

午膳 Lunch
套餐 Set Menu $ 1,600-3,400
點菜 À la carte $ 1,400-7,600
晚膳 Dinner
套餐 Set Menu $ 2,500-4,500
點菜 À la carte $ 1,400-7,600

■ 營業時間 **OPENING HOURS**

午膳 Lunch 11:30-14:00
晚膳 Dinner 18:30-21:30

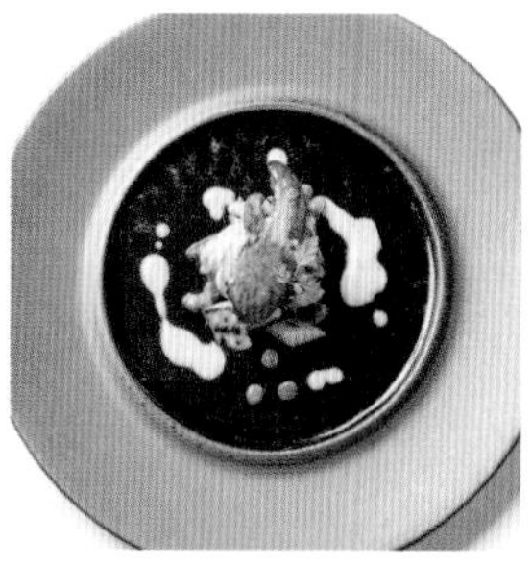

教父牛排
DANNY'S STEAKHOUSE

牛排屋 · 時尚

Steakhouse • Contemporary Décor

餐廳選用頂級美國乾式熟成牛肉及澳洲和牛，懷著無比熱情的廚師對火候和烹調時間掌握得宜，並選擇以荔枝木烹調，使肉品帶有獨特的香氣，其中熱門的老饕牛排軟嫩多汁，令人再三回味。配菜也非常出眾——自製酸種麵包令人難以抗拒，佐以特調燒烤醬的薯條和甜品亦不能錯過。服務細心周到，且價錢並非高不可攀。

Known as Taiwan's 'godfather of steaks', the eponymous owner certainly knows what makes the best steaks. Prime cuts of U.S. dry-aged and Australian Wagyu beef are grilled perfectly to your desired doneness over lychee wood in a broiler from the U.S. and then rested properly before being served. Even the homemade sourdough, french fries and desserts are hard to find fault with. Given the quality of the food and service, prices are more than reasonable.

TEL. 02 8501 1838

中山區樂群三路58號

58 Lequn 3rd Road, Zhongshan

■ 價錢 **PRICE**

午膳 Lunch
套餐 Set Menu $ 1,280-3,200
晚膳 Dinner
套餐 Set Menu $ 2,150-3,760

■ 營業時間 **OPENING HOURS**

午膳 Lunch 12:00-14:30
晚膳 Dinner 18:00-21:30

TEL. 02 2521 2518

中山區中山北路二段39巷3號B1
(晶華酒店)

B1, Regent Hotel, 3, Lane 39, Section 2, Zhongshan North Road, Zhongshan

www.impromptu.com.tw

■ 價錢 **PRICE**
晚膳 Dinner
套餐 Set Menu $ 2,580

■ 營業時間 **OPENING HOURS**
晚膳 Dinner 17:30-20:30

■ 休息日期 **ANNUAL AND WEEKLY CLOSING**
週一休息
Closed Monday

IMPROMPTU BY PAUL LEE

創新菜 · 前衛

Innovative · Trendy

霧面玻璃門後是開放式廚房和吧檯座位，在這可一覽廚房團隊的精妙合作。餐廳僅設一個逾十道菜的嚐味菜單，主廚盼顧客能以最開放舒適心情用餐，享受他以在地食材、不受料理方式所限呈現的臺灣風味，故只會在用餐完畢才將菜單交到食客手上。菜色不定期更換，幸運的話將能嚐到主廚引以為傲的自製乾拌麵。

Ask to sit at the counter so you can watch the team in front of your eyes prepare every course in the expansive open kitchen. It serves a creative 10+ course tasting menu that changes from time to time, and uses influences from around the world. One standout is white chocolate bread pudding with nitro foie gras – an intriguing contrast of textures and an unusual combination that works; round it out with their rich and fragrant milk tea blend.

明福台菜海產

MING FU

臺灣菜 · 簡樸

Taiwanese • Simple

來到明福，一定會被餐廳熱絡的氣氛感染。這裡主要提供家常臺灣菜，份量適合和親朋好友分享，尤其是須預訂的招牌菜一品佛跳牆，其用料與傳統有別，以松茸、銀杏、鮑魚等食材取代炸排骨酥和芋頭，湯頭呈清澈琥珀色且滋味鮮甜。此外，野菜山蘇與烏魚腱料理都是熱門菜色。但座位有限，建議訂位。

A bustling spot for home-style food, Ming Fu serves big portions best shared with friends and family. The signature 'Buddha jumps over the wall' must be pre-ordered; it's an amber-coloured soup, simmered for five hours with chicken, pork, abalone, matsutake mushrooms, water chestnuts etc. The mullet tripe with fried garlic is crisp and perfect with drinks. There are only six tables so booking is highly recommended.

TEL. 02 2562 9287

中山區中山北路二段137巷18之1號

18-1, Lane 137, Section 2, Zhongshan North Road, Zhongshan

■ 價錢 PRICE

午膳 Lunch
點菜 À la carte $ 1,500-2,000
晚膳 Dinner
點菜 À la carte $ 1,500-2,000

■ 營業時間 OPENING HOURS

午膳 Lunch 12:00-13:00
晚膳 Dinner 18:00-20:00

■ 休息日期 ANNUAL AND WEEKLY CLOSING

除夕至初五休息
Closed CNY eve to fifth day of CNY

渥達尼斯磨坊 N
MOLINO DE URDÁNIZ

時尚歐陸菜 · 新潮

European Contemporary • Chic

西班牙El Molino de Urdániz 首間海外分店，由兩位於本店受訓的主廚共同領軍，並延續本店風格，以嚐味菜單帶領饕客上山下海。建議晚間光臨，十二道菜色交替穿插呈現陸上與海洋的食材滋味，並融入日式元素和新鮮香草，道道精巧細膩。甜點之後，每天更有不同的隱藏版甜點，為饗宴寫上完美句點。

The first branch outside Spain of this famous name is helmed by two head chefs who honed their skills at the flagship. Central to the original concept is the 12-course tasting menu which takes diners on a poetic culinary journey across the sea and the mountains, punctuated by subtle Japanese influences and liberal use of fresh herbs. The second dessert course is a sweet surprise that changes daily and rounds off the meal perfectly.

TEL. 02 2500 6770

中山區建國北路一段61號 (慕舍酒店)

GF, Hotel MVSA, 61, Section 1, Jianguo North Road, Zhongshan

www.hotelmvsa.com

■ 價錢 **PRICE**

午膳 Lunch
套餐 Set Menu $ 2,280
晚膳 Dinner
套餐 Set Menu $ 3,680

■ 營業時間 **OPENING HOURS**

午膳 Lunch 12:00-13:30
晚膳 Dinner 18:00-20:30

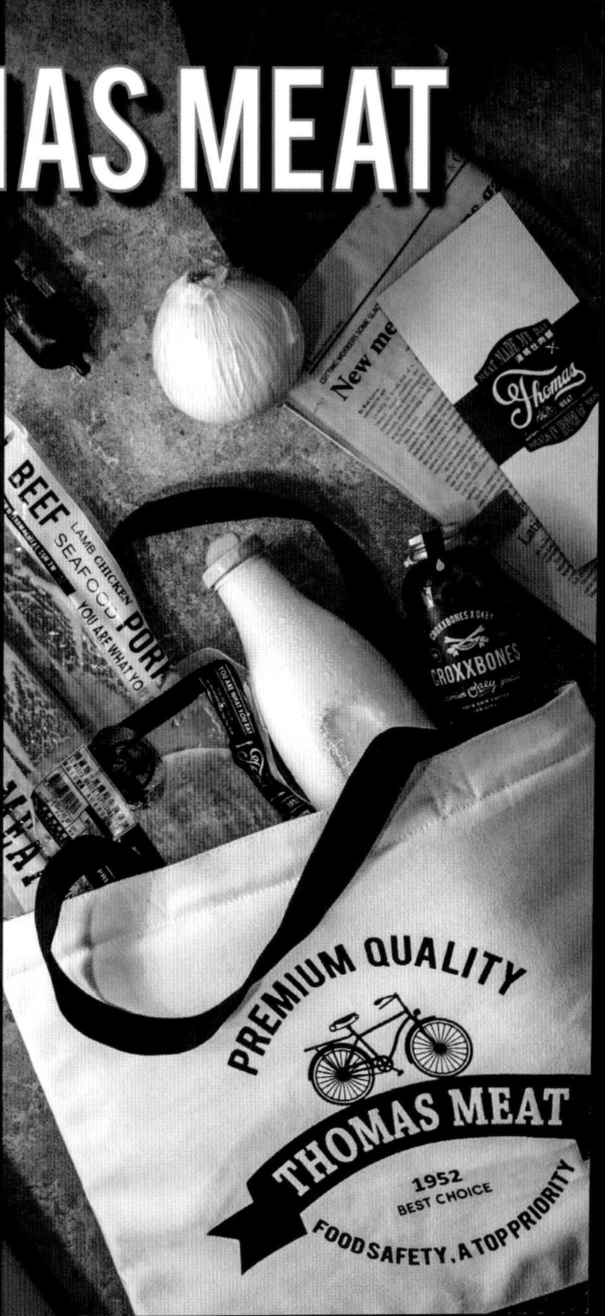
BEEF
LAMB CHICKEN
SEAFOOD
PORK
CROXXBONES
PREMIUM QUALITY
THOMAS MEAT
1952
BEST CHOICE
FOOD SAFETY, A TOP PRIORITY

明壽司 Ⓝ
SUSHI AKIRA

壽司·友善

Sushi • Friendly

開業超過十年，於2018年重新裝潢，用餐氣氛熱絡。然而料理特色始終如一，提供江戶前風格壽司，採用一致比例的紅醋和白醋製作醋飯。食材多源自日本，並以江戶前的做法，善用魚類放置時間作適度熟成。例如黑鮪魚會依情況放置四至五天。設有板前包廂，既可保有隱私，又能夠觀賞壽司製作過程。

With over 20 years of experience, the sushi chef makes diners feel right at home with his warm and gentle personality. This favourite among locals for over a decade had a makeover in 2018, but what remains constant is the Edomae sushi made with the chef's precise blend of red vinegars and the finest fish aged according to his experience. The room with counter seats allows for more privacy without missing any of the action.

TEL. 02 2596 1069

中山區雙城街25巷6之3號

6-3, Lane 25, Shuangcheng Street, Zhongshan

■ 價錢 PRICE

午膳 Lunch
套餐 Set Menu $ 2,500-3,500
晚膳 Dinner
套餐 Set Menu $ 3,500-4,500

■ 營業時間 OPENING HOURS

午膳 Lunch 12:00-14:00
晚膳 Dinner 18:00-22:00

■ 休息日期 ANNUAL AND WEEKLY CLOSING

農曆新年3天、週一午膳、週六午膳及週日休息
Closed 3 days CNY, Monday lunch, Saturday lunch and Sunday

TEL. 02 2581 8380

中山區新生北路二段60之5號

60-5, Section 2, Xinsheng North Road, Zhongshan

■ 價錢 **PRICE**

午膳 Lunch
套餐 Set Menu $ 3,000-5,000
晚膳 Dinner
套餐 Set Menu $ 5,000-7,000

■ 營業時間 **OPENING HOURS**

午膳 Lunch 12:00-13:00
晚膳 Dinner 18:00-20:00

■ 休息日期 **ANNUAL AND WEEKLY CLOSING**

農曆新年6天、元旦及週一休息
Closed 6 days CNY, New Year's Day and Monday

鮨隆
SUSHI RYU

壽司 · 簡約

Sushi • Minimalist

壽司吧檯以數百年加拿大木材製造，一室淡雅，是傳統壽司店風格。餐廳2017年才開業，可主廚兼老闆有穩紮經驗，師從日本師傅，曾先後效力城中多家知名壽司店近三十年。選料嚴謹，米飯以北海道七星米及三種日本醋混合而成，且每週多次從日本各地進口新鮮海產。只供應無菜單料理，其中秋冬供應的鮟鱇魚肝壽司是廚師拿手之作。

Having had almost 30 years' experience working in renowned sushi restaurants in Taipei, the owner-chef opened here in 2017. The décor is traditionally Japanese, with solid wood countertops imported from Canada. He insists on shipping the fish from Japan three times a week and his rice is seasoned with three different kinds of vinegar. Only omakase menus are available; the monk fish liver sushi is a standout.

天香樓
TIEN HSIANG LO

杭州菜 · 時尚

Hang Zhou • Contemporary Décor

餐室經重新裝潢，以金屬屏風仿楊柳、湖影，營造杭州風情。食物方面，完美呈現出杭州菜重手工的特點，宋嫂魚羹、天香東坡肉、龍井蝦仁均非常出色。主廚亦會選用在地食材，創造出別具特色的獨門菜，例如糅合經典菜色火膧神仙鴨和魚丸湯特色的神仙鴨魚丸湯。此外亦設有侍茶師，提供以茶配餐的最佳建議。

The chef honours Hangzhou traditions with precision and meticulous preparation. His unique creation Fairy Duck soup combines two Hangzhou classics, namely fish ball soup and braised duck with ham. From time to time, he also adds new items made with local ingredients to the menu to keep it fresh. The dining room got a facelift in 2019 and now features a white-grey palette and brushed brass accents. Ask the tea sommelier to pair tea with your food.

TEL. 02 2597 1234

中山區民權東路二段41號B1
(亞都麗緻大飯店)

B1, The Landis, 41, Section 2, Minquan East Road, Zhongshan

taipei.landishotelsresorts.com

■ 價錢 **PRICE**

午膳 Lunch
套餐 Set Menu $ 2,000-8,800
點菜 À la carte $ 800-2,000
晚膳 Dinner
套餐 Set Menu $ 2,000-8,800
點菜 À la carte $ 800-2,000

■ 營業時間 **OPENING HOURS**

午膳 Lunch 12:00-13:00
晚膳 Dinner 18:00-20:30

阿城鵝肉 (中山)
A CHENG GOOSE (ZHONGSHAN)

臺灣菜 · 簡樸

Taiwanese · Simple

提起鵝肉餐廳，阿城總是榜上有名。土城總店已經營二十餘年，此分店於2010年開業，是上班族或小家庭用餐的熱門地點。鵝肉選用重四至五斤的雲林鵝，有白斬及煙燻兩種口味，煙燻為招牌之選，推薦口感較嫩的後半段鵝腿肉。此外，魯鵝胗及杏鮑菇香腸也不能錯過；韭菜下水、麻辣血和黃金筍風味絕佳。

Opened in 2010, this restaurant is a branch of the flagship shop in Tucheng. Its famous goose is sourced from Yunlin County and is served two ways – boiled or smoked, the latter being the signature dish most customers prefer. Diners can also choose the cut; the breast is leaner and boneless whereas the leg is juicier and more tender. Also try their braised gizzards, spicy blood pudding and king oyster mushroom sausage.

TEL. 02 2541 5238

中山區吉林路105號

105 Jilin Road, Zhongshan

www.acheng.com.tw

■ 價錢 **PRICE**

點菜 À la carte $ 200-500

■ 營業時間 **OPENING HOURS**

11:30-21:00

■ 休息日期 **ANNUAL AND WEEKLY CLOSING**

除夕至初五休息

Closed CNY eve to fifth day of CNY

阿國切仔麵 N

A KUO NOODLES

麵食 · 簡樸

Noodles • Simple

於2019年重返第一代的舊址經營，繼續提供樸實家常的老滋味。老闆將一隻隻盛有油麵的笊籬陸續放於熱水中快速擺動，燙熟的麵條轉眼置身於以大骨和排骨熬煮半天的湯頭中，上放綠豆芽和自製油蔥酥，一碗古早切仔麵就此誕生，湯鮮味醇，別要錯過。也不妨配上一碟外酥內嫩的炸紅燒肉或每天現滷的滷蹄膀。

This shop is named after the traditional staple Tshek-a-mi – greased noodles, bean sprouts and crispy scallion in a flavoursome clear broth made daily with pork bones and simmered for hours. Other recommendations include steamed rice with crispy scallion, braised pork hock, and dumplings tossed in chilli oil. Try also their crispy deep-fried pork belly marinated in red yeast rice for extra aroma.

TEL. 02 2531 0009

中山區錦西街20號

20 Jinxi Street, Zhongshan

■ 價錢 **PRICE**

點菜 À la carte $ 100-300

■ 營業時間 **OPENING HOURS**

11:00-20:00

■ 休息日期 **ANNUAL AND WEEKLY CLOSING**

除夕至初五及週二休息

Closed CNY eve to fifth day of CNY and Tuesday

TEL. 02 2536 4459

中山區錦州街16號

16 Jinzhou Street, Zhongshan

■ 價錢 **PRICE**

午膳 Lunch
點菜 À la carte $ 400-500
晚膳 Dinner
點菜 À la carte $ 600-800

■ 營業時間 **OPENING HOURS**

午膳 Lunch 11:30-13:50
晚膳 Dinner 17:30-20:50

■ 休息日期 **ANNUAL AND WEEKLY CLOSING**

除夕至初三休息
Closed CNY eve to third day of CNY

人和園

JEN HO YUAN

滇菜 · 簡樸

Yunnanese • Simple

人和園自1956年創立，祖籍雲南的老闆娘每年都會帶員工回鄉考察，以確保菜餚符合滇菜精髓。在此可嚐到多款手工考究的菜色，推薦選用本地黑毛豬的大薄片，採豬頰肉川燙、冷凍再切片而成；雞油豌豆也是必點，豌豆每天購入並由員工親手揀選，配上以老母雞與大骨熬製一天的高湯，湯頭清澈，豌豆清甜脆口；豇豆鑲百花和須預訂的汽鍋雞均值得一試。

Authentic Yunnan fare has been served here since 1956, including dishes that entail painstaking preparations. The pre-order-only steam pot chicken is a free-range bird that is steamed and stewed in its own juices without adding water. The sliced pork cheek cold appetiser, and green peas in chicken fat also stand out. But the true showstopper is string beans stuffed with minced shrimp, for the intriguing contrast of textures and layered flavours.

茂園

MAO YUAN

臺灣菜 · 舒適

Taiwanese · Cosy

自1971年開業的茂園現由第二代掌舵，工作人員均是服務多年的老臣子。兩層高的餐廳適合不同大小宴席。友善的服務生會把客人帶至海鮮冰櫃前，細心介紹招牌菜及當日的時令海鮮，並因應用餐人數建議合適份量，好讓客人多嚐幾道菜。蒜泥鮮蚵和鹽冬瓜蒸時令魚等都是馳名菜色，白斬雞也值得一試。

Service is friendly and attentive at this home-style joint which has been serving the neighbourhood with old-time local delicacies since 1971. Most diners pick the catch of the day at the seafood stand; otherwise, a chalkboard menu next to it lists all their signature dishes, such as baby oysters with garlic and steamed seasonal fish with preserved winter melon. Portion sizes can be adjusted according to the number in your party.

TEL. 02 2752 8587

中山區長安東路二段185號

185, Section 2, Chang'an East Road, Zhongshan

www.maoyuan.tw

■ 價錢 PRICE

午膳 Lunch
點菜 À la carte $ 600-1,000
晚膳 Dinner
點菜 À la carte $ 600-1,000

■ 營業時間 OPENING HOURS

午膳 Lunch 11:30-13:50
晚膳 Dinner 17:30-20:20

■ 休息日期 ANNUAL AND WEEKLY CLOSING

除夕至初四休息
Closed CNY eve to fourth day of CNY

美麗餐廳
MIREI

臺灣菜・溫馨

Taiwanese • Family

TEL. 02 2521 0698
中山區錦州街146號
146 Jinzhou Street, Zhongshan

■ 價錢 **PRICE**
晚膳 Dinner
點菜 À la carte $ 800-1,000

■ 營業時間 **OPENING HOURS**
晚膳 Dinner 17:30-20:30

■ 休息日期 **ANNUAL AND WEEKLY CLOSING**
農曆新年4天及週二休息
Closed 4 days CNY and Tuesday

由老闆母親開設的美麗餐廳開業逾二十年，常客不少。精簡的菜單刻在收銀櫃檯後的竹牌子上，只見菜名不見價錢，因為店家會按用餐人數調整份量。若有意多嚐幾道菜，記得於點菜時提出。依古法秘方每天新鮮製作的燉湯是食客們一再光臨的原因之一。除此以外，粉肝白斬雞和依古方料理的魯腸也值得一讚。

Opened over 20 years ago, this neighbourhood shop has a loyal following. The second-generation owners stick with their family recipes for that authentic Taiwanese taste. Regulars come for the double-boiled chicken soup simmered for hours, pork chitterlings braised in soy sauce, and steamed chicken with velvety pork liver. Most dishes can be ordered in smaller portions if you want to sample the variety on offer.

My 灶
MY TSAO

臺灣菜 · 經典

Taiwanese • Classic Décor

餐廳名取「賣走(別走)」的諧音，有留住客人之意。裝潢以五六十年代街景為藍本，在懷舊路燈的映照下，恍似進入時光隧道，回到半世紀前的臺灣。廚師選用的均為上等食材，且標榜不過度調味，以呈現食材原味。菜單頗精簡，廚師會將每天精選寫於白板上。滷肉飯、炸軟絲丸拼小二雞卷和滷豬腳都值得一試。

This nostalgic shop is styled after a local back street circa 1950 and serves traditional Taiwanese cuisine with a modern twist. The chef tries to re-create old-time flavours and lets the ingredients shine by holding back on the seasoning. The menu is small, with daily recommendations written on the board. The quintessential Taiwanese ground pork rice is a big hit. Also try marinated pork knuckles, deep-fried chicken rolls, and squid balls.

TEL. 02 2522 2697

中山區松江路100巷9之1號

9-1, Lane 100, Songjiang Road, Zhongshan

■ 價錢 **PRICE**

午膳 Lunch
點菜 À la carte $ 500-1,000
晚膳 Dinner
點菜 À la carte $ 500-1,000

■ 營業時間 **OPENING HOURS**

午膳 Lunch 11:30-13:30
晚膳 Dinner 17:30-20:30

■ 休息日期 **ANNUAL AND WEEKLY CLOSING**

初三至初六休息
Closed third to sixth day of CNY

TEL. 02 2551 1111

中山區中山北路二段63號2樓

2F, Ambassador Hotel, 63, Section 2, Zhongshan North Road, Zhongshan

www.ambassador-hotels.com

■ 價錢 **PRICE**

午膳 Lunch
套餐 Set Menu $ 1,800
點菜 À la carte $ 800-1,500
晚膳 Dinner
套餐 Set Menu $ 1,800
點菜 À la carte $ 800-1,500

■ 營業時間 **OPENING HOURS**

午膳 Lunch 11:00-14:00
晚膳 Dinner 17:30-21:00

國賓粵菜廳

AMBASSADOR CANTON COURT

粵菜 · 舒適

Cantonese · Cosy

整齊有致的茶壺一列列掛在牆上，既有趣又不失中國味道，樸實中顯心思。顧名思義，餐廳以粵菜為主，技巧扎實不花巧，菜單上羅列的品項眾多，包括招牌菜花膠濃湯煲土雞和花雕雞油蒸龍蝦。點心亦是叫好之作，由經驗豐富的點心廚師負責，不僅於早午餐時段應市，連晚間時段亦有供應。

This simple dining room blends a modern décor with traditional Chinese tones, while teapots on the walls add fun touches to that theme. Just like its name, the food shows solid accomplished skills without being over-embellished. Regulars come for the chicken soup with dried fish maw and steamed lobster with Shaoxing wine and chicken oil. Exquisite Cantonese dim sum made in-house is served all day.

國賓川菜廳
AMBASSADOR SZECHUAN COURT

川菜・典雅

Sichuan • Elegant

開業至今逾五十載，在2019年重新裝潢，其挑高設計、柔亮色調和精緻的餐具，令環境更高雅舒適。廚師團隊多次赴四川考察，增添四十多道全新菜餚。其中貢椒鮑魚以南非鮑魚佐以古代視為貢品的四川花椒烹調，味道極麻，餘韻在舌尖散開，滋味難以忘懷。菜單上標示了辣菜餚的辛辣程度供顧客考量，十分貼心。

Its glorious history stretches back to 1966 but in 2019 this famous restaurant had a makeover and now the high-ceilinged room comes in soft hues, affording comfort and elegance. The kitchen team also took the chance to travel to Sichuan to refresh its skills and subsequently added 45 new items to the menu. Spicy food lovers should try South African abalone braised in Sichuan pepper sauce – complex aromas intertwined with a lingering, tingly sensation.

TEL. 02 2551 1111

中山區中山北路二段63號12樓

12F, Ambassador Hotel, 63, Section 2, Zhongshan North Road, Zhongshan

www.ambassador-hotels.com

■ 價錢 **PRICE**

午膳 Lunch
套餐 Set Menu $ 2,000-2,500
點菜 À la carte $ 1,000-2,000
晚膳 Dinner
套餐 Set Menu $ 2,000-2,500
點菜 À la carte $ 1,000-2,000

■ 營業時間 **OPENING HOURS**

午膳 Lunch 11:30-14:00
晚膳 Dinner 17:30-21:00

ANIMA

時尚歐陸菜・友善

European Contemporary • Friendly

TEL. 02 2541 6901

中山區中原街40號

40 Zhongyuan Street, Zhongshan

■ 價錢 **PRICE**

午膳 Lunch
點菜 À la carte $ 800-2,200
晚膳 Dinner
套餐 Set Menu $ 1,680

■ 營業時間 **OPENING HOURS**

午膳 Lunch 12:00-13:45
晚膳 Dinner 18:00-20:30

■ 休息日期 **ANNUAL AND WEEKLY CLOSING**

週一至週四午膳休息
Closed Monday to Thursday lunch

義籍主廚曾於多個國家工作，其料理融合歐陸和日本技法，溫和細膩。來到臺灣，他決定採用在地食材，並根據當天的採買品項規劃菜單。其中一道菜糅合了馬鈴薯和地瓜葉這兩種常見食材，迸發出新滋味。主廚也擅於呈現臺灣牛軟嫩可口的一面。套餐有七至八道菜，價格實惠，加上環境舒適，深受年輕顧客喜愛。

This 20-seater dining concept boasts a casual, relaxed vibe. Having worked around the world and in a famous Japanese restaurant, the Italian chef seamlessly blends European techniques with the restrained finesse of Japanese fare. The reasonably priced 7- or 8-course menu is based on local ingredients available that day. Sweet potato ravioli stands out in particular – diced potato sandwiched in sweet potato leaves, tempura-crusted and deep-fried.

雞家莊 (長春路)
CHI CHIA CHUANG (CHANGCHUN ROAD)

臺灣菜 · 傳統

Taiwanese · Traditional

雞家莊除了深受遊客青睞，亦甚得上班族歡心。原為雞販的老闆對雞隻素有研究，嚴選五至六個月大、未生過蛋的雞隻做菜，取其皮細肉嫩。想多嚐幾種風味可點選三味雞，包括了烏骨雞、白斬雞及燻雞；此外，以嫩豆腐及雞丁調製的雞家豆腐亦是廚師得意之作；餐後的雞蛋布丁也是顧客再訪之因。

Chicken features heavily on the menu and the owner is picky about them – he uses only pullets from 5 to 6 months old for their tender meat. Diners' favourites include 'Three Taste Chicken' – a trio of Silkie chicken, steamed and smoked chicken – and 'Chi Chia Chuang Dough-Foux', velvety tofu with diced chicken. Even steamed rice is cooked with chicken broth. Their homemade egg pudding is the perfect way to end a meal.

TEL. 02 2581 5954

中山區長春路55號

55 Changchun Road, Zhongshan

■ 價錢 **PRICE**

點菜 À la carte $ 600-800

■ 營業時間 **OPENING HOURS**

11:30-21:30

■ 休息日期 **ANNUAL AND WEEKLY CLOSING**

除夕至初四休息

Closed CNY eve to fourth day of CNY

TEL. 02 8502 7689

中山區植福路215號

215 Zhifu Road, Zhongshan

■ 價錢 PRICE

午膳 Lunch
套餐 Set Menu $ 1,200-5,000
點菜 À la carte $ 800-4,000
晚膳 Dinner
套餐 Set Menu $ 2,300-5,000
點菜 À la carte $ 800-4,000

■ 營業時間 OPENING HOURS

午膳 Lunch 11:30-13:30
晚膳 Dinner 17:30-20:30

鐵板教父謝樂觀 Ⓝ

IRON CHEF TEPPANYAKI

鐵板燒・時尚

Teppanyaki • Contemporary Décor

主廚烹調鐵板燒近五十年，首創將養生概念融入鐵板燒料理，並採用在地食材和苦茶油，以及少油少鹽的烹調手法，令客人吃得更健康。入座後，可以欣賞一下牆上的藝術品，然後享用以多種有機蔬果製成的五色拿鐵。設多種套餐，其中美國沙朗牛肉捲多汁可口，值得推薦。也不要錯過爆米花與舒芙蕾等鐵板現做甜點。

Along with his choreographed performance and impressive skills, Chef Hsieh with almost 50 years of experience on the griddle is also passionate about Chinese medicine. That's why his food is lightly seasoned and cooked in tea seed oil instead of butter. The prix-fixe menus emphasize dietary needs according to the time of the year, without sacrificing gastronomic pleasure. Signatures include U. S. beef sirloin roll, popcorn and soufflé made on the spot.

想想廚房
JOSEPH BISTRO

印度菜・舒適

Indian • Cosy

簡樸的灰色牆壁和地板、線條俐落的木製桌椅，輕鬆的氛圍與一般印度餐廳大相逕庭。餐廳提供以海鮮為主的南印度料理。主廚曾於十多個國家工作，認為香料醬汁是菜色關鍵，故堅持親自調配，為每種食材搭配不同配方；除了仰賴家傳秘方，更憑藉自身敏銳的味覺和嗅覺。不少食材由農場直送，亦自行種植香草。餐廳設有最低消費。

This simple dining room with blonde wood and bare concrete exudes a laid-back feel. The chef embraces a farm-to-table concept and even grows his own herbs and mixes his own spice blends. As opposed to the norm in other Indian restaurants, Western produce is used and specific spices are paired with specific ingredients. The menu rotates every three to four months, but popular dishes are always kept on. A minimum charge applies.

TEL. 02 2508 1329

中山區松江路69巷13號

13, Lane 69, Songjiang Road, Zhongshan

■ 價錢 PRICE

午膳 Lunch
點菜 À la carte $ 1,000-1,200
晚膳 Dinner
點菜 À la carte $ 1,000-1,200

■ 營業時間 OPENING HOURS

午膳 Lunch 11:30-13:00
晚膳 Dinner 17:30-20:00

■ 休息日期 ANNUAL AND WEEKLY CLOSING

週一及週日休息
Closed Monday and Sunday

林家蔬菜羊肉爐
LIN'S VEGETABLE LAMB HOTPOT

火鍋・友善

Hotpot • Friendly

TEL. 02 2592 5174

中山區吉林路327號

327 Jilin Road, Zhongshan

■ 價錢 **PRICE**

晚膳 Dinner

點菜 À la carte $ 1,000-1,200

■ 營業時間 **OPENING HOURS**

晚膳 Dinner 16:00-00:30

■ 休息日期 **ANNUAL AND WEEKLY CLOSING**

除夕至初五休息

Closed CNY eve to fifth day of CNY

怕了羊肉的羶味嗎？這餐館的蔬菜羊肉爐可能會合你心意。店家選用本地溫體現宰太監羊，每個羊肉爐都含有半斤帶皮羊肉和半斤蔬菜，湯底則以貝類與羊骨熬成，加上各式蔬菜、枸杞和薑絲，湯清味醇全無羶味，尤合滋補身心。別忘了多點一份生羊肉片。此外，其他羊肉料理如滷羊腳、炒刈菜羊肉等也值得一嚐。

Lamb hotpot here differs from others thanks to its special soup base which is fragrant and nourishing – it's made with shellfish, lamb bones, goji berries and ginger, plus mustard cabbage stems in winter or white radish in summer. Order an extra portion of sliced lamb belly or loin to be blanched in the soup. Lamb trotters braised in spiced marinade are also worth trying. Choose between the wood-clad dining room and al fresco seating.

米香
MIPON

臺灣菜・豪華

Taiwanese • Luxury

主廚烹調臺菜逾三十年，經典菜餚自然難不到他，魚皮白菜魯、三杯雞腿肉等都處理得恰到好處。愛周遊列國的主廚更為菜餚注入不少創新想法，例如推薦菜口水雞乃從臺式白斬雞變化而成，在白斬雞上淋上以蒜頭、辣椒、味醂、檸檬汁、豆醬等調製而成的醬汁，酸酸甜甜別有特色。綴以水晶燈的空間富麗堂皇，落地大窗更令環境通透明亮。

Crystal chandeliers and stone trimmings contrast starkly with the rustic faux-bamboo chairs in the high-ceilinged dining room. Head chef Chen has over 30 years of experience and is keen to put a new twist on Taiwanese classics. Mouth-watering chicken dressed in soybean paste, lemon juice, mirin, garlic and chilli surprises with its exotic tropical overtones. Classics such as "Three-cup" chicken drumstick and stewed Chinese cabbage with fish skin also impress.

TEL. 02 7722 3391

中山區樂群二路55號3樓
(美福大飯店)

3F, Grand Mayfull Hotel, 55 Lequn 2nd Road, Zhongshan

www.grandmayfull.com

■ 價錢 **PRICE**

午膳 Lunch
套餐 Set Menu $ 2,500-3,800
點菜 À la carte $ 1,800-2,500
晚膳 Dinner
套餐 Set Menu $ 3,000-3,800
點菜 À la carte $ 1,800-2,500

■ 營業時間 **OPENING HOURS**

午膳 Lunch 11:30-14:00
晚膳 Dinner 18:00-21:00

TEL. 02 6602 5678

中山區敬業四路168號4樓
(維多麗亞酒店)

4F, Grand Victoria Hotel, 168 Jingye 4th Road, Zhongshan

www.168prime.com.tw

■ 價錢 **PRICE**

午膳 Lunch
套餐 Set Menu $ 1,080-4,800
點菜 À la carte $ 2,000-7,100
晚膳 Dinner
套餐 Set Menu $ 1,900-5,100
點菜 À la carte $ 2,000-7,100

■ 營業時間 **OPENING HOURS**

午膳 Lunch 12:00-14:30
晚膳 Dinner 18:00-21:30

N°168 Prime牛排館 (中山)
N°168 PRIME STEAKHOUSE (ZHONGSHAN)

牛排屋 · 時尚

Steakhouse • Contemporary Décor

2018年底重新裝潢後的空間以寶藍色為主調，投射在地板上的168字樣與橡木堆起的牆面相映成趣。餐廳提供美國牛、澳洲9+和牛和日本A5宮崎和牛，每件均使用夢幻橡木烤箱烘烤，帶著淡淡炭火香氣，十分可口。推薦美國神戶肋眼牛排及澳洲9+和牛肋眼牛排。店內輕快的音樂令氣氛輕鬆；服務團隊友善而周到。

Remodelled in 2018, this dining room now boasts an ultramarine colour scheme dotted by oak logs and panels. Top-quality U. S. Kobe ribeye, Australian grade 9+ and Japanese Miyazaki A5 Wagyu are grilled to perfection in an oak wood-fired oven imbuing steaks with a lovely smokiness. The set menu with starter, soup, main and dessert represents good value. Service is smooth, prompt and friendly and the open kitchen keeps your eyes entertained.

頁小館
PAGE

國際菜・法式小餐館

International • Bistro

吉他、唱片和各種與音樂相關的紀念品散落四周，道出了其中一位合伙人的音樂人背景。在精挑細選的樂韻襯托下，廚師在開放式廚房烹調不拘一格的國際菜色，蒜味薯條、桶仔桂丁雞燉飯皆是巧手之作，手工蘋果派卷配自製冰淇淋更是不容錯過。酒單上除了葡萄酒，也有多種日本清酒和手工啤酒。

This laid-back modern bistro dotted with music memorabilia speaks loudly of the passions of one of its owners - food and music. The blue and white dining room with an open kitchen sets the mood for a food and music journey. The globally inspired menu covers all bases. Try their signature fries with mayo; grilled chicken risotto; and house-made apple pie with ice cream. A good selection of sake and Mikkeller craft beers are available.

TEL. 02 2532 8003

中山區北安路595巷20弄4號

4, Alley 20, Lane 595, Bei'an Road, Zhongshan

www.restaurant-page.com

■ 價錢 **PRICE**

午膳 Lunch
點菜 À la carte $ 600-1,600
晚膳 Dinner
點菜 À la carte $ 600-1,600

■ 營業時間 **OPENING HOURS**

午膳 Lunch 11:30-14:00
晚膳 Dinner 17:30-20:45

■ 休息日期 **ANNUAL AND WEEKLY CLOSING**

小年夜至初三休息
Closed 2 days before CNY to third day of CNY

巴黎廳1930x高山英紀 N

PARIS 1930 DE HIDEKI TAKAYAMA

時尚法國菜 · 典雅

French Contemporary • Elegant

環境典雅奢華，無論是吊燈、名貴餐具還是精心設計的桌布，都一絲不苟，適合正式宴會。日籍主廚融合了日本美學及法式烹調技巧，並使用臺灣茶品與食材，創造出令人驚豔的美食，例如野菇清湯燉蛋運用了普洱茶，口味清新。套餐內包含多款海鮮菜色，而蔬果千層及甜點福岡八女抹茶奶油千層皆是主廚的得意之作。

Seafood is very much the focus at this elegantly dressed restaurant whose muted décor and quality tableware exude comfort and luxury. The Japanese chef from Fukuoka also cleverly incorporates local tea into his cooking. The signature dish of marinated vegetables layered with sushi rice with avocado puree not only pleases the eyes but also the palate. The mille-feuille with white chocolate matcha cream is warm, crisp and flaky.

TEL. 02 2597 1234

中山區民權東路二段41號2樓
(亞都麗緻大飯店)

2F, The Landis, 41, Section 2, Minquan East Road, Zhongshan

taipei.landishotelsresorts.com

■ 價錢 **PRICE**

午膳 Lunch
套餐 Set Menu $ 1,200-3,000
晚膳 Dinner
套餐 Set Menu $ 2,400-6,000

■ 營業時間 **OPENING HOURS**

午膳 Lunch 12:00-13:30
晚膳 Dinner 18:00-21:00

■ 休息日期 **ANNUAL AND WEEKLY CLOSING**

週二至週五午膳及週一休息
Closed weekday lunch and Monday

Robin's 鐵板燒
ROBIN'S TEPPANYAKI

鐵板燒 · 經典

Teppanyaki · Classic Décor

餐廳以已故資深外場人員命名，老饕皆熟知這家鐵板燒的所在。套餐選擇琳瑯滿目，當中不乏美國頂級牛排，還有日本與澳洲和牛。於席前為客人烹調的廚師均經驗豐富，對於食材的料理時間，以至客人的用餐節奏均了然於胸。肉類以外，海鮮的處理也甚具水準。嗜杯中物者會對其酒單感到稱心。

One of the best known teppanyaki places in town, named after a long-serving maître d', enjoys an enthusiastic local following. The show-stopping teppan tricks are something to behold, but they don't outshine the perfectly cooked seafood, premium steaks from the U. S., or the Wagyu from Japan and Australia. The six-course dinner unfolds according to your pace as experienced chefs time things just right. An excellent wine list also features.

TEL. 02 2523 8000

中山區中山北路二段39巷3號2樓
(晶華酒店)

2F, Regent Hotel, 3, Lane 39, Section 2, Zhongshan North Road, Zhongshan

www.regenttaiwan.com

■ 價錢 **PRICE**

午膳 Lunch
套餐 Set Menu $ 2,250-5,100
晚膳 Dinner
套餐 Set Menu $ 2,800-5,900

■ 營業時間 **OPENING HOURS**

午膳 Lunch 12:00-14:00
晚膳 Dinner 18:00-21:30

TEL. 02 2561 1246

中山區中山北路二段42巷6號

6, Lane 42, Section 2, Zhongshan North Road, Zhongshan

■ 價錢 **PRICE**

午膳 Lunch
套餐 Set Menu $ 2,000-5,000
晚膳 Dinner
套餐 Set Menu $ 3,000-6,000

■ 營業時間 **OPENING HOURS**

午膳 Lunch 12:00-13:30
晚膳 Dinner 18:00-20:30

■ 休息日期 **ANNUAL AND WEEKLY CLOSING**

週一休息
Closed Monday

笹鮨
SASA

壽司 · 簡約

Sushi • Minimalist

餐廳環境各項細節盡顯老闆心思，不論是椅子的高度、腳踏的寬度、或桌子的深度均經過精心計算，為求顧客用餐時舒適自在。食材主要自日本豐洲市場進口，並按種類施以不同的熟成和處理，例如鮪魚肚經櫻花木燻製，生筋子經去膜和醃製。餐廳定期邀請日本廚師作客，以提升員工技術。

The owner gave serious thought to every detail in this shop. Most of the fish is flown straight from Tokyo's Toyosu market and aged for different periods of time to enhance taste and texture. Tuna belly is smoked with cherry wood; salmon roe is removed from skeins and cured in-house; and rare and highly prized catches such as tuna from Oma and Tenjyo amberjack are also sourced. Only omakase menus are served.

欣葉台菜 (創始店)

SHIN YEH TAIWANESE CUISINE

臺灣菜·溫馨

Taiwanese • Family

說起臺菜餐館，欣葉必定榜上有名。多年來，規模變大了，從只供應清粥小菜，至成為宴席菜的場地，店東希望將家庭的味道帶給客人的心願始終未變。到欣葉必嚐其手工菜色——菜脯蛋以筷子邊煮邊攪拌翻鍋，做法獨特；杏仁豆腐由三位師傅人手鮮製，口感軟糯；其他招牌菜還有煎豬肝和以手工見稱的潤餅等。

A household name in Taiwanese cuisine since 1977, it specialises in authentic home-style cooking that seems simple, but requires scrupulous care - just try the egg omelette with dried radish, pan-seared pork liver and flatbread rolls. Even their almond tofu dessert is made by three chefs from scratch. This branch boasts 110 tables and is ideal for banquets and parties of all sizes.

TEL. 02 2596 3255

中山區雙城街34之1號

34-1 Shuangcheng Street, Zhongshan

www.shinyeh.com.tw

■ 價錢 **PRICE**

套餐 Set Menu $ 800-2,000
點菜 À la carte $ 600-1,400

■ 營業時間 **OPENING HOURS**

11:00-23:00

旬採 (中山)
SHUN SAI (ZHONGSHAN)

日本菜·舒適

Japanese • Cosy

TEL. 02 2521 9679

中山區中山北路二段50巷3號

3, Lane 50, Section 2, Zhongshan North Road, Zhongshan

■ 價錢 **PRICE**

午膳 Lunch
套餐 Set Menu $ 1,200-6,600
晚膳 Dinner
套餐 Set Menu $ 2,000-6,600

■ 營業時間 **OPENING HOURS**

午膳 Lunch 11:30-13:30
晚膳 Dinner 17:30-20:30

■ 休息日期 **ANNUAL AND WEEKLY CLOSING**

小年夜至初五及週日休息
Closed 2 days before CNY to fifth day of CNY and Sunday

室內設計由日本人操刀，採用加拿大雲杉木餐桌搭配硅藻土牆身，簡潔自然。大部分食材由日本各地進口，包括製作壽司飯的米，海產則多來自豐洲市場，主廚喜以時令食材入饌，幸運的話有機會嚐到活生生的香箱蟹。無菜單料理中的熱食比例較高，如偏愛生食或欲全選握壽司，便需於訂位時告知店家。

The Canadian spruce table-tops and diatomite walls exude simple, natural beauty. The omakase menu carries an unusually high proportion of cooked food, but can be customised to accommodate the cravings of raw fish lovers. Most produce originates from Japan and is shipped straight from Tokyo's Toyosu market. Sushi rice is seasoned with akazu vinegar to complement the fatty fish. Ask for seasonal specialities such as kobako crab.

晶華軒

SILKS HOUSE

粵菜・經典

Cantonese • Classic Décor

入口處是一條長長的書法走廊，鐵畫銀鉤的草書字體刻滿玻璃，感覺優雅而傳統。於2019年新上任的香港主廚和點心師傅將菜單改頭換面，專精於粵式佳餚。西施泡飯為主廚拿手好菜，招牌蜜汁叉燒亦是熱門菜色。另外，點心滋味出眾，建議一嚐晶瑩蝦餃和紅裳脆皮蝦腸粉。如果想享有私人空間，不妨預訂包廂。

The Chinese calligraphy etched and backlit on glass screens in the corridor befits the elegant cuisine. In 2019, the Hong Kong head chef and dim sum chefs trimmed down the menu to accentuate the best of the best. The exquisite har gow sports springy prawns glistening under the translucent skin; prawns and fried dough stick enrobed in red rice roll gives a delightful mix of textures; and Xishi soup rice and char siu pork also stand out.

P

TEL. 02 2523 8000

中山區中山北路二段39巷3號3樓
(晶華酒店)

3F, Regent Hotel, 3, Lane 39, Section 2, Zhongshan North Road, Zhongshan

www.regenttaiwan.com

■ 價錢 **PRICE**

午膳 Lunch
套餐 Set Menu $ 1,580-1,880
點菜 À la carte $ 800-4,000
晚膳 Dinner
套餐 Set Menu $ 2,280-2,680
點菜 À la carte $ 800-4,000

■ 營業時間 **OPENING HOURS**

午膳 Lunch 11:30-14:00
晚膳 Dinner 17:30-21:00

TEL. 02 2781 5137

中山區八德路二段174巷5號

5, Lane 174, Section 2, Bade Road, Zhongshan

■ 價錢 **PRICE**

午膳 Lunch
點菜 À la carte $ 600-1,000
晚膳 Dinner
點菜 À la carte $ 800-1,500

■ 營業時間 **OPENING HOURS**

午膳 Lunch 11:30-13:30
晚膳 Dinner 17:30-20:30

■ 休息日期 **ANNUAL AND WEEKLY CLOSING**

除夕至初一休息
Closed CNY eve to first day of CNY

田園海鮮

TIEN YUAN SEAFOOD

海鮮 · 友善

Seafood • Friendly

占地四層的田園建立最初為路邊攤販，至今已由第三代接棒，並成為擁有十多間大大小小包廂的熱門聚餐場所。海鮮每日由澎湖及基隆運抵，店內不設菜單，食客需到海鮮檯上挑選當日時令海鮮，資深的點菜大姊會按人數及食材建議料理方式。必點菜餚包括紅糟鰻及龍蝦三明治。

It started off as a street hawker stall and the third-generation owner still runs the place like it was – there is no menu. Live seafood in the tank is shipped from Penghu and Keelung – just have a look and take your pick; the experienced servers will suggest the portion sizes, cooking methods and the accompanying condiments. Recommended specialities include fried eel in red yeast rice sauce and lobster sandwich. Private rooms are available.

桃花林
TOH-KA-LIN

粵菜・經典

Cantonese • Classic Décor

紅色為主調的中式桌椅和滿牆的瓷器擺設使餐廳洋溢著傳統韻味，玻璃屏風和吊燈又添上少許現代元素，典雅中不失時尚。菜單方面，偏於粵菜風味，燒味深受顧客喜愛，其中港式蜜汁叉燒滋味細膩，值得一試。同時提供多樣化的個人套餐以供選擇，當中不乏海參、鮑魚等高檔食材之搭配，適合商務聚會或宴請。

This outpost of the 50-year-old Tokyo namesake boasts elegant Chinese décor with opulent modern touches. The elaborate menu is mostly Cantonese, with barbecue meats especially popular with diners - try the honey-glazed barbecued pork for its fine texture and robust flavour. A number of single-portioned set menus are available; many include luxury ingredients like sea cucumber and abalone making them perfect for business meals or entertainment.

TEL. 02 2181 5136

中山區南京東路一段9號3樓
(大倉久和大飯店)

3F, Okura Prestige Hotel, 9, Section 1, Nanjing East Road, Zhongshan

www.okurataipei.com.tw

■ 價錢 **PRICE**

午膳 Lunch
套餐 Set Menu $ 1,200-5,200
點菜 À la carte $ 1,000-5,500
晚膳 Dinner
套餐 Set Menu $ 2,000-5,200
點菜 À la carte $ 1,000-5,500

■ 營業時間 **OPENING HOURS**

午膳 Lunch 11:30-14:00
晚膳 Dinner 18:00-21:30

ZHONGSHAN 中山區

TEL. 02 2592 3355

中山區雙城街25巷15號

15, Lane 25, Shuangcheng Street, Zhongshan

www.tuttobello.com.tw

■ 價錢 **PRICE**

午膳 Lunch
套餐 Set Menu $ 3,600
點菜 À la carte $ 2,500-3,000
晚膳 Dinner
套餐 Set Menu $ 3,800-5,200
點菜 À la carte $ 3,500-4,500

■ 營業時間 **OPENING HOURS**

午膳 Lunch 12:00-13:30
晚膳 Dinner 18:00-21:30

■ 休息日期 **ANNUAL AND WEEKLY CLOSING**

小年夜至初三休息
Closed 2 days before CNY to third day of CNY

TUTTO BELLO

時尚義大利菜・舒適

Italian Contemporary • Cosy

來自香港的主廚兼老闆移居臺灣逾三十年，具天賦的他以上乘的材料和恰到好處的烹調技巧，將經典義大利菜色演化為外表精緻、賣相時尚的菜餚，推薦檸檬辣椒烘菌菇、煎干貝和手工義大利麵條等。團隊致力令每個環節都完美無瑕，酒單羅列不少法國和義國名釀，所選用的酒杯款式多樣，盡顯心思。

A smart Italian restaurant where the owner and his team strive to ensure that "everything is perfect". The cuisine is firmly based upon classic dishes but is interpreted by the talented chef in a light, modern style. Well-presented dishes show care, quality ingredients and well-judged subtlety, especially with their flavours; the homemade pasta is a highlight. A substantial wine list includes some impressive French and Italian producers.

ZHONGSHAN 中山區

YORU

時尚歐陸菜 · 簡約

European Contemporary · Minimalist

日文Yoru是指「夜晚」，寓意大家能在這裡享受美好的晚上。因此，儘管裝潢走極簡風格，但服務熱情溫暖，令人愜意。全餐廳僅設板前座位，配合西式手法和日式窯燒，炮製出多款特色料理。提供單一套餐，以日本和牛作主菜食材，其他菜色則按當季時令變化，其中厚切牛舌深受好評。但必須提前訂位。

The cement façade and walls are softened by a wood counter and the warm service, which comes courtesy of a young team. Guests sit at the counter and interact with the chefs so it resembles a sushi-ya, but European touches are obvious in the cooking and the plating. The omakase menu features plenty of Japanese Wagyu, mostly grilled in a Japanese stone oven, while the thickly sliced gyutan is a favourite of many. Reservations are mandatory.

TEL. 02 2776 0322

中山區八德路二段332巷16號

16, Lane 332, Section 2, Bade Road, Zhongshan

■ 價錢 **PRICE**

晚膳 Dinner
套餐 Set Menu $ 3,950-4,950

■ 營業時間 **OPENING HOURS**

晚膳 Dinner 18:00-19:30

■ 休息日期 **ANNUAL AND WEEKLY CLOSING**

除夕至初三及週一休息
Closed CNY eve to third day of CNY and Monday

TEL. 02 2503 0303

中山區合江街41巷4號

4, Lane 41, Hejiang Street, Zhongshan

■ 價錢 **PRICE**

午膳 Lunch
套餐 Set Menu $ 2,500
晚膳 Dinner
套餐 Set Menu $ 3,500-4,500

■ 營業時間 **OPENING HOURS**

午膳 Lunch 12:00-13:00
晚膳 Dinner 18:00-20:00

■ 休息日期 **ANNUAL AND WEEKLY CLOSING**

除夕至初五及週日休息
Closed CNY eve to fifth day of CNY and Sunday

彧割烹
YU KAPO

日本菜・友善

Japanese • Friendly

位於寧靜巷弄的彧割烹於2018年開業，老闆兼料理長包辦設計，整個空間以木材為主，板前座位採用整片不修邊的南洋檜木製成。餐廳於中午提供生食與握壽司為主的套餐，晚間才供應主推的割烹料理。海鮮六成來自東京和北海道，其中以季節性魚類所作的釜飯為招牌菜。團隊年輕親切，讓人感到賓至如歸。

Hidden down a quiet alley is this restaurant furnished prominently with untreated cypress wood that feels warm and cosy. Kappo menus are only offered at dinner, while nigiri sushi is served at lunch. The signature kamameshi is made with seasonal fish, such as eel in winter. Chargrilled Kagoshima Wagyu steak dressed in sukiyaki sauce has a subtle smoky scent to it with a spot-on salty-sweet balance. Young servers and chefs deliver precise and friendly service.

luo yun/iStock

酒店
HOTELS

美福

GRAND MAYFULL

豪華・時尚

Luxury • Contemporary

糅合中義風格建成的瑰麗花崗岩建築，讓人難以置信是於2016年落成的酒店。兩座高聳塔樓內是146間高雅房間；其中的落地窗、大理石浴室與特設衣帽間，均給予豪華的住宿體驗。附設的餐廳提供義、粵、臺、日美食。如果想進一步提升入住質素，務必挑選具陽臺並可俯瞰露天泳池的房間，景觀優美亦較寧靜。

Opened in 2016, the twin palatial granite towers house 146 elegant rooms, with floor-to-ceiling windows, marble-clad bathrooms, walk-in closets and hand-painted murals. Quality bedding and linen add to the luxurious experience. Guests can choose from a variety of restaurants: all-day international, Italian, Cantonese, Taiwanese and Japanese. Ask for a room overlooking the outdoor pool.

TEL. 02 7722 3399
www.grandmayfull.com

中山區樂群二路55號
55 Lequn 2nd Road, Zhongshan

146 客房/Rooms $ 7,600-8,000
20 套房/Suites $ 25,000

餐廳推薦/Recommended restaurants:
米香 **Mipon**

TEL. 02 2523 1111
www.okurataipei.com.tw

中山區南京東路一段9號
9, Section 1, Nanjing East Road, Zhongshan

201 客房/**Rooms** $ 6,500-15,000
7 套房/**Suites** $ 17,500-26,250

餐廳推薦/**Recommended restaurants:**
桃花林 Toh-Ka-Lin

大倉久和
OKURA PRESTIGE

豪華・典雅

Luxury • Elegant

瑰麗堂皇的日式風格酒店——貼切地形容了大倉久和大飯店。這座水晶高樓矗立於城市中心，光潔明亮的大理石大堂、雄偉的吊燈顯出令人讚嘆的氣派。208間房間同樣出眾，糅合東西風格裝飾，三米高的樓頂配以高層房間獨享由南到北的山巒城市景觀，是極致愉悅。附設的水療空間與頂樓露天泳池提供讓人放鬆身心的服務。

Comfort is at the core of this glass-clad tower in the city centre. It makes a statement with its marble lobby with a majestic chandelier, and understated yet tasteful rooms with 3-metre high ceilings and marble bathrooms. Rooms on higher floors have mountain views to the north and city views to the south. The spa has separate pools for women and men, alongside a rooftop pool.

晶華
REGENT

豪華・經典

Luxury • Classic

名店侍立、匯聚設計師品牌店，甫進入酒店範圍已感受到其奢華氣派。裡外一致，全種類房間均飄散出高雅氣息，裝潢布置富麗豪華，倘入住雲天露臺客房更能尊享私人陽臺。餐飲選擇目不暇給，包含牛排屋、粵菜、日本菜等。吃膩了豐富大餐，也可於一樓的Azie伴著樂聲淺嚐下午茶，甚或到頂樓享受芳療放鬆身心。

Fashionistas need not leave this luxury hotel to splurge as its galleria is home to world-class designer stores. All rooms exude classic elegance and corner suites also sport a private terrace. Dining options abound – choose between a steakhouse, Cantonese, Japanese or buffet. Afternoon tea at the atrium lounge Azie is also a delight. Those feeling weary can recharge at the Magnolia spa.

TEL. 02 2523 8000
www.regenttaiwan.com

中山區中山北路二段39巷3號
3, Lane 39, Section 2, ZhongShan North Road, Zhongshan

478 客房/**Rooms** $ 7,000-14,900
60 套房/**Suites** $ 15,400-25,200

餐廳推薦/**Recommended restaurants:**
Impromptu by Paul Lee
晶華軒 Silks House
Robin's 鐵板燒 Robin's Teppanyaki

Big_Suttawat/iStock

萬華區
中正區

WANHUA & ZHONGZHENG

萬華區 WANHUA
中正區 ZHONGZHENG

餐廳 RESTAURANTS

✿✿

請客樓

THE GUEST HOUSE

淮揚菜及川菜・時尚

Huai Yang & Sichuan・Contemporary Décor

本以俱樂部形式經營的請客樓於2005年才對外開放，簡單的布置說明了餐廳將心思全貫注在食物之上，其手工菜口碑甚佳，廚師擅於將簡單的菜色精緻地呈現，質感及味道均十分出色，特別推薦核桃棗煎餅。以川揚菜為基礎的菜色融合臺灣味道，包括香濃燉湯、麻油雞飯、紅麴豬尾、千層百頁豆腐等。設多間供宴客的包廂 。

Formerly a members-only dining club, it excites not with its décor, but with its food. Impressive skills transform seemingly simple dishes into tasteful presentations revealing great textures and taste. The menu is largely Huai Yang and Sichuan in origin, but with a Taiwanese twist. Signature dishes include double-boiled soups, chicken rice with sesame oil, pork tail braised in red yeast rice, and millefeuille tofu skin.

TEL. 02 2321 1818

中正區忠孝東路一段12號17樓
(喜來登大飯店)

17F, Sheraton Grand Hotel, 12, Section 1, Zhongxiao East Road, Zhongzheng

www.sheratongrandtaipei.com

■ 價錢 **PRICE**

午膳 Lunch
套餐 Set Menu $ 1,980-4,280
點菜 À la carte $ 1,200-3,500
晚膳 Dinner
套餐 Set Menu $ 2,680-4,280
點菜 À la carte $ 1,800-3,500

■ 營業時間 **OPENING HOURS**

午膳 Lunch 11:30-14:00
晚膳 Dinner 18:00-21:00

山海樓

MOUNTAIN AND SEA HOUSE

臺灣菜 · 傳統

Taiwanese • Traditional

TEL. 02 2351 3345

中正區仁愛路二段94號

94, Section 2, Ren'ai Road, Zhongzheng

www.mountain-n-seahouse.com

■ 價錢 PRICE

午膳 Lunch
套餐 Set Menu $ 980-4,680
點菜 À la carte $ 1,500-2,000
晚膳 Dinner
套餐 Set Menu $ 1,980-4,680
點菜 À la carte $ 2,000-2,500

■ 營業時間 OPENING HOURS

午膳 Lunch 11:30-14:00
晚膳 Dinner 17:30-21:00

推開厚沉的大門，氣勢非凡的大堂彷彿把時光拉回1930年，師承蓬萊閣老師傅的主廚復原當年的傳統臺菜菜色，並精緻化呈現。熱門的金銀燒豬採用養殖二十一天的正黑豬，低溫烘烤十二小時後再高溫烤至外皮酥脆，並佐以四種醬料享用；肚包雞則把餡料塞入土雞，再以豬肚包覆燉煮。菜餚多屬手工菜，建議先從網頁查看預訂菜色。

Complete with a courtyard and a high-ceilinged foyer, this luxurious mansion evokes the glamorous days of the 1930s in both its décor and its food. The must-try roast suckling pig uses only 21-day-old hogs, slow-cooked for 12 hours and roasted until crisp and golden. Another speciality, deboned chicken braised in pork tripe, takes six hours to prepare. Both the pig and chicken need pre-ordering. Fried rice with mullet roe is also unmissable.

大三元
THREE COINS

粵菜 · 經典

Cantonese • Classic Décor

開業近半世紀的大三元現由第三代掌舵。建築物外牆飾以饒有氣勢的書法，店內裝潢古雅，藝文氣氛濃厚，難怪成為政商名人聚會的熱門場所。這兒提供的廣東菜帶點臺式元素，鮮茄大鮮鮑以乾、鮮番茄和九層塔入饌，清新可喜；創意菜海鮮烤木瓜則將干貝、鮑魚、日本魚板等放入剖半木瓜中烤製；苦茶油雞湯也蠻受歡迎。

Celebrating 40+ years of glorious history, this family business is now helmed by the third generation. The oversized Chinese calligraphy on the exterior and art pieces in the interior impart a sense of high culture. The menu is classic Cantonese, with occasional Taiwanese touches, such as the simple but tasty steamed abalone with dried and fresh tomatoes. Seafood baked in papaya provides an interesting mix of flavours and textures.

TEL. 02 2381 7180

中正區衡陽路46號

46 Hengyang Road, Zhongzheng

www.3coins.com.tw

■ 價錢 **PRICE**

午膳 Lunch
點菜 À la carte $ 500-1,500
晚膳 Dinner
點菜 À la carte $ 1,000-1,500

■ 營業時間 **OPENING HOURS**

午膳 Lunch 11:30-14:00
晚膳 Dinner 17:30-21:00

■ 休息日期 **ANNUAL AND WEEKLY CLOSING**

初一休息
Closed first day of CNY

阜杭豆漿
FU HANG SOY MILK

點心・簡樸

Dim Sum • Simple

TEL. 02 2392 2175

中正區忠孝東路一段108號2樓28號(華山市場)

Stall 28, 2F, Huashan Market, 108, Section 1, Zhongxiao East Road, Zhongzheng

■ 價錢 PRICE
點菜 À la carte $ 30-100

■ 營業時間 OPENING HOURS
05:30-12:30

■ 休息日期 ANNUAL AND WEEKLY CLOSING
週一休息
Closed Monday

這中式早餐店藏匿於華山市場二樓，即便不設座位依然門庭若市，吸引顧客排隊久候的是燒餅、油條與飯糰夾蛋等點心，招牌厚燒餅油條於店內以窯烤爐新鮮現做，是必點品項；鹹豆漿也值得一嚐。顧客可至公共座位區享用或外帶，僅營業至中午，建議饕客們提早前來。

This breakfast stall in Huashan Market constantly attracts long queues so come early for your morning fix. The crowds are here just for the food – their deep-fried dough stick, freshly roasted buns from a tandoor oven, egg crepes, and savoury or sweet soy milk have been the quintessential breakfast for many local. Seats are available in a food court setting. Many also order to go.

老山東牛肉家常麵店

LAO SHAN DONG HOMEMADE NOODLES

麵食 · 簡樸

Noodles · Simple

於1949年開業，以其手工刀切麵條和牛肉湯俘擄了不少食客的心。牛肉麵湯頭以臺灣牛骨及十種特調的中藥材熬製；現切麵條口感彈牙，吸附滿滿紅燒湯汁，佐以本地與澳洲滷牛肉，滋味十足。每款小菜均當天現做，其中山東泡菜脆口清爽；豬頭肉晶凍以細火慢燉六小時而成，晶瑩剔透，均是熱門之選。

This household name in the beef noodle scene has been attracting a loyal following with its ribbon noodles and beef broth since 1949. Beef bones and a blend of Chinese herbs give the broth its flavour and depth. Noodles are cut and cooked to order and local and Australian beef is simmered in the broth for hours until tender, so slurping up the broth gives you a burst of flavours. Cold sides such as pork ear in aspic and pickled cabbage are made fresh daily.

TEL. 02 2389 1216

萬華區西寧南路70號B1之15室
(萬年商業大樓)

Shop 15, B1, 70 Xining South Road, Wanhua

■ 價錢 **PRICE**

點菜 À la carte $ 150-250

■ 營業時間 **OPENING HOURS**

10:30-21:30

■ 休息日期 **ANNUAL AND WEEKLY CLOSING**

農曆除夕休息
Closed CNY eve

雙月食品 (青島東路)

MOONMOONFOOD (QINGDAO EAST ROAD)

臺灣菜 · 簡樸

Taiwanese • Simple

TEL. 02 3393 8953

中正區青島東路6之2號

6-2 Qingdao East Road, Zhongzheng

www.moonmoonfood.com

■ 價錢 **PRICE**

午膳 Lunch
點菜 À la carte $ 300-500
晚膳 Dinner
點菜 À la carte $ 300-500

■ 營業時間 **OPENING HOURS**

午膳 Lunch 11:00-14:00
晚膳 Dinner 17:00-20:00

■ 休息日期 **ANNUAL AND WEEKLY CLOSING**

農曆除夕、初五及週日休息
Closed CNY eve, fifth day of CNY and Sunday

名為雙月，取其雙雙對對、團圓圓滿之意，正好配合其出品的古早味藥膳。菜色均按老闆媽媽的傳統配方烹調，並堅持使用上等食材，例如招牌雞湯，做法是先將湯熬好，再將每早新鮮運到的溫體仿土雞放入烹煮，以保持雞肉嫩滑；另一熱門之選何首烏燉雞，使用的中藥均從產地直接取得，確保品質上乘。雙月油飯通常很早售罄，不想失望而回便得早點前來。

The family feel is obvious in this shop serving healthy home-style cooking. Their signature chicken soup is made daily with freshly slaughtered free-range chicken; the stock is simmered for hours and extra chicken is added at the end to keep it juicy and tender. The herbal variety of the soup with He Shou Wu is considered a health booster. Fresh milkfish is also delivered daily and painstakingly de-boned before cooking. Don't miss their glutinous oil rice.

牛店精燉牛肉麵

NIU TIEN BEEF NOODLES

麵食・簡樸

Noodles • Simple

工業風裝潢加上整齊制服的服務生，這家麵店無疑是走較精緻路線。牛肉麵的湯頭採用法式清湯製法、以多種牛骨部位與西式香料熬製，滋味清爽甘甜；而麵條則為自家生產，以家常麵做成拉麵口感，顧客更可挑選軟硬度。招牌滿漢牛肉麵包含牛腱、牛筋和牛肚三個部位，更附以辣醬油，是以同時可嚐到兩種風味。

This hip shop, with its faux industrial décor, sources beef foreshank from Australia and New Zealand and braises it for seven hours in a consommé made from beef bones, mirepoix and herbs. The soup has depth and a sweet undertone. Noodles are handmade to have a springy texture like ramen – you can even specify your preferred noodle consistency. Try the Manchurian-Chinese beef noodle soup to sample different cuts all at once.

TEL. 02 2389 5577

萬華區昆明街91號

91 Kunming Street, Wanhua

■ 價錢 **PRICE**

午膳 Lunch
點菜 À la carte $ 200-450
晚膳 Dinner
點菜 À la carte $ 200-450

■ 營業時間 **OPENING HOURS**

午膳 Lunch 11:30-14:30
晚膳 Dinner 17:00-20:00

■ 休息日期 **ANNUAL AND WEEKLY CLOSING**

農曆新年4天及週一休息
Closed 4 days CNY and Monday

祥和蔬食 (中正)
SERENITY (ZHONGZHENG)

素食·簡樸

Vegetarian • Simple

TEL. 02 2357 0377

中正區鎮江街1巷1號

1, Lane 1, Zhenjiang Street, Zhongzheng

■ 價錢 **PRICE**

午膳 Lunch
套餐 Set Menu $ 200
點菜 À la carte $ 200-500
晚膳 Dinner
點菜 À la carte $ 300-1,000

■ 營業時間 **OPENING HOURS**

午膳 Lunch 11:00-13:45
晚膳 Dinner 17:00-20:30

■ 休息日期 **ANNUAL AND WEEKLY CLOSING**

除夕至初一休息
Closed CNY eve to first day of CNY

這是全臺首家四川風味的素菜餐廳，半露天的格局令室內明亮寬敞，牆壁綴以來自各地的佛教壁畫，環境更添祥和。所有菜色均不含蔥蒜，其中塔香脆腸赫赫有名，是一道以杏鮑菇作主食材的功夫菜，其他特色菜還有清蒸臭豆腐、鹽酥杏鮑菇、宮保素雞丁等。由天麻等中藥材熬製的養生鍋與佛跳牆須經長時間燉煮，建議於兩天前預訂。

The first Sichuan vegetarian restaurant in Taiwan is jointly helmed by a chef specialising in vegetarian cooking and another well versed in Sichuan cuisine. As half of the shop is enclosed in glass panes, it feels airy and bright. Must-try items include basil-scented vegetarian crisp tripe, bean sprouts in truffle pâté, steamed stinky tofu, fried king oyster mushrooms and Gong Bao vegetarian chicken. No garlic or onion is used in any dish.

一甲子餐飲 Ⓝ

YI JIA ZI

小吃・簡樸

Small eats • Simple

位於艋舺祖師爺廟旁的臺南風味小店，至今已傳承了三代。老闆每天選用肥瘦均勻的五花肉，佐以自製小黃瓜、酸菜、滷豆乾，以及口感出眾的南部米，製作出招牌焢肉飯。此外，滷肉飯、刈包與麻豆碗粿也是店內熱門小吃，後者更限量供應。如果想嚐嚐北部口味，可以來一碗沙茶味道濃厚的豬血湯佐餐。

The third generation owners of this family shop insist on re-creating authentic Tainan flavours. The must-try stewed pork belly shows alternate layers of fat and meat and comes with pickles and marinated dried tofu on a bed of steamed Tainan rice; or you can order a gua bao sandwich with pork. Pork blood curd soup is seasoned with shacha sauce for a rich and complex flavour; Madou rice cake is also popular but come early before they run out.

TEL. 02 2311 5241

萬華區康定路79號

79 Kangding Road, Wanhua

www.yi-jia-zi.com

■ 價錢 **PRICE**

點菜 À la carte $ 55-150

■ 營業時間 **OPENING HOURS**

09:00-19:00

■ 休息日期 **ANNUAL AND WEEKLY CLOSING**

農曆新年10天、清明節、端午節、中秋節及週日休息

Closed 10 days CNY, Qingming Festival, Dragon Boat Festival, Mid-Autumn Festival and Sunday

TEL. 02 2396 3186

中正區濟南路一段2之1號1-2樓
(臺大校友會館)

1-2F, 2-1, Section 1, Ji'nan Road, Zhongzheng

www.suhung.com.tw

■ 價錢 **PRICE**
午膳 Lunch
點菜 À la carte $ 400-800
晚膳 Dinner
點菜 À la carte $ 400-800

■ 營業時間 **OPENING HOURS**
午膳 Lunch 11:30-13:00
晚膳 Dinner 17:30-20:00

蘇杭 (中正)
SU HUNG (ZHONGZHENG)

江浙菜・舒適

Jiangzhe • Cosy

供應江浙菜及上海點心的蘇杭擁四家餐廳,而位於濟南路的為總店。東坡肉是人氣菜色,五花肉以金蘭醬油做的滷汁燜上六至八小時,酥而不爛,濃郁入味。除此之外,杭州老鴨煲、花雕黃魚等亦是廚師拿手之作。點心方面,絲瓜蝦仁湯包和蔥油餅也甚得顧客歡心,不妨一試。

This bustling place is the flagship of a four-shop chain serving Jiangzhe and Shanghainese cuisine. What it lacks in ambience, it makes up with its food. Their famous dongpo pork is braised in Taiwanese soy sauce for 6 to 8 hours until flavoursome and tender. Other signature dishes include Hangzhou duck pot, braised fish head, and drunken yellow croaker. Try also their xiao long bao with shrimp and angled luffa filling, and green onion flatbread.

台南担仔麵

TAINAN TAN TSU MIEN SEAFOOD

海鮮・典雅

Seafood • Elegant

別因店名以為這是吃擔仔麵的小店，這可是高檔臺式海鮮餐廳的始祖。顧客可在瑰麗的水晶燈下，使用歐洲名貴餐具享用一頓高雅舒適的海鮮饗宴。熱門的清蒸龍蝦選用基隆野生珠龍蝦，僅以少許淡味醬油提味，完美呈現出臺式海鮮的「清、淡、鮮」好滋味。小巧的擔仔麵、五味九孔與蟹黃焗白菜也不容錯過，冬季莫忘細啖烏魚子。

It feels somewhat surreal in a bustling market to suddenly find yourself in a baroque-style palatial dining room, dotted by European tableware. However, the seafood is cooked in an unmistakably Taiwanese way. Try their steamed wild-caught lobster seasoned with a dash of soy. Blanched abalone in five-flavour sauce is extremely tender and aromatic, while baked Chinese cabbage with crab roe bursts with seafood flavours. Finish off with their signature danzai noodles.

TEL. 02 2308 1123
萬華區華西街31之1號
31-1 Huaxi Street, Wanhua
www.seafoodtaipei.com.tw

■ 價錢 **PRICE**
午膳 Lunch
套餐 Set Menu $ 2,200-5,100
點菜 À la carte $ 1,200-1,500
晚膳 Dinner
套餐 Set Menu $ 2,200-5,100
點菜 À la carte $ 2,000-2,500

■ 營業時間 **OPENING HOURS**
午膳 Lunch 11:30-13:30
晚膳 Dinner 15:30-21:00

■ 休息日期 **ANNUAL AND WEEKLY CLOSING**
初一休息
Closed first day of CNY

辰園
THE DRAGON

粵菜 · 時尚

Cantonese • Contemporary Décor

TEL. 02 2321 1818

中正區忠孝東路一段12號B1
(喜來登大飯店)

B1, Sheraton Grand Hotel, 12, Section 1, Zhongxiao East Road, Zhongzheng

www.sheratongrandtaipei.com

■ 價錢 **PRICE**

午膳 Lunch
套餐 Set Menu $ 1,980-3,380
點菜 À la carte $ 1,200-2,800
晚膳 Dinner
套餐 Set Menu $ 1,980-3,380
點菜 À la carte $ 1,200-2,800

■ 營業時間 **OPENING HOURS**

午膳 Lunch 11:30-14:00
晚膳 Dinner 18:00-21:00

選址地下一樓無減餐廳的吸引力，深棕色木屏風配以同色系的牆身，拼合出帶中國色彩的餐室，傳統中不失時尚，寬敞的環境加上舒適的靠背椅更適合宴客和商務聚餐。菜色由多位擅長廣東菜的廚師負責，叫好之作眾多，包括須預訂的脆皮先知鴨、限量供應的廣式片皮鴨、脆皮叉燒和金瑤炒龍筋，難怪總是座無虛席。

Pre-booking is recommended at this spacious restaurant boasting a contemporary décor, with Chinese details, tan wood finishes and comfy chairs, which add to the feeling of serenity. The kitchen is run by experienced chefs specialising in Cantonese cuisine. Signature dishes include stir-fried pork tendons in XO sauce, crispy barbecued pork, roasted baby duck (pre-order needed) and Cantonese-style Peking duck (in strictly limited quantities).

鈺善閣
YU SHAN GE

素食 · 舒適

Vegetarian • Cosy

鈺善閣經營逾十五年，提倡五感合一與平衡，店內以自然景物營造出具禪意美感的空間。餐廳提供素食懷石料理，每道菜均以花材裝飾，擺盤猶如藝術品；強調不過度烹調與調味，蔬食的原始風味得以呈現。不要錯過胡汁猴排，以黑胡椒醬燉煮過的猴頭菇，多汁而具彈性。設有含九道菜的個人套餐，推薦「鈺善」及「鈺鼎」套宴。

For over 15 years, this vegetarian restaurant has been enchanting customers with dishes that satisfy all five senses and echo with the Zen-inspired décor. There are several nine-course prix fixe menus to choose from, all crafted in a Japanese kaiseki style that emphasises artistic plating. Natural flavours are accentuated with minimal seasoning and cooking. Monkey head mushrooms in black pepper sauce is a standout dish with its meat-like texture and juiciness.

TEL. 02 2394 5155

中正區北平東路14號

14 Beiping East Road, Zhongzheng

www.yu-shan-ge.com.tw

■ 價錢 **PRICE**

午膳 Lunch
套餐 Set Menu $ 698-4,998
點菜 À la carte $ 1,500-2,000
晚膳 Dinner
套餐 Set Menu $ 1,298-4,998
點菜 À la carte $ 1,500-2,000

■ 營業時間 **OPENING HOURS**

午膳 Lunch 11:30-13:30
晚膳 Dinner 17:30-20:00

萬華區 WANHUA
中正區 ZHONGZHENG

夜市
NIGHT MARKETS

公館夜市 Gongguan

位於臺北市南區的主要道路之間，交通方便；且鄰近多家高上學府，各種小吃和零售店深受學生及觀光客歡迎。

Located between the streets of Taipei and the university district, this market consists of many snack and retail stalls.

雄記蔥抓餅 HSIUNG CHI SCALLION PANCAKE

蔥抓餅餅皮外脆內嫩，搭配特製的蜂蜜芥末醬和九層塔，香味四溢，毫不油膩。

Crispy on the outside, soft on the inside, the pancake matches perfectly with the honey mustard and basil.

中正區羅斯福路四段108巷2號

2, Lane 108, Section 4, Luosifu Road, Zhongzheng

價錢 **PRICE:** $ 25-65

營業時間 **OPENING HOURS:** 16:30-00:30

週三休息 **Closed Wednesday**

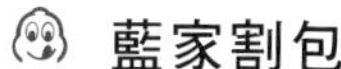

藍家割包 LAN CHIA GUABAO

夾著花生粉、香菜、酸菜與滷肉的割包口感鬆軟，味道具層次，更可自選滷肉的肥瘦度。

Buns stuffed with ground peanuts, coriander, pickles and braised pork build layers of textures and flavours.

中正區羅斯福路三段316巷8弄3號

3, Alley 8, Lane 316, Section 3, Luosifu Road, Zhongzheng

價錢 **PRICE:** $ 55-175

營業時間 **OPENING HOURS:** 11:00-00:00

週一休息 **Closed Monday**

華西街夜市 Huaxi Street

臺灣首座觀光夜市，牌樓建築與紅色宮燈富傳統特色。昔日以殺蛇表演聞名，現多轉型為蛇料理。兩旁店家皆為老字號，深受遊客歡迎。

This was the first night market to open in Taiwan. It has a traditional feel and the decades-old shops make it popular with tourists.

昶鴻麵點 N
CHANG HUNG NOODLES

開業近半世紀，以招牌湯麵及古早風味的菊花肉麵最受歡迎。小菜中，白斬土雞及豬尾巴為熱門之選。

For almost 50 years, regulars have been coming for its pork cheek noodle soup, boiled chicken and pork tail.

萬華區華西街15號171號攤
Stall 171, 15 Huaxi Street, Wanhua
價錢 **PRICE:** $ 100-200
營業時間 **OPENING HOURS:** 12:00-20:00

小王煮瓜
WANG'S BROTH

有「黑金」之稱的滷肉飯入口黏稠，甜而不膩。清湯瓜仔肉湯頭清香回甘，肉塊更保有嚼勁。

As well as minced pork and pickled cucumber in broth, try their steamed rice with 'black gold' pork sauce.

萬華區華西街17之4號153號攤
Stall 153, 17-4 Huaxi Street, Wanhua
價錢 **PRICE:** $ 100-200
營業時間 **OPENING HOURS:** 09:00-20:00

源芳刈包 N
YUAN FANG GUABAO

經營逾一甲子，刈包皮為店家特製，搭配軟嫩多汁的滷五花肉和配料，令人回味再三。四神湯也濃郁鮮美。

An over-60-year-old shop selling buns stuffed with marinated pork belly, pickles, ground peanuts and coriander.

萬華區華西街17之2號161號攤
Stall 161, 17-2 Huaxi Street, Wanhua
價錢 **PRICE:** $ 45-100
營業時間 **OPENING HOURS:** 12:00-22:00
週一休息 **Closed Monday**

南機場夜市 Nanjichang

曾為機場，後被改建並發展成夜市。雖名夜市但全日皆有攤檔，且大都是屹立數十年的老字號，以食店居多。

Originally an airport, it was converted into a park and then a night market later on. Despite its name, stalls tend to also open in the morning and afternoon.

臭老闆 現蒸臭豆腐
STINKY TOFU BOSS

適合素食者。軟嫩的臭豆腐散發著淡淡九層塔香氣，可謂一大享受。

Silky and porous, the vegan stinky tofu is steamed to order with mushrooms and basil adding extra aroma.

中正區中華路二段313巷6號

6, Lane 313, Section 2, Zhonghua Road, Zhongzheng

價錢 **PRICE:** $ 70-150

營業時間 **OPENING HOURS:** 11:30-22:30

週三休息 **Closed Wednesday**

無名推車燒餅
UNNAMED CLAY OVEN ROLL

沒有招牌的推車停駐夜市尾段，常常人龍不斷。販售四款古早味餅食，推薦甜酥餅與長燒餅。

This push cart near the end of the market always attracts a queue. Try their sweet pastry and long shaobing.

中正區中華路二段311巷

Lane 311, Section 2, Zhonghua Road, Zhongzheng

價錢 **PRICE:** $ 12-15

營業時間 **OPENING HOURS:** 16:00-20:00

週三休息 **Closed Wednesday**

吾旺再季 Ⓝ

WU WANG TSAI CHI

松青潤餅易名後搬至巷弄之內，繼續提供包著紅燒肉、素排骨酥等餡料的潤餅，滋味依然。

Rechristened and moved into an alley, but expect the same tasty popiah roll with 10 different fillings that are packed with layered flavours.

中正區中華路二段313巷29號

29, Lane 313, Section 2, Zhonghua Road, Zhongzheng

價錢 **PRICE:** $ 50

營業時間 **OPENING HOURS:** 15:30-21:30

除夕至初五及週一休息

Closed CNY eve to fifth day of CNY and Monday

阿男麻油雞

A NAN SESAME OIL CHICKEN

提供四季合宜的養生麻油雞，現場可以添湯；雞腿七時多便售罄，宜早點抵達免撲空。

It serves revitalising sesame oil chicken soup all year round. Come early as chicken legs often run out by 7 pm.

中正區中華路二段311巷34號

34, Lane 311, Section 2, Zhonghua Road, Zhongzheng

價錢 **PRICE:** $ 70-150

營業時間 **OPENING HOURS:** 17:00-22:00

除夕至初五及週一休息

Closed CNY eve to fifth day of CNY and Monday

玉米家烤玉米

CORN HOUSE GRILLED CORN

選用雲林小農生產的玉米，配以店家調配的粉料烤製，有原味、新孜然及地獄勁辣三種口味。

Sweet corn from Yunlin city is grilled and coated in spice mix - choose between original, cumin or fiery hot.

中正區中華路二段311巷

Lane 311, Section 2, Zhonghua Road, Zhongzheng

價錢 **PRICE:** $ 60-90

營業時間 **OPENING HOURS:** 18:00-23:30

南機場夜市
Nanjichang

山內雞肉
SHAN-NEI CHICKEN

皮爽肉嫩，份量頗多，十分超值。關門時間不定，若要點選雞腿，建議八時前到達。

Good-value steamed chicken is feted for its springy skin and juicy flesh. Come before 8 pm for chicken legs.

中正區中華路二段307巷20之3號

20-3, Lane 307, Section 2, Zhonghua Road, Zhongzheng

價錢 **PRICE:** $ 70-150

營業時間 **OPENING HOURS:** 11:00-20:00

週六休息 **Closed Saturday**

caoyu36/iStock

酒店
HOTELS

喜來登
SHERATON GRAND

商務・現代

Business • Modern

商務旅程重視的一環是交通便利，鄰近臺北車站的喜來登大飯店滿足了此要求。酒店空間開揚現代，共占十三層的房間亦整潔舒適。入住首席客房可享有更大空間，行政套房則提供管家服務及可享用特設貴賓廳。酒店內各家餐廳包羅自助餐、牛排屋、中菜、泰菜等菜餚。

Conveniently located close to the main station, this hotel is aimed primarily at business travellers. Public areas are spacious and modern, while rooms are spotless and cosy. Opt for a Premier room for more space, or an Executive room for butler service and exclusive access to the lounge. Restaurants offer a wide selection of dining options: buffet, steak, Chinese and Thai.

TEL. 02 2321 5511
www.sheratongrandtaipei.com

中正區忠孝東路一段12號
12, Section 1, Zhongxiao East Road, Zhongzheng

640 客房/Rooms $ 12,000-14,000
48 套房/Suites $ 22,000-198,000

餐廳推薦/Recommended restaurants:
辰園 The Dragon
請客樓 The Guest House

Tuomas_Lehtinen/iStock

松山區
南港區

SONGSHAN & NANGANG

松山區 **SONGSHAN**
南港區 **NANGANG**

餐廳 RESTAURANTS

雅閣
YA GE

粵菜・經典

Cantonese • Classic Décor

穿過置滿中式古董擺設的小長廊，方正的空間飾以華麗布藝和木屏風，格調典雅，大型吊燈吸引眾人目光。厚甸甸的菜單上羅列多款經典粵菜，傳統中又不失主廚個人風格，不少更是桌邊烹調。海鮮種類繁多，例如阿拉斯加蟹、澎湖龍蝦等，秋季時分還設有大閘蟹菜單。推薦脆皮雞及蔥燒遼參。

A narrow corridor with Asian antiques leads to this square-shaped and classically-styled Cantonese restaurant on the 3rd floor of the Mandarin Oriental. Semi-private booths on the sides and at the back are the ones to go for. The vast choice includes various set menus (such as hairy crab when in season) and an array of Cantonese classics, some with a personal twist added by the experienced chef. Service is efficient and formal.

TEL. 02 2715 6788

松山區敦化北路158號3樓
(文華東方酒店)

3F, Mandarin Oriental Hotel, 158 Dunhua North Road, Songshan

www.mandarinoriental.com/taipei

■ 價錢 **PRICE**

午膳 Lunch
套餐 Set Menu $ 1,580-8,800
點菜 À la carte $ 1,200-3,500
晚膳 Dinner
套餐 Set Menu $ 3,980-8,800
點菜 À la carte $ 2,000-3,500

■ 營業時間 **OPENING HOURS**

午膳 Lunch 12:00-14:30
晚膳 Dinner 18:00-22:00

TEL. 02 8712 6689

松山區南京東路四段61號

61, Section 4, Nanjing East Raod, Songshan

www.dianshuilou.com.tw

■ 價錢 **PRICE**

午膳 Lunch
套餐 Set Menu $ 1,380
點菜 À la carte $ 600-800
晚膳 Dinner
套餐 Set Menu $ 1,380
點菜 À la carte $ 600-800

■ 營業時間 **OPENING HOURS**

午膳 Lunch 11:00-14:00
晚膳 Dinner 17:30-21:00

點水樓 (松山)

DIAN SHUI LOU (SONGSHAN)

江浙菜・傳統

Jiangzhe • Traditional

小橋流水、木雕窗花、骨董藝品為餐廳添了古色古香的江南韻味。命名為點水樓，乃因餐廳對自家茶水點心引以為傲，事實上，除了江南美點水準上乘，其江浙名菜亦甚得饕客青睞，西湖醋魚、點水烤方等招牌菜多得不勝枚舉。廚師大量採用在地食材，並按季節設計時令菜色。菜餚更設大、中、小盤份量，甚為周到。

Diners are greeted with sumptuous modern Chinese furnishings and antique art pieces; the bridges, water features, carved screens and lanterns are reminiscent of a traditional Chinese garden. Ingredients are mostly from Taiwan and the kitchen specialises in Jiangsu, Shanghai and Zhejiang cuisines; the menu changes seasonally to include the freshest produce. Must-try items include Xihu fish in sweet vinegar glaze, and braised pork.

欣葉小聚今品 (南港)
SHIN YEH SHIAO JU (NANGANG)

臺灣菜・舒適

Taiwanese • Cosy

欣葉名下專攻小家庭的品牌，菜餚專為二至四人小型聚會而設，並迎合健康飲食潮流，調味上較少油和鹽，且提供多樣蔬食料理。菜單上除了有菜脯蛋、紅蟳米糕等傳統臺菜，也有融入創意的新菜色，如以糯米椒炒皮蛋的青龍皮皮挫。高聳的天花，配合整片落地窗讓陽光灑落，視野遼闊且典雅溫馨。

A sister concept spun off from the household brand, it caters to small groups and families with a menu designed for sharing, and champions low-fat and low-sodium Taiwanese cooking. Signatures such as stir-fried thousand-year eggs with green chillies, and omelette with angled luffa and dried scallops are original recipes not found elsewhere. The airy and elegant space is bathed in daylight and adorned with wood and neutral greys.

TEL. 02 2785 1819

南港區經貿二路166號
(中國信託金融園區A棟)

166 Jingmao 2nd Road, Nangang

www.shinyeh.com.tw

■ 價錢 **PRICE**

午膳 Lunch
點菜 À la carte $ 500-700
晚膳 Dinner
點菜 À la carte $ 500-700

■ 營業時間 **OPENING HOURS**

午膳 Lunch 11:00-14:20
晚膳 Dinner 17:00-20:50

北平陶然亭
TAO LUAN TING ROAST PEKING DUCK PALACE

京菜・溫馨

Beijing Cuisine • Family

TEL. 02 2778 7805

松山區復興北路86號2樓

2F, 86 Fuxing North Road, Songshan

■ 價錢 **PRICE**

午膳 Lunch
點菜 À la carte $ 500-1,000
晚膳 Dinner
點菜 À la carte $ 500-1,000

■ 營業時間 **OPENING HOURS**

午膳 Lunch 11:00-14:00
晚膳 Dinner 17:00-21:00

■ 休息日期 **ANNUAL AND WEEKLY CLOSING**

除夕至初四休息
Closed CNY eve to fourth day of CNY

經營半世紀，陶然亭堅持製作傳統而富自家特色的烤鴨，採用來自宜蘭、不施打抗生素的紅面番鴨，這種鴨較櫻桃鴨多養一百天，肉質肥嫩。每日送抵的鴨會風乾一天才送入專用炭爐燻烤，皮薄香脆，除了配以鮮擀餅皮享用，更可一鴨多吃。烤鴨以外，現包現煎的蘿蔔絲餅飽滿多汁，值得一試。

The third-generation owner still makes Peking duck the way his grandpa did over 50 years ago. Antibiotic-free Muscovy ducks from Yilan County are kept 100 days more than their counterparts for extra fattiness. Delivered daily and air-dried for a day to crisp up the skin before roasting in a wood oven, each duck is carved into 36 pieces and served with flatbread. Don't miss the made-to-order pan-fried shredded radish dumplings with a soupy filling.

醉楓園小館

TSUI FENG YUAN

粵菜·簡樸

Cantonese • Simple

彭主廚一直遵從叔公的料理配方，雖然與彭家園的廚師師承同一人，大家的手法還是大相逕庭。其芋泥香酥鴨、瓊山豆腐特別出色。冬季記得一試羊腩火鍋或魚頭火鍋，前者以澳洲草羊、甘蔗頭、老薑和南乳熬煮；後者強調原汁原味，與坊間用沙茶醬的做法有別。服務生訓練有素，且記住客人喜好。假期前後特別繁忙，建議訂位。

At this sister restaurant to Peng Family, the chef insists on cooking Cantonese food exactly the way his great uncle did. Lamb belly hot pot is a winter speciality made with Australian lamb, red bean curd, sugarcane and ginger. Equally popular is crispy duck stuffed with mashed taro, steamed egg white custard with scallops and fish head hot pot. Service is friendly and warm and reservations are recommended on holidays.

TEL. 02 2577 9528

松山區八德路三段8巷5號

5, Lane 8, Section 3, Bade Road, Songshan

■ 價錢 **PRICE**

午膳 Lunch
點菜 À la carte $ 300-400
晚膳 Dinner
點菜 À la carte $ 400-500

■ 營業時間 **OPENING HOURS**

午膳 Lunch 11:30-13:20
晚膳 Dinner 17:30-20:00

TEL. 02 2715 6868

松山區敦化北路158號6樓
(文華東方酒店)

6F, Mandarin Oriental Hotel, 158 Dunhua North Road, Songshan

www.mandarinoriental.com/taipei

■ 價錢 **PRICE**
午膳 Lunch
套餐 Set Menu $ 1,280-1,680
點菜 À la carte $ 2,400-3,800
晚膳 Dinner
套餐 Set Menu $ 1,980-2,380
點菜 À la carte $ 2,400-3,800

■ 營業時間 **OPENING HOURS**
午膳 Lunch 12:00-14:30
晚膳 Dinner 17:30-22:00

■ 休息日期 **ANNUAL AND WEEKLY CLOSING**
週一休息
Closed Monday

BENCOTTO

義大利菜 · 新潮

Italian • Chic

於義大利成長的主廚經驗豐富，不僅採用義式料理手法，更重視食材的品質，約八成食材均選自臺灣。培根帕瑪森乳酪蛋黃麵餃和綜合香料烤鴿肉都是招牌菜色；經長時間發酵的自家製麵包也不容錯過。超過四百款的餐酒中不乏義國珍釀，可請侍酒師或經理為你作出最佳搭配。

The Tuscan chef, with over 10 years of experience, took over in 2018. His menu showcases a farm-to-table concept, accentuating the natural flavours of organic produce, most of which is sourced locally. The tasting menu changes four times a year to reflect seasonality. The house-made long-fermented bread is a must, while signatures like ravioli alla carbonara and piccione Toscano are well matched by over 400 labels of mostly Italian wines.

50/50 CUISINE FRANÇAISE

時尚法國菜・時尚

French Contemporary •
Contemporary Décor

簡約淨雅的門楣，在寧靜的住宅區特別引人注目，而室內裝潢同樣時尚，深淺不一的木紋條拼湊成的牆面和大理石地板使餐廳有著輕鬆氣氛。餐廳名字傳達了廚師的理念——傳統與創新各占一半。食材一半取自臺灣，其餘則選自法國及其他地區。招牌菜包括羊肚菌菇麵捲及製作需時兩天的龍蝦濃湯。

The sleek and minimalistic shop front stands out in this quiet residential community and is matched by the equally chic interior, with its multi-coloured wood panelling and white marbled floor. Its name reflects its culinary philosophy - half traditional and half creative. The good-value 7-course menu offers a choice of dishes and showcases the chef's ambition. Try their morel mushroom cannelloni and lobster bisque.

TEL. 02 2765 3727
松山區富錦街448號
448 Fujin Street, Songshan

■ 價錢 PRICE
午膳 Lunch
套餐 Set Menu $ 1,480
晚膳 Dinner
套餐 Set Menu $ 2,200-3,700

■ 營業時間 OPENING HOURS
午膳 Lunch 12:00-13:30
晚膳 Dinner 18:00-20:00

■ 休息日期 ANNUAL AND WEEKLY CLOSING
週三至週四午膳、週一及週二休息
Closed Wednesday to Thursday lunch, Monday and Tuesday

先進海產店
HSIEN CHIN SEAFOOD

海鮮・友善

Seafood • Friendly

來自基隆的新鮮海產陳列於門前小冰櫃中，顧客挑選食材後，服務人員會建議料理方式。推薦店家的改良版蚵嗲，取大香菇放上東石鮮蚵、肉末和韭菜末，再抹上麵糊油炸，外酥內嫩且多汁。香烤紅喉魚也不俗，簡單的碳烤方式突顯了魚的鮮甜和油脂。海產以外，嫩煎豬肝為必點菜餚。菜色口味偏重，但能應需求調整。

The owner himself shops daily for the freshest seafood in Keelung. Simply pick your favourite from the fridge and servers will recommend the best cooking method. Chargrilled rosy seabass seduces with its lush oily flesh and natural umami, while oyster fritters with ground pork and mushrooms are crispy on the outside and juicy on the inside. Other signatures include steamed leopard coral grouper, and pan-fried pork liver.

TEL. 02 2578 4397

松山區延吉街23巷5號

5, Lane 23, Yanji Street, Songshan

■ 價錢 **PRICE**

晚膳 Dinner
點菜 À la carte $ 600-800

■ 營業時間 **OPENING HOURS**

晚膳 Dinner 17:30-00:30

■ 休息日期 **ANNUAL AND WEEKLY CLOSING**

除夕至初五及週一休息
Closed CNY eve to fifth day of CNY and Monday

老乾杯 (松山)
KANPAI CLASSIC (SONGSHAN)

燒烤 · 舒適

Barbecue • Cosy

乾杯集團的分店均不離三大特色：選用頂級日本和牛、供應獨家代理的日本吟釀酒滿壽泉、採用北海道七星米製作釜飯。其和牛從日本整頭進口，再切割成小份送達各店。服務人員對牛肉瞭若指掌，且都通過燒烤技巧考核，確保能將牛肉烹調至最佳狀態。此店燈光布置巧妙，別具氣氛，吧檯位置則可近距離觀賞燒烤過程。

Like others in the chain, the menu here features premium Wagyu beef, exclusive Ginjo sake rice wine, and Nanatsuboshi rice from Hokkaido cooked in a kama pot. Whole cows are imported from Japan and butchered into more than 30 different cuts before being shipped to the various branches, where servers are trained to grill the meat meticulously. This moodily lit branch has counter seats where diners can watch the transformation on their own grill at close range.

TEL. 02 2713 9000

松山區慶城街29號

29 Qingcheng Street, Songshan

www.kanpaiclassic.com.tw

■ 價錢 **PRICE**

午膳 Lunch
套餐 Set Menu $ 580-980
點菜 À la carte $ 900-1,000
晚膳 Dinner
點菜 À la carte $ 1,500-2,000

■ 營業時間 **OPENING HOURS**

午膳 Lunch 11:30-14:00
晚膳 Dinner 17:00-22:30

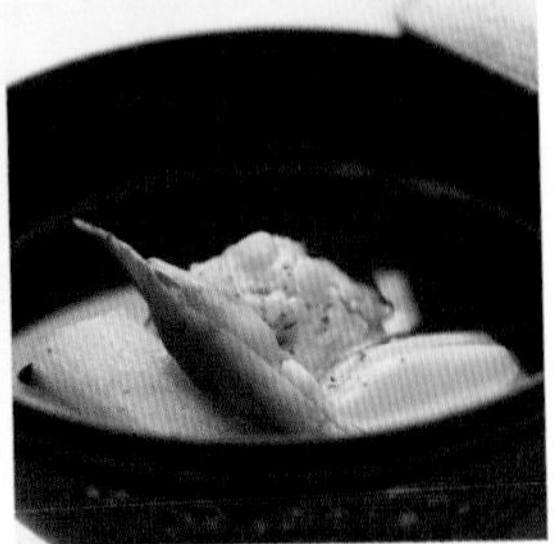

TEL. 02 2718 1188

松山區民生東路三段111號B1
(西華飯店)

B1, Sherwood Hotel, 111, Section 3, Minsheng East Road, Songshan

www.sherwood.com.tw

■ 價錢 **PRICE**

午膳 Lunch
套餐 Set Menu $ 2,000-2,500
點菜 À la carte $ 2,000-5,000
晚膳 Dinner
套餐 Set Menu $ 3,000-4,000
點菜 À la carte $ 3,000-6,000

■ 營業時間 **OPENING HOURS**

午膳 Lunch 12:00-14:00
晚膳 Dinner 18:00-21:00

■ 休息日期 **ANNUAL AND WEEKLY CLOSING**

除夕至初三及週日休息
Closed CNY eve to third day of CNY and Sunday

小馬
KOUMA

日本菜・時尚

Japanese • Contemporary Décor

饕客對小馬趨之若鶩，其聞名遐邇的顧問廚師固然是其中一個原因，而叫人去而復返，則全因那優質上乘的在地食材、一絲不苟的處理和傳統道地的日本風味。四款餐單中有一半以和牛為主食材。只得七個座位和少量包廂，細小的規模確保服務細緻周到。供佐餐的清酒和葡萄酒選擇不俗。

An intimate restaurant with 7 counter seats and several private rooms, it sources the best ingredients from around Taiwan with a few imported from Japan. Two of the fixed price menus feature Wagyu beef, in a hot pot or fried, while the other two are skewed towards sushi and raw fish. Quality ingredients are mostly prepared in traditional ways, delivering authentic tastes. Service is excellent and the wine and sake lists extensive.

蘿莎娜小廚房
LA LOCANDA

義大利菜・友善

Italian • Friendly

餐廳只設三十多個座位，廚師從義大利或葡萄牙進口主要食材，並取用在地的蔬菜及魚料，各款麵包、義大利麵和義式冰淇淋均為手工製作。招牌菜包括燉煮章魚、義式香腸寬麵及碳烤美國豬排；用餐之餘不妨來一杯義國佳釀。菜單定期更換，主廚更可按需求設計不同的菜單，使用餐體驗更為獨特。

Apart from house-made bread, pasta and gelato, flexibility is also part of the appeal here – the chef is happy to make your favourite pasta even if it's not on the menu. Vegetables and fish from local markets, along with cheeses and olive oil from Europe, are put to use in signature items like slow-cooked octopus, or tagliatelle with mushrooms and sausage. The menu changes regularly and the exclusively Italian wine list is also worth checking out.

TEL. 02 2579 2922

松山區八德路三段12巷52弄18號

18, Alley 52, Lane 12, Section 3, Bade Road, Songshan

■ 價錢 **PRICE**

午膳 Lunch
套餐 Set Menu $ 350-600
點菜 À la carte $ 800-3,000
晚膳 Dinner
點菜 À la carte $ 800-3,000

■ 營業時間 **OPENING HOURS**

午膳 Lunch 11:30-14:00
晚膳 Dinner 17:30-21:00

■ 休息日期 **ANNUAL AND WEEKLY CLOSING**

農曆新年4天及週二休息
Closed 4 days CNY and Tuesday

L先生
MONSIEUR L

時尚法國菜・親密

French Contemporary • Intimate

TEL. 02 8770 5505

松山區民生東路四段131巷21號

21, Lane 131, Section 4, Minsheng East Road, Songshan

www.monsieur-l.com.tw

■ 價錢 PRICE

午膳 Lunch
套餐 Set Menu $ 880-1,380
晚膳 Dinner
套餐 Set Menu $ 1,880-2,680

■ 營業時間 OPENING HOURS

午膳 Lunch 11:30-13:30
晚膳 Dinner 18:00-20:30

■ 休息日期 ANNUAL AND WEEKLY CLOSING

除夕至初五及週二休息
Closed CNY eve to fifth day of CNY and Tuesday

選址綠意盎然的民生東路，予人舒適之感。L是東主的名字，他同時經營時尚的蘭餐廳，兩者相比，這兒的布置更顯古典。精煉的法式料理風格現代、賣相不凡，且融入日本元素。滋味豐富的晚間套餐含六道菜色，午餐時間人潮不斷，菜單選項更具彈性。開放式廚房讓你窺見廚師團隊大顯身手的過程。

This neighbourhood restaurant on a tree-lined street is furnished in a more classical style than its hip sister Orchid. Its accomplished French cuisine is flavoursome, well presented and modern in style while showing some Japanese influences. The 6-course dinner menu offers some choice, while the lunch menu is even more flexible and is when the restaurant is busiest. Diners can watch the chefs at work in the open kitchen.

PASTI TRATTORIA Ⓝ

義大利菜・溫馨

Italian • Family

店內裝潢出自主廚夫婦之手，牆上不乏義大利地圖及各種食材介紹，彰顯兩位對料理的熱愛。他們擅長利用新鮮食材，佐以橄欖油和香料，烹調出傳統義大利美食。所有海鮮均購自漁港，並根據時令頻繁地更換菜單。熱門菜色有阿瑪菲烤白帶魚捲煙燻起司、米蘭大象耳朵，以及老闆娘親手製作的西西里黃檸檬凍。

The chef couple have a passion for Italy and have covered every wall with photos and maps of their favourite country. Seafood is big on the menu which changes every couple of days to reflect availability. The no-frills food may not always be photogenic, but the quality and flavours more than make up for that. Try their grilled silverfish rolls stuffed with smoked cheese and pork scallopini. The zesty lemon jelly will transport you instantly to the Amalfi coast.

TEL. 02 2785 1588
南港區中南街30號
30 Zhongnan Street, Nangang
www.pastitrattoria.com

■ 價錢 PRICE
午膳 Lunch
點菜 À la carte $ 1,200-4,000
晚膳 Dinner
點菜 À la carte $ 1,200-4,000

■ 營業時間 OPENING HOURS
午膳 Lunch 12:00-12:30
晚膳 Dinner 18:00-19:30

■ 休息日期 ANNUAL AND WEEKLY CLOSING
除夕至初四、週二午膳、週一及週四休息
Closed CNY eve to fourth day of CNY, Tuesday lunch, Monday and Thursday

TEL. 02 2712 6828

松山區敦化北路166號5樓 (文華精品)

5F, THE ARCADE, 166 Dunhua North Road, Songshan

■ 價錢 **PRICE**

午膳 Lunch
套餐 Set Menu $ 9,800
晚膳 Dinner
套餐 Set Menu $ 9,800

■ 營業時間 **OPENING HOURS**

午膳 Lunch 12:00-12:30
晚膳 Dinner 18:00-20:30

■ 休息日期 **ANNUAL AND WEEKLY CLOSING**

新年3天及週一休息
Closed 3 days New Year and Monday

鮨增田 N

SUSHI MASUDA

壽司・新潮

Sushi • Chic

與東京鮨增田跨海合作，坐落文華精品五樓，環境幽靜。由東京料理長增田勵於日本採買食材，副主廚小杉秀樹則在此掌廚，提供單一價位、包含熱菜及壽司的無菜單料理。醋飯由兩種日本米及其米醋調製而成，來自青森縣的黑鮪魚赤肉細緻光滑，值得細味。食材均來自日本，故於當地新年及豐洲市場停市時休息。

Mosaic tiles, mirrors and a chandelier with hundreds of floating glass balls make this dining room hipper than most sushi spots. This joint venture by its Tokyo namesake and The Arcade is helmed by Chef Kosugi and supervised by Chef Masuda, the head chef at the Tokyo flagship who also sources ingredients for this outpost, mostly from Toyosu Market. Don't miss the maguro from Aomori prefecture with its silky texture and lovely sheen. Omakase only.

鮨翁 N

SUSHI WOU

壽司・簡約

Sushi • Minimalist

從歷史悠久的備前燒裝飾，到餐具擺設，都是料理長從日本帶回來的珍藏品，令這家壽司專門店更添韻味。料理長嚮往職人精神，故每年前往日本考察，並遵循傳統江戶前壽司風格，沒有花俏的陪襯食材，但處理手法細緻。推薦用昆布處理過的縞蝦，其肉質滑嫩，鮮味十足。另外，春子鯛、小鰭和穴子等也甚具水準。

This low-key sushi-ya boasts a spectacular collection of unglazed bizen ware. The head chef visits Japan regularly, both for inspiration and to bring home these exquisite pieces. He doesn't talk much behind the counter but instead stays highly focused on his actions. Besides fish commonly seen on Edomae sushi, such as kasugodai, kohada and anago, if you're lucky you may get to taste kombu-marinated Akashimamo shrimps – velvety and bursting with umami.

TEL. 0922 222 775
松山區敦化北路155巷110號
110, Lane 155, Dunhua North Road, Songshan

■ 價錢 **PRICE**
晚膳 Dinner
套餐 Set Menu $ 5,000

■ 營業時間 **OPENING HOURS**
晚膳 Dinner 18:30-19:30

■ 休息日期 **ANNUAL AND WEEKLY CLOSING**
除夕至初五及週日休息
Closed CNY eve to fifth day of CNY and Sunday

但馬家涮涮鍋 (本館)
TAJIMAYA SHABU SHABU

涮涮鍋 · 型格

Shabu-shabu • Design

TEL. 02 2712 1606

松山區敦化北路166號5樓 (文華精品)

5F, THE ARCADE, 166 Dunhua North Road, Songshan

■ 價錢 PRICE

午膳 Lunch
套餐 Set Menu $ 1,280-7,600
點菜 À la carte $ 1,300-4,000
晚膳 Dinner
套餐 Set Menu $ 1,280-7,600
點菜 À la carte $ 1,300-4,000

■ 營業時間 OPENING HOURS

午膳 Lunch 11:30-13:30
晚膳 Dinner 17:30-22:00

老闆認為吃火鍋是跟好友、家人相聚的親密時光，客人應好好享受用膳過程，不應費心處理食材，因此一切會由店員代為打點。食材方面，除了有在地蔬菜和海鮮，亦有多款日本蟹和不受時節所限的菲律賓花龍蝦等，牛肉更是直接從日本的但馬牛供應商取貨。客人更可點整條活魚分享，別忘了品嚐鮮甜味美的雜炊。

The owner believes hot pot dinner is the perfect occasion for diners to chat and have a good time. That's why the servers here cook the food for them so that they won't be distracted from their conversations. Apart from local seafood and veggies, he also imports Wagyu and Tajima beef directly from Japan to ensure the quality. If you feel like splurging a little, order a whole fish or a Filipino lobster to share.

日本橋玉井
TAMAI

日本菜 · 舒適

Japanese • Cosy

日本橋玉井主打以星鰻為主的料理，選用與臺灣一般使用品種不同的野生星鰻，且全由日本冷凍進口。餐廳製作的菜色主要分為滷煮及香烤兩大類，即作壽司之用或香烤。其中穴子西京燒是將鰻魚用京都味噌醃製至少一晚再作香烤，製作用心。穴子握壽司則是餐廳推薦菜色，另外烤起司穴子也值得一試。

The first branch outside Japan serves wild-caught anago (sea eel) in almost every possible way: simmered in sweet soy, grilled kabayaki-style, battered and deep-fried, rolled in egg omelette, or marinated in white miso before being grilled. The medium-sized lacquered box set includes both simmered and kabayaki eel with condiments such as green onion, wasabi, sesame, pepper and yuzu zest. Also try their anago nigiri sushi.

TEL. 02 2719 6660

松山區復興北路313巷23號

23, Lane 313, Fuxing North Road, Songshan

www.anago-tamai.com

■ 價錢 **PRICE**

午膳 Lunch
套餐 Set Menu $ 320-1,690
點菜 À la carte $ 700-1,300
晚膳 Dinner
套餐 Set Menu $ 390-1,690
點菜 À la carte $ 700-1,300

■ 營業時間 **OPENING HOURS**

午膳 Lunch 11:30-14:00
晚膳 Dinner 17:30-20:45

■ 休息日期 **ANNUAL AND WEEKLY CLOSING**

除夕至初三休息
Closed CNY eve to third day of CNY

TEL. 02 2719 6689

松山區敦化北路158號5樓 (文華精品)

5F, THE ARCADE, 158 Dunhua North Road, Songshan

www.thaiandthai.com.tw

■ 價錢 **PRICE**

午膳 Lunch
點菜 À la carte $ 900-2,000
晚膳 Dinner
點菜 À la carte $ 900-2,000

■ 營業時間 **OPENING HOURS**

午膳 Lunch 11:30-14:30
晚膳 Dinner 17:30-21:00

THAI & THAI

泰國菜 · 型格

Thai · Design

欲嚐傳統泰國菜，多數人會立時想起這家歷史悠久的餐廳。於2015年遷到文華精品現址，餐廳裝潢與所在商場同樣典雅高貴，佇立於餐室中央的雕像製作細緻精巧，令人不禁駐足欣賞。富經驗的泰籍廚師團隊料理的菜餚風味道地，滋味無窮。體貼周到的服務亦使人心滿意足。

Having served authentic Thai food in Taipei for many years, this restaurant re-opened in this elegant mall behind the Mandarin Oriental in 2015. It matches its surroundings by having a beautifully appointed interior complete with an impressive sculpture. The experienced Thai chef delivers what Thai food is renowned for on all fronts, alongside charming service.

VII-photo/iStock

松山區 **SONGSHAN**
南港區 **NANGANG**

夜市
NIGHT MARKETS

饒河街夜市
Raohe Street

於1987年開業，是首個由政府規劃的觀光夜市，全長只有六百米，攤位非常集中。各式小吃，以至百貨及傳統表演一應俱全。

Opened in 1987 and the first tourist night market managed by the government. The market isn't too big and the 600m street is easy to navigate.

阿國滷味
A KUO LU WEI

位處夜市入口，售賣各式滷味，其中鴨翅和脆腸大受歡迎，亦推薦爽脆清甜的玉米筍。

It sells a range of items braised in a spiced marinade. Try their duck wings, pork uterus and baby sweetcorn.

松山區饒河街226號
226 Raohe Street, Songshan
價錢 **PRICE:** $ 50-300
營業時間 **OPENING HOURS:** 17:00-00:00
週一休息 **Closed Monday**

紅燒牛肉麵牛雜湯
BEEF NOODLES AND BEEF ENTRAILS SOUP

店面欠牌匾，須認明牛頭圖樣。牛雜湯口感豐富。乾拌麵以肉燥搭配醬油膏，滋味讓人無法忘懷。

Look for the comic cow head on the unnamed cart. Beef offal soup and dry noodles with meat sauce are both good.

松山區饒河街63號
63 Raohe Street, Songshan
價錢 **PRICE:** $ 80-300
營業時間 **OPENING HOURS:** 17:00-00:00
週三休息 **Closed Wednesday**

饒河街夜市
Raohe Street

陳董藥燉排骨 Ⓝ
CHEN TUNG PORK RIBS MEDICINAL HERBS SOUP

屹立三十餘年，以豬肋骨及中藥材燉煮而成的湯頭呈琥珀色，清甜溫潤。喜愛滋補者可來一客藥燉羊肉。

Running for over 30 years, it's famous for pork ribs stewed in herbal stock. Lamb is recommended in winter.

松山區饒河街160號
160 Raohe Street, Songshan
價錢 **PRICE:** $ 80-120
營業時間 **OPENING HOURS:** 16:00-00:00

福州世祖胡椒餅
FUZHOU BLACK PEPPER BUN

胡椒餅現做現賣，皮薄香脆，餡料肉汁淋漓且充滿辛香胡椒味。極受歡迎，常見人龍。

Freshly made crusty buns burst with pork juices and pepperiness. Expect a queue.

松山區饒河街249號
249 Raohe Street, Songshan
價錢 **PRICE:** $ 55
營業時間 **OPENING HOURS:** 15:30-00:00

麻糬寶寶
MOCHI BABY

檔主帶著透明廚櫃在此經營十多年，所賣的小麻糬每天鮮做，口感軟糯且帶糯米香。

The transparent case houses gooey mocha – they're freshly made every day and have a strong sticky rice fragrance.

松山區饒河街111號前
111 Raohe Street, Songshan
價錢 **PRICE:** $ 30-60
營業時間 **OPENING HOURS:** 16:00-23:30

東發號
TUNG FA HAO

由顏老先生於1937年創立，繼承的女兒繼續以清湯烹煮蚵仔麵線，成品鮮甜甘美。

The second-generation owner makes tasty baby oyster vermicelli soup the same way as her father did when he started in 1937.

松山區饒河街94號

94 Raohe Street, Songshan

價錢 **PRICE:** $ 60-100

營業時間 **OPENING HOURS:** 08:30-00:00

松山區 SONGSHAN
南港區 NANGANG

酒店
HOTELS

文華東方
MANDARIN ORIENTAL

奢華・典雅

Grand Luxury • Elegant

坐落於商業中心地段，古雅的建築內蘊藏着1,700件藝術品，走進明亮的大理石大堂，等待客人的是優越的服務；尊貴高雅旅程所必需的應有盡有。房間內的吊燈明示著極致奢華的布置，精製皮革傢俱與手繪牆紙畫龍點睛。酒店內有六所餐廳，供客人在富麗的環境下享用多國菜色。附設的水療中心有極多樣化的療程服務供選用，在奢華環境中提供清新的體驗。

Its exclusive address, an exceptional level of service and the 1,700 art pieces on display match its classy architectural motifs. Rooms are luxuriously furnished with exquisite leather details and hand-painted wallpaper. Afternoon tea at the opulent Jade Lounge is an event in itself. Don't miss the tranquil spa with a myriad of treatments. Rooms on the 17th floor have the highest ceilings.

TEL. 02 2715 6888
www.mandarinoriental.com/taipei

松山區敦化北路158號
158 Dunhua North Road, Songshan

256 客房/**Rooms** $ 9,500-18,500
47 套房/**Suites** $ 22,500-31,500

餐廳推薦/**Recommended restaurants:**
雅閣 Ya Ge
Bencotto

S

精品酒店・型格

Boutique Hotel • Design

酒店名稱饒有深意，是以知名藝人的藝名冠名。風格逕走大膽破格精品酒店路線，並邀得法國設計師著手打造修飾。房間裝潢選用簡約主義，所有房型貫徹白色主調，明亮而具現代感；設開放式浴室，鏡子的置放亦增加了空間感。酒店設有供應歐陸菜餚的餐廳。

Anyone from a Chinese-speaking community should be familiar with the muse of this hotel – a renowned Taiwanese actress and singer. Owned by her husband, this bold and distinctive boutique hotel is styled by designer Philippe Starck. Rooms are minimalistic, with open-plan bathrooms and a white palette; mirrors add to the feeling of space.

TEL. 02 2712 1777
www.shotel.com

松山區敦化北路150號
150 Dunhua North Road, Songshan

103 客房/Rooms $ 6,000-8,000
2 套房/Suites $ 13,200-16,000

zhudifeng/iStock

J. Warburton Lee/hemis.fr

大安區

DA'AN

餐廳 RESTAURANTS

LOGY

時尚亞洲菜・*前衛*

Asian Contemporary • Trendy

承襲其東京姊妹店的裝潢風格，以混凝土灰黑色調搭配板前座位，予人沉穩且神秘之感。其無菜單套餐包含約十道菜，每兩個月更換一次。日籍主廚強調使用在地食材和亞洲元素，以日本料理手法呈現亞洲菜的多元風貌。例如拿手菜茶碗蒸，首次菜單融入了臺式風味，除了加入牛肉清湯，更以芹菜及當歸葉的冰沙提味。顧客必須於網路預約訂位。

Opened in 2018, this 13-seater restaurant is a spin-off from the celebrated Florilège in Tokyo. The dimly-lit concrete interior adds to the intriguing ambiance. On the menu, local ingredients are finessed by modern techniques and strong Asian influences. Egg custard in beef consommé with celery sorbet; and aiyu jelly, cocoa juice and nata de coco particularly stand out. The prix-fixe menu changes every two months. Online booking only.

TEL. N/A

大安區安和路一段109巷6號

6, Lane 109, Section 1, Anhe Road, Da'an

logy.tw

■ 價錢 **PRICE**

午膳 Lunch
套餐 Set Menu $ 3,750
晚膳 Dinner
套餐 Set Menu $ 3,750

■ 營業時間 **OPENING HOURS**

午膳 Lunch 12:00-12:30
晚膳 Dinner 18:00-19:30

■ 休息日期 **ANNUAL AND WEEKLY CLOSING**

週三午膳、週一及週二休息
Closed Wednesday lunch, Monday and Tuesday

TEL. 02 2775 1239

大安區仁愛路四段371號

371, Section 4, Ren'ai Road, Da'an

■ 價錢 **PRICE**

午膳 Lunch
套餐 Set Menu $ 3,000
晚膳 Dinner
套餐 Set Menu $ 5,000

■ 營業時間 **OPENING HOURS**

午膳 Lunch 12:00-15:00
晚膳 Dinner 18:00-22:00

■ 休息日期 **ANNUAL AND WEEKLY CLOSING**

元旦、除夕至初六、週二至週五午膳及週三休息
Closed New Year's Day, CNY eve to sixth day of CNY, Tuesday to Friday lunch and Wednesday

鮨天本
SUSHI AMAMOTO

壽司·簡約

Sushi · Minimalist

鮨天本位置略為隱蔽，卻為一眾老饕所認識。秉承傳統壽司店設計，板前座位由加拿大檜木所組成，僅能容納十二位客人。謙虛和善的料理長天本先生由九州進口漁獲，輔以來自豐洲市場的海鮮，並以長野的天然水按特定配方烹煮壽司米飯。無菜單料理套餐共二十道菜，其中包含約十二件時令手握壽司。

You have to book months in advance and it's not easy to find, but the food will be well worth the effort. The classically decorated sushi-ya has 12 seats at a solid cypress counter. The humble and friendly chef imports the seasonal fish mostly from Kyushu, and some from Tokyo, to be hand-pressed on sushi rice cooked in natural spring water from Nagano. There are 20 courses in the prix-fixe omakase menu, including 12 pieces of nigiri.

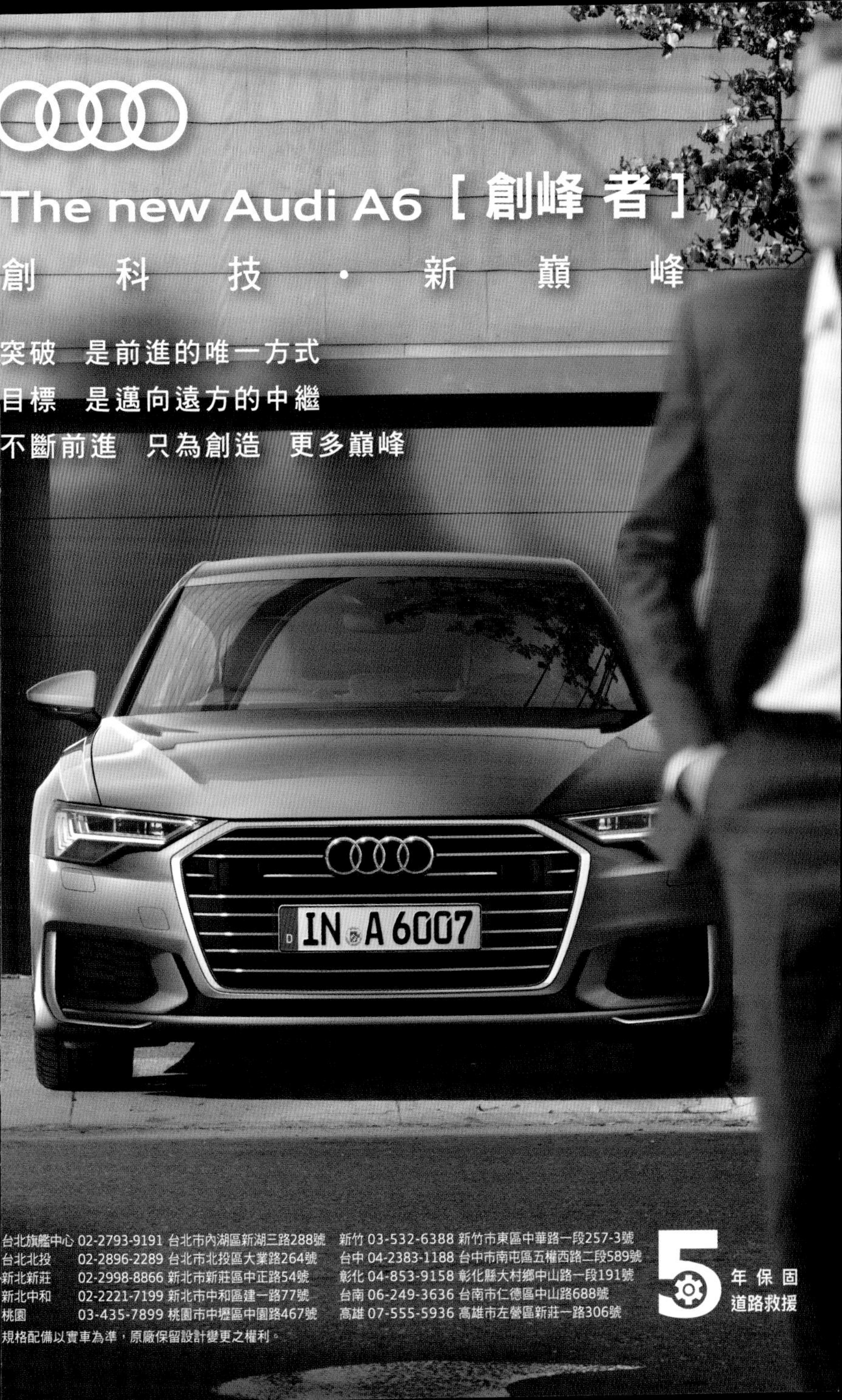

The new Audi A6 [創峰者]
創 科 技 · 新 巔 峰
突破 是前進的唯一方式
目標 是邁向遠方的中繼
不斷前進 只為創造 更多巔峰
IN A 6007
台北旗艦中心 02-2793-9191 台北市內湖區新湖三路288號
台北北投 02-2896-2289 台北市北投區大業路264號
新北新莊 02-2998-8866 新北市新莊區中正路54號
新北中和 02-2221-7199 新北市中和區建一路77號
桃園 03-435-7899 桃園市中壢區中園路467號
新竹 03-532-6388 新竹市東區中華路一段257-3號
台中 04-2383-1188 台中市南屯區五權西路二段589號
彰化 04-853-9158 彰化縣大村鄉中山路一段191號
台南 06-249-3636 台南市仁德區中山路688號
高雄 07-555-5936 高雄市左營區新莊一路306號
規格配備以實車為準，原廠保留設計變更之權利。
5 年保固 道路救援

大腕
DA-WAN

燒烤・友善

Barbecue • Friendly

曾於大阪工作的店東對牛肉部位的切割瞭如指掌，並挑選最優質的食材待客。牛肉九成為來自日本的A5級和牛，到店後進行熟成最少三星期，並由老闆定期培訓和考核的廚師團隊進行分割、修切、調味和燒烤。團隊更會每日嚴選限量供應的特定部位，設計成隱藏版菜單。

This is heaven for beef lovers – 21-day aged beef is trimmed, seasoned and grilled to your liking over Bincho charcoal right in front of your counter seat. The menu features mostly A5-grade Wagyu from Japan alongside a small Australian selection. The owner once worked in Osaka and knows his beef inside out. Ask about the secret menu of rare cuts handpicked daily by the chef. The enthusiastic servers and chefs deliver friendly, attentive service.

TEL. 02 2711 0179

大安區敦化南路一段177巷22號

22, Lane 177, Section 1, Dunhua South Road, Da'an

www.dawan.com.tw

■ 價錢 **PRICE**

晚膳 Dinner

點菜 À la carte $ 2,600-4,700

■ 營業時間 **OPENING HOURS**

晚膳 Dinner 18:00-23:00

■ 休息日期 **ANNUAL AND WEEKLY CLOSING**

除夕至初四休息

Closed CNY eve to fourth day of CNY

謙安和
KEN ANHE

日本菜·典雅

Japanese · Elegant

TEL. 02 2700 8128

大安區安和路一段127巷4號

4, Lane 127, Section 1, Anhe Road, Da'an

■ 價錢 **PRICE**

午膳 Lunch
套餐 Set Menu $ 4,500
晚膳 Dinner
套餐 Set Menu $ 6,800

■ 營業時間 **OPENING HOURS**

午膳 Lunch 12:00-14:30
晚膳 Dinner 18:00-22:00

■ 休息日期 **ANNUAL AND WEEKLY CLOSING**

農曆新年7天、週一及週日休息
Closed 7 days CNY, Monday and Sunday

謙安和中午供應以生食為主的手握壽司套餐，晚間則是割烹料理。不論哪種料理，不時不食是廚師和知軍雄的烹調宗旨，菜單根據時令食材和當日新鮮到店的魚類而定；昆布和柴魚高湯更是每日鮮煮。主廚亦強調食材與配料的味道融合，所以其以新潟米煮的壽司飯會與不同的醋作調和，以帶出不同食材的鮮味。

The Japanese chef is well known for his insistence on freshness and the skilful juxtaposition of different flavours. Only omakase menus are served and the exact items depend on the catch of the day. The menus feature prominently raw fish and nigiri sushi at lunch, while more cooked kappo dishes are served at night. Precise attention is paid to every detail, down to the blended vinegar in the sushi rice and the kelp bonito stock.

吉兆割烹壽司
KITCHO

壽司・簡約

Sushi • Minimalist

其名取自一日本燒酒名稱，由兩位熱愛壽司的臺灣主廚所經營。他們希望能讓臺灣人吃到媲美日本名店的上乘壽司，故裝潢亦秉承日本壽司店的簡樸，氣氛更為輕鬆。食物以生食及手握壽司為主，也會按客人需求提供熟食，只需於訂位時說明。由於兼營日本清酒代理，餐廳會按時令提供不同的清酒佐餐，亦會邀請日本廚師當客座主廚。

The interior follows Japanese tradition with pale wood, warm lighting and fabric-wrapped panels. Niigata rice is seasoned with three vinegars, including akazu that gives depth and umami. The owner also imports sake and the list changes constantly to match the seasonal ingredients available. This relaxed sushi spot also serves cooked dishes if pre-ordered. Note that it is not related in any way to its namesake in Tokyo.

TEL. 02 2771 1020

大安區忠孝東路四段181巷48號

48, Lane 181, Section 4, Zhongxiao East Road, Da'an

■ 價錢 **PRICE**

午膳 Lunch
套餐 Set Menu $ 3,500-7,000
晚膳 Dinner
套餐 Set Menu $ 4,500-7,000

■ 營業時間 **OPENING HOURS**

午膳 Lunch 12:00-13:30
晚膳 Dinner 18:00-20:40

■ 休息日期 **ANNUAL AND WEEKLY CLOSING**

除夕至初五及週日休息
Closed CNY eve to fifth day of CNY and Sunday

TEL. 02 2732 6616

大安區敦化南路二段174號

174, Section 2, Dunhua South Road, Da'an

www.longtail.com.tw

■ 價錢 **PRICE**

晚膳 Dinner
套餐 Set Menu $ 1,880-2,880
點菜 À la carte $ 1,400-2,800

■ 營業時間 **OPENING HOURS**

晚膳 Dinner 18:00-00:00

■ 休息日期 **ANNUAL AND WEEKLY CLOSING**

除夕至初四及週二休息
Closed CNY eve to fourth day of CNY and Tuesday

LONGTAIL

創新菜 · 前衛

Innovative · Trendy

在寫意而富格調的酒吧輕呷一口雞尾酒，是開始晚餐的絕佳方法。小酌一杯後，你可繼續在此用餐，或移師到主餐室，甚至廚房邊的榻榻米餐桌上。主廚選用在地或環球優質食材，菜色賣相不甚花巧，味道和質感卻呈現有趣的對比，精湛技巧毋庸置疑。海膽海苔脆飯、油封鴨肉餃及法式咖椰吐司都是巧手之作，服務人員更可為你配搭雞尾酒。

More ambitious than its sister Chou Chou, this is the brainchild of owner-chef Lam who spent years in some of the world's best kitchens. The menu changes every three months and features local seasonal produce alongside the finest ingredients from around the world. Specialities include uni on crispy rice, foie gras and duck confit dumpling, and Kaya French toast with espresso ice cream. Cocktail pairings are also available.

MUME

時尚歐陸菜・前衛

European Contemporary • Trendy

名稱在拉丁文解作梅花，像在呼應著餐盤上林林總總的花卉和香草。主廚精於北歐烹調技巧，兩個價位的套餐皆融合了在地時令食材和斑斕的花草，每道菜色都美豔如畫。餐廳門面低調而富型格，店內雖然燈光暗淡，用餐氣氛卻輕鬆友善。不妨搭配一杯帶有臺灣風味的雞尾酒佐餐。

In line with its name (the Latin word for 'plum blossom'), the relaxed and friendly MUME generously garnishes dishes with fresh herbs and flowers – in somewhat stark contrast to the dimly-lit faux-industrial interior of the restaurant itself. On the menu, Taiwanese ingredients are melded with Nordic influences and modern techniques are used effectively to create dishes that provide contrasts in tastes and textures.

TEL. 02 2700 0901

大安區四維路28號

28 Siwei Road, Da'an

www.mume.tw

■ 價錢 PRICE

晚膳 Dinner

套餐 Set Menu $ 2,680-3,880

■ 營業時間 OPENING HOURS

晚膳 Dinner 18:00-21:00

■ 休息日期 ANNUAL AND WEEKLY CLOSING

元旦休息

Closed New Year's Day

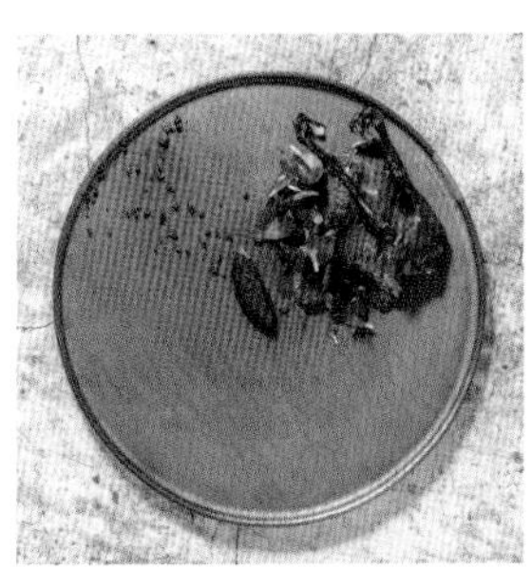

鮨野村
SUSHI NOMURA

壽司 · 簡約

Sushi • Minimalist

TEL. 02 2707 7518

大安區仁愛路四段300巷19弄4號

4, Alley 19, Lane 300, Section 4, Ren'ai Road, Da'an

■ 價錢 **PRICE**

午膳 Lunch
套餐 Set Menu $ 2,000-6,000
晚膳 Dinner
套餐 Set Menu $ 5,000-10,000

■ 營業時間 **OPENING HOURS**

午膳 Lunch 12:00-13:00
晚膳 Dinner 18:00-19:30

■ 休息日期 **ANNUAL AND WEEKLY CLOSING**

元旦、初一及週一休息
Closed New Year's Day, first day of CNY and Monday

來臺多年的大廚野村先生專司江戶前壽司，單是米飯已反映他的要求極高：為達滿意效果，採用來自四國水主町的有機越光米及北海道七星米，並以富士山泉水烹調，調味用上赤醋及白醋，以特別配方混合。他對魚生片的掌控和熟成度了解亦十分透徹，自家醃製的亮皮魚和星鰻值得細味。用餐區裝潢雖簡約，備前燒食具卻顯露了他對細節的講究。

Good sushi starts with the rice – here it's a mix of Koshihikari from Kakomachi and Nanatsuboshi from Hokkaido, cooked in Mount Fuji spring water and seasoned with a blend of akazu and regular sushi vinegar. Chef Nomura, who moved to Taiwan years ago, sets the bar high for every detail of the dining experience – the fish is aged properly and sliced skilfully. The marinated silver-skinned fish and the anago are not to be missed.

四川吳抄手 (大安)
CHILI HOUSE (DA'AN)

川菜・簡樸

Sichuan • Simple

以四川道地小吃吳抄手命名，每一道菜均顯露出老闆對家鄉的思念——麻辣鍋以六十多種中藥和香料熬製，溫和而不油膩；水煮牛及西柿酸魚以自家發酵的牛番茄入菜，酸中帶果香；紅油抄手以豬後腿肉和獨家配方的抄手皮製作。從小小的麵食店擴展至現今的菜館規模，足證其製作用心，菜色更會按季節更迭。

This aptly named Sichuan restaurant started out as a small noodle shop over 60 years ago. Its signature pork dumplings in red oil are made with pork hind shank wrapped in custom-made dumpling skins. Homemade fermented beefsteak tomatoes lend a fruity tanginess to Shuizhu beef and fish poached in sour tomato soup. Mala hotpot made with over 60 different Chinese herbs and spices is mild in taste without being greasy. The menu changes every season.

TEL. 02 2772 1707

大安區忠孝東路四段250之3號

250-3, Section 4, Zhongxiao East Road, Da'an

■ 價錢 **PRICE**

午膳 Lunch

點菜 À la carte $ 300-500

晚膳 Dinner

點菜 À la carte $ 500-1,000

■ 營業時間 **OPENING HOURS**

午膳 Lunch 11:30-14:15

晚膳 Dinner 17:30-21:15

■ 休息日期 **ANNUAL AND WEEKLY CLOSING**

除夕至初一休息

Closed CNY eve to first day of CNY

TEL. 02 2321 8928

大安區信義路二段194號

194, Section 2, Xinyi Road, Da'an

www.dintaifung.com.tw

■ 價錢 **PRICE**

點菜 À la carte $ 350-450

■ 營業時間 **OPENING HOURS**

11:00-21:00

■ 休息日期 **ANNUAL AND WEEKLY CLOSING**

除夕至初一休息

Closed CNY eve to first day of CNY

鼎泰豐 (信義路)

DIN TAI FUNG (XINYI ROAD)

滬菜 · 簡樸

Shanghainese · Simple

樓高四層的餐廳共設330個座位，由分別在一樓的點心廚房及四樓的料理廚房服務客人。提供餛飩、粽子及點心等滬式食品，其中小籠包和紅油抄手也是受歡迎之選。此店的部分菜色只在臺灣供應，例如只限此店和101店的泡菜。門外有禮盒發售，從糕點至調味料色色俱全。人客眾多，唯假日不接受訂位。

It's now a renowned international chain famous for its xiao long bao and authentic Shanghainese fare, but this 330-seater four-storey flagship is where the story began back in 1972. It offers exclusive dishes not available outside of Taiwan, such as pickled cabbage, porcini mushroom soup, stir-fried bird's nest fern, and noodles with minced oxtail sauce. Those running out of local notes can even pay with certain foreign currencies.

清真中國牛肉麵食館 (大安)
HALAL CHINESE BEEF NOODLES (DA'AN)

麵食 · 親切

Noodles • Neighbourhood

傲立超過六十年，其清燉牛肉麵遠近馳名，牛肉選用臺灣溫體牛，湯頭清香而帶濃重牛骨香味，秘訣是湯頭從不關火，年月將它變得濃而不膩。除牛肉麵，其現做的東北斤餅配炒牛肉絲也是招牌菜色。店家更販售自製牛肉乾，唯產量不多，若不致電預訂便得碰碰運氣。

For his restaurant with over 60 years of history, the owner insists on using only Taiwanese beef that has never been frozen for the best flavour and texture. The beef stock is simmered all day to develop deep flavours without any greasiness. Apart from their signature braised beef noodle soup, also try fried-to-order flatbread, which is stuffed with stir-fried shredded beef. The beef jerky is also good but is only available in strictly limited quantity.

TEL. 02 2721 4771

大安區延吉街137巷7弄1號

1, Alley 7, Lane 137, Yanji Street, Da'an

■ 價錢 **PRICE**

午膳 Lunch
點菜 À la carte $ 155-300
晚膳 Dinner
點菜 À la carte $ 155-300

■ 營業時間 **OPENING HOURS**

午膳 Lunch 11:30-14:00
晚膳 Dinner 17:00-20:30

■ 休息日期 **ANNUAL AND WEEKLY CLOSING**

除夕至初三休息
Closed CNY eve to third day of CNY

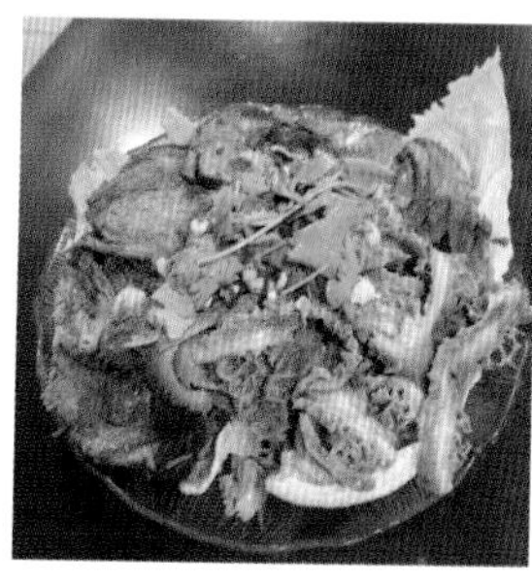

杭州小籠湯包 (大安)
HANG ZHOU XIAO LONG BAO (DA'AN)

點心・傳統

Dim Sum • Traditional

老闆黃氏兄弟與楊主廚師承上海師傅，主張販售樸實且真材實料的小籠包。招牌小籠湯包包皮僅以麵粉及水所做，不含添加物，每天現擀，並以新鮮豬後腿肉作餡，皮薄多汁而不油膩。豆沙鍋餅餅皮帶芝麻與餅皮酥香，內餡混合兩種豆沙，入口絲滑，也值得一試。餐廳採自助式服務，價格親民。

This popular soup dumpling shop was born over 20 years ago after its owners were taught how to make xiao long bao by a Shanghainese chef. Only the freshest pork hind leg cuts are used as the filling and the dumpling 'skin' is made simply with flour and water. Their soup-squirting dumplings are also known for their lightness. The red bean pancake uses two kinds of red beans in its silky filling which is complemented by a crisp sesame pastry crust.

TEL. 02 2393 1757

大安區杭州南路二段17及19號

17 & 19, Section 2, Hangzhou South Road, Da'an

www.thebestxiaolongbao.com

■ 價錢 **PRICE**

點菜 À la carte $ 350-600

■ 營業時間 **OPENING HOURS**

11:00-21:30

■ 休息日期 **ANNUAL AND WEEKLY CLOSING**

除夕至初六休息

Closed CNY eve to sixth day of CNY

好公道金雞園 (大安)
HAO KUNG TAO CHIN CHI YUAN (DA'AN)

滬菜 · 簡樸

Shanghainese • Simple

餐廳前一盤盤的點心和蒸籠是其標記。占地兩層的好公道裝潢簡單，樸實的桌椅無礙饕客興致。開業四十餘年一直提供上海小菜點心，各種菜品皆手工現做，其菜肉蒸餃皮薄多汁，內含剁碎的青江菜與豬肉餡，一口咬下香氣四溢，絕對不容錯過。此外，黃金十八摺小籠包、蟹黃小包與油豆腐細粉也值得品嚐。

Just look for the bamboo steamers stacked up high at the entrance to find this simple, two-storey shop. It isn't the ambiance that appeals to diners, it's the food – for over 40 years everything on the menu has been made by hand. Try their xiao long bao boasting 18 pleats on each bun, and their steamed pork and bok choy dumplings with wafer-thin skin and juicy fillings. Mung bean vermicelli soup with fried tofu and crab roe buns are also recommended.

TEL. 02 2341 6980

大安區永康街28之1號

28-1, Yongkang Street, Da'an

■ 價錢 **PRICE**

點菜 À la carte $ 100-150

■ 營業時間 **OPENING HOURS**

09:30-20:40

■ 休息日期 **ANNUAL AND WEEKLY CLOSING**

農曆新年5天及週三休息

Closed 5 days CNY and Wednesday

TEL. 02 2704 5152

大安區東豐街60號

60 Dongfeng Street, Da'an

■ 價錢 PRICE

午膳 Lunch
點菜 À la carte $ 300-500
晚膳 Dinner
點菜 À la carte $ 300-800

■ 營業時間 OPENING HOURS

午膳 Lunch 11:30-13:45
晚膳 Dinner 17:30-20:30

彭家園

PENG FAMILY

粵菜・溫馨

Cantonese • Family

規模不大的餐廳屬家族生意，紅地毯、水晶吊燈加上中式掛畫，是典型粵菜餐館格局，服務多年的店員令餐廳充溢親切感。來自香港的大廚兼店東扎根臺灣三十多年，致力為顧客帶來不賣弄花巧的傳統廣東味道。他對烹調的時間拿捏準確，尤其擅長清蒸海鮮菜色，此外，芋泥酥鴨、瓊山豆腐和螃蟹粉絲煲也是推薦之選。

The owner-chef moved to Taiwan from Hong Kong over 35 years ago to bring authentic Cantonese cooking to the island. The décor of his family-run restaurant may be rather old-school but the crystal ceiling lamps, red carpet and Chinese paintings are welcoming and familiar. Seafood dishes, such as silky egg white custard with scallops, fried crab with glass noodles in a clay pot, and steamed seafood, are particularly prized.

榮榮園

RONG RONG YUAN

浙江菜・友善

Zhejiang • Friendly

成立於1965年的榮榮園已走過半世紀時光，雖現已無法再看到創辦人的身影，但跟隨他三十個年頭的首席徒弟確保餐廳繼續傳承浙江老滋味。經典菜色繁多，烤排骨為必嚐之選，豬子排和洋蔥以小火燒六小時，輕觸即骨肉分離，汁濃味香，搭配光餅更是一絕。鐵板牛尾也不容錯過。服務親切得讓你猶如置身家中般舒適。

The chef has been at the helm here for 30 years and each dish is prepared the same way as it was when the shop opened in 1965. The must-try braised pork ribs are slow-cooked in an onion broth for six hours until the meat falls off the bone – the perfect match for the guangbing flatbread. Other signatures include oxtail on a sizzling hotplate, dongpo pork with red yeast rice, and Beggar's chicken. Most items need pre-ordering. Service is warm and homely.

TEL. 02 2703 8822

大安區信義路四段25號

25, Section 4, Xinyi Road, Da'an

■ 價錢 **PRICE**

午膳 Lunch
點菜 À la carte $ 500-1,000
晚膳 Dinner
點菜 À la carte $ 500-1,000

■ 營業時間 **OPENING HOURS**

午膳 Lunch 11:30-13:50
晚膳 Dinner 17:30-20:50

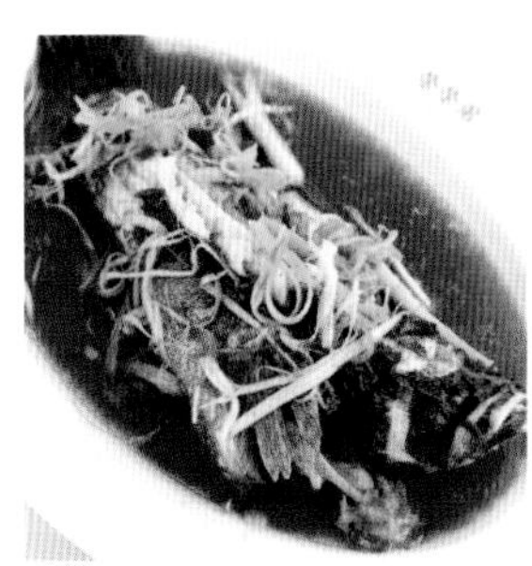

泰姬 N

TAJ

印度菜·異國風情

Indian • Exotic Décor

裝潢用色大膽，使用印度裝飾品、花布與大象圖案作點綴，加上印度音樂，充滿異國風情。餐廳所用的香料甚至廚師團隊，也是老闆在當地物色回來。食物方面，以北印菜為主，並獲得官方的清真認證。招牌菜包括泰姬火紅乳酸碳烤雞、黑扁豆咖哩，別忘了點上一客麥香四溢的全麥碳烤餅佐餐，加倍滿足。

Bold colours, patchwork and ethnic prints abound in this bustling halal restaurant serving Northern Indian cuisine. The Pakistani owner shops for spices and recruits chefs from India to ensure the cooking aligns with his vision. He is also keen on hosting Indian cultural events at weekends. Signatures include tandoori chicken, and dal Makhani (black lentil curry). Don't forget to order wholemeal tandoori roti to go with the food.

TEL. 02 8773 0175

大安區市民大道四段48巷1號

1, Lane 48, Section 4, Civic Boulevard, Da'an

■ 價錢 **PRICE**

午膳 Lunch
點菜 À la carte $ 500-800
晚膳 Dinner
點菜 À la carte $ 500-800

■ 營業時間 **OPENING HOURS**

午膳 Lunch 12:00-14:30
晚膳 Dinner 17:30-22:00

天下三絕

TIEN HSIA SAN CHUEH

麵食 · 友善

Noodles · Friendly

欲於水晶燈下邊啖紅酒邊嚐牛肉麵，天下三絕可滿足心願。店家所選用的牛肉來自美國和澳洲；麵條則以澳洲黃金小麥製作，有三種不同寬度；湯頭用上牛大骨、牛肋排、四種酸度的番茄等熬煮八小時而成，香醇清甜且富層次。特別推薦天下三絕牛肉麵，網羅四個牛肉部位，是為極品享受。逢週三點選主食可獲贈一杯紅酒。

As opposed to the typical cramped noodle shop, this one is lavish and glam. Better still, it also delivers in terms of taste – the signature beef noodle soup with oxtail, shank, tendon and heel muscle lets you sample a range of beef textures. The broth is made with beef backbones and ribs plus four kinds of tomatoes and two kinds of onions for extra depth and dimension. The marinated meat platter, appetisers and pork rib rice are also well made.

TEL. 02 2741 6299

大安區仁愛路四段27巷3號

3, Lane 27, Section 4, Ren'ai Road, Da'an

www.noodle3.com

■ 價錢 **PRICE**

午膳 Lunch
點菜 À la carte $ 300-500
晚膳 Dinner
點菜 À la carte $ 300-500

■ 營業時間 **OPENING HOURS**

午膳 Lunch 11:30-14:20
晚膳 Dinner 17:30-20:20

■ 休息日期 **ANNUAL AND WEEKLY CLOSING**

農曆新年4天休息
Closed 4 days CNY

TEL. 02 2351 1051

大安區金山南路二段31巷17號

17, Lane 31, Section 2, Jinshan South Road, Da'an

www.beefnoodle-master.com

■ 價錢 **PRICE**

午膳 Lunch
點菜 À la carte $ 150-450
晚膳 Dinner
點菜 À la carte $ 150-450

■ 營業時間 **OPENING HOURS**

午膳 Lunch 11:00-15:30
晚膳 Dinner 16:30-21:00

■ 休息日期 **ANNUAL AND WEEKLY CLOSING**

除夕至初五休息
Closed CNY eve to fifth day of CNY

永康牛肉麵

YONG-KANG BEEF NOODLE

麵食 · 親切

Noodles · Neighbourhood

千萬不要在飢腸轆轆時光臨此店，因為餓著肚子站在輪候隊伍中更是難受。其川味牛肉麵赫赫有名，濃郁的湯頭以大骨熬製，鹹辣帶勁。招牌紅燒牛肉麵選用半筋半肉的澳洲牛腱和在地牛肉，熬煮超過四小時，肉味濃，軟嫩而不失嚼勁。多種小菜也值得一試，尤其推薦滷五香豆腐，味道香濃令人欲罷不能。

Another shop where one always sees long queues, it sells beef shin and tendon noodle soups with heavy seasoning slightly on the spicy side. Australian beef is used for its meaty flavour and is braised in an intense Sichuanese stock for over 4 hours. An array of cold appetizers are also available at reasonable prices, with the marinated five-spice tofu being the highlight – every hole in the tofu is saturated with the flavourful marinade.

BAAN Ⓝ

泰國菜 · 新潮

Thai • Chic

本店位於曼谷，提供家庭風味的泰國中部菜餚，所有醬料與咖哩均手工製作。為了呈現當地特色，總店的泰籍主廚每年都會來訪視察。推薦菜色眾多，包括香茅拌蝦、綠咖哩燉牛肉，以及口感酥脆、以新鮮蝦隻烹製的金錢蝦餅。此外，酸辣海鮮湯是主廚的家鄉菜，值得一試。店內裝潢新穎，並選用無毒環保餐具，適合約會聚餐。

Chicly decorated Baan is an outpost of a Bangkok-based restaurant and serves home-style cooking from central Thailand, hence its name which translates as "home". Signatures include spicy shrimp salad, braised beef green curry, and spicy-sour pork belly and egg stew. The chef makes Tom Yum seafood soup in his home-town style – with red chilli paste and coconut milk. All sauces and curries are hand-made in-house.

TEL. 02 2711 0528

大安區敦化南路一段233巷15號

15, Lane 233, Section 1, Dunhua South Road, Da'an

■ 價錢 PRICE

午膳 Lunch
點菜 À la carte $ 1,000-1,200
晚膳 Dinner
點菜 À la carte $ 1,000-1,200

■ 營業時間 OPENING HOURS

午膳 Lunch 11:30-14:00
晚膳 Dinner 17:30-21:30

■ 休息日期 ANNUAL AND WEEKLY CLOSING

初四至初五休息
Closed fourth to fifth day of CNY

CHOU CHOU

法國菜 · 小酒館

French • Brasserie

TEL. 02 2773 1819

大安區忠孝東路四段170巷6弄22號

22, Alley 6, Lane 170, Section 4, Zhongxiao East Road, Da'an

www.chouchou.com.tw

■ 價錢 PRICE

午膳 Lunch
套餐 Set Menu $ 1,080-1,780
晚膳 Dinner
套餐 Set Menu $ 1,580-2,580

■ 營業時間 OPENING HOURS

午膳 Lunch 11:30-14:00
晚膳 Dinner 18:00-21:30

■ 休息日期 ANNUAL AND WEEKLY CLOSING

農曆新年5天及週二休息
Closed 5 days CNY and Tuesday

經過重新裝潢，以黑色百葉窗搭配米色與咖啡色調，令用餐環境帶有濃烈法國情懷。廚房前的大理石吧檯被保留下來，客人可以在此欣賞主廚精湛的料理技巧。菜單上盡是融入當代元素的法國菜餚，從洋蔥湯到爐烤乾式熟成胭脂鴨胸，一切應有盡有。推薦油封鴨腿和烤全雞，但後者需要三天前預訂，可於訂位時提出。

After being remodelled in 2019, this dining room now exudes French bistro chic – a beige-tan colour scheme punctuated by black blinds. The marble counter seats overlooking the open kitchen are for those who want to be close to the culinary action. The prix-fixe menu offers laudable choices of updated bistro classics: onion soup, roasted dry-aged duck breast, duck confit, roast chicken and apple tart. Prices remain wallet-friendly.

DA'AN 大安區

EPHERNITÉ

時尚法國菜・友善

French Contemporary • Friendly

由曾居於法國的夫妻檔經營，餐廳提倡「產地直送」理念，著重採購在地食材，並與陽明山農夫合作，栽種獨家的農產品每天運抵餐廳。包含三道菜的菜單每天隨當日食材更迭，顧客抵達一刻方會從服務人員口中得知菜色。以法式料理為基調的菜餚賣相精緻，其中每天新鮮預備的蔬菜凍令人回味。另外可以預訂設九道菜的季節菜單。

The décor seamlessly blends faux-industrial style with minimalist chic. Owned and run by a couple who once lived in France, it champions a farm-to-table concept using fresh produce grown on the fringes of the city. The owner-chef honed her skills at world famous L'Astrance so classic French techniques underpin all her ambitious creations – the vegetable terrine made daily stands out. You can also pre-order the 9-course seasonal menu.

TEL. 02 2732 0732

大安區安和路二段233號

233, Section 2, Anhe Road, Da'an

www.ephernite.com

■ 價錢 **PRICE**

晚膳 Dinner
套餐 Set Menu $ 1,800-5,000

■ 營業時間 **OPENING HOURS**

晚膳 Dinner 18:30-20:30

■ 休息日期 **ANNUAL AND WEEKLY CLOSING**

除夕至初六、週一及週二休息
Closed CNY eve to sixth day of CNY, Monday and Tuesday

TEL. 02 2707 3348

大安區敦化南路二段63巷24號

24, Lane 63, Section 2, Dunhua South Road, Da'an

www.gentaipei.com

■ 價錢 **PRICE**

晚膳 Dinner
點菜 À la carte $ 1,300-1,500

■ 營業時間 **OPENING HOURS**

晚膳 Dinner 17:30-21:00

■ 休息日期 **ANNUAL AND WEEKLY CLOSING**

週日休息
Closed Sunday

GĒN CREATIVE

創新菜 · 友善

Innovative • Friendly

三位合伙人分別來自臺灣、韓國和瓜地馬拉，以「根」為名，在美式風格料理中融入三人的家鄉味，並依據每季的在地食材，變化菜色口味。菜單分為開胃小點、地、海、陸及甜點五類，若二人共享不妨從每個類別中各挑其一。推薦半熟澎湖紅甘和墨式究好豬戰斧豬排，後者選用人道飼養的臺灣豬，其肉質軟嫩，別具風味。

The word Gēn is the transliteration of the Chinese word for root, a homage paid to the ethnic origins of the three chefs, namely Guatemala, Taiwan and Korea. Their creative fusion fare is divided into Snacks, Earth, Sea, Land and Sweets on the menu. Most portion sizes are big enough to share between two. Don't miss their amberjack tataki and tomahawk pork chop, the latter using humanely raised local meat.

驥園川菜
GI YUAN

川菜・簡樸

Sichuan • Simple

饕客來到驥園，都是為了一嚐那招牌砂鍋雞湯！此菜做法耗時，先用老母雞熬製十小時成高湯，再放入新鮮土雞肉、火腿、干貝與豬腳熬煮兩小時，湯色乳白且味道香濃。菜單上除了常見川菜如乾煸四季豆、宮保雞丁外，廚師更以多種食材搭配不同料理手法，如豆酥、麻辣、京醬肉絲等，口味多元。餐廳人潮不絕，建議提前訂位。

Regulars come for the signature chicken soup casserole – it takes 10 hours to make the milky rich chicken stock before free-range chicken, ham, dried scallops and pork trotters are added and cooked for two more hours. Other famed Sichuan dishes are also on the menu, such as dry-fried French beans and Kungpao chicken. Some dishes can be customised with condiments of your choice. It's always busy so early reservations are recommended.

P

TEL. 02 2708 3110

大安區敦化南路一段324號

324, Section 1, Dunhua South Road, Da'an

■ 價錢 PRICE

午膳 Lunch
套餐 Set Menu $ 500-900
點菜 À la carte $ 600-1,200
晚膳 Dinner
點菜 À la carte $ 800-1,500

■ 營業時間 OPENING HOURS

午膳 Lunch 11:30-13:30
晚膳 Dinner 17:30-20:00

■ 休息日期 ANNUAL AND WEEKLY CLOSING

除夕至初一休息
Closed CNY eve to first day of CNY

隱丹廚
HIDDEN BY DN

時尚西班牙菜 · 時尚

Spanish Contemporary · Contemporary Décor

TEL. 0909 849 937

大安區延吉街261號

261 Yanji Street, Da'an

■ 價錢 **PRICE**

午膳 Lunch
套餐 Set Menu $ 999
晚膳 Dinner
套餐 Set Menu $ 2,399

■ 營業時間 **OPENING HOURS**

午膳 Lunch 12:00-13:30
晚膳 Dinner 18:00-20:00

■ 休息日期 **ANNUAL AND WEEKLY CLOSING**

除夕至初四、週一午膳及週日休息
Closed CNY eve to fourth day of CNY, Monday lunch and Sunday

這小餐館由西班牙籍主廚及其妻子共同經營，妻子是外場總帥，凡事親力親為的主廚則專注研發菜色。菜單不缺創意巧思，融合經典西班牙風味和現代烹調技藝，且巧用在地食材，各式海鮮直送自宜蘭大溪港，亦少不了每日新鮮採購的時令食材。清一色西班牙佳釀的酒單不乏精彩之作，餐廳更不定期舉行葡萄酒晚宴。

The Spanish owner-chef worked at the legendary Arzak and El Bulli before opening this cosy restaurant to showcase his contemporary take on Spanish cuisine, using the best Taiwanese ingredients. Seafood from Daxi Harbour in Yilan is prominently featured in his prix-fixe tasting menu, which expertly renders classic Spanish flavours with modern techniques and artful presentations, perfectly complemented by the Spanish wines on offer.

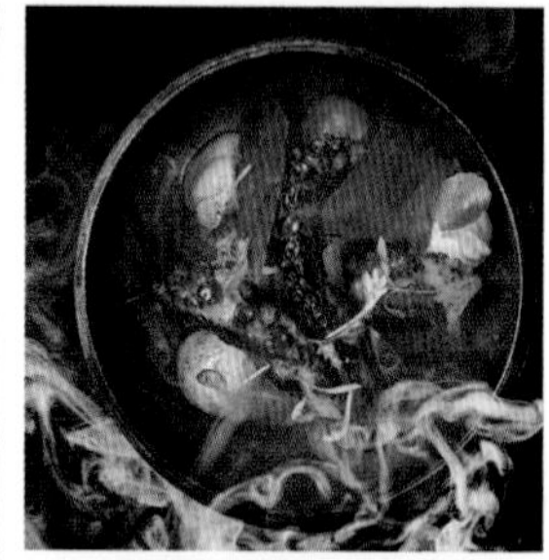

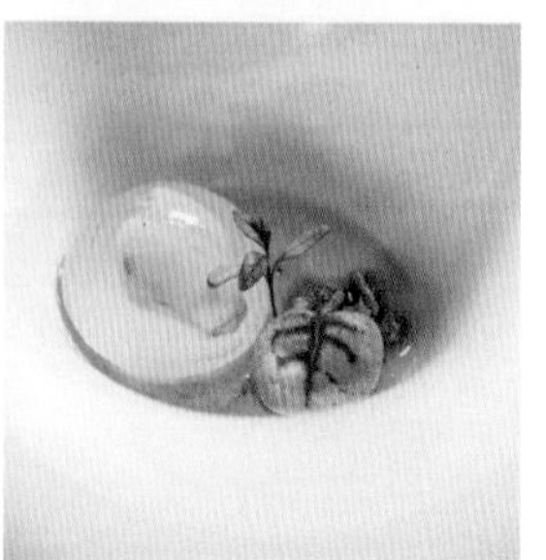

INDULGE

創新菜・法式小餐館

Innovative • Bistro

淺色高背皮革座椅的用餐區，帶有時尚氣息。菜單亦充滿趣味，以臺灣環島鐵道的路線方式呈現，把西式菜餚與各地火車站做連結，並將臺灣飲食文化融入其中，讓客人體驗各種相異的飲食風格。餐後不妨到別具型格的地下室淺酌一番，出色的酒吧團隊設計了一系列以五行為概念的雞尾酒，值得一試。

The ground floor features cream leather seats and award-winning mixologists creating concoctions with a five-element theme behind a glitzy bar, whereas the lower floor has a bistro feel to it. But no matter where you're seated, the same menu prevails – Western dishes reinvented with culinary references to places along the rail line around Taiwan. Cooking is honest and rustic and comes with a refined edge, robust flavours and balanced spicing.

TEL. 02 2773 0080

大安區復興南路一段219巷11號

11, Lane 219, Section 1, Fuxing South Road, Da'an

www.indulge-life.com

■ 價錢 **PRICE**

午膳 Lunch
套餐 Set Menu $ 380-700
晚膳 Dinner
點菜 À la carte $ 1,000-1,500

■ 營業時間 **OPENING HOURS**

午膳 Lunch 11:30-14:00
晚膳 Dinner 18:00-23:30

TEL. 02 2741 7115

大安區光復南路346巷48號

48, Lane 346, Guangfu South Road, Da'an

www.jekitchen.tw

■ 價錢 **PRICE**

午膳 Lunch
套餐 Set Menu $ 980-1,280
晚膳 Dinner
套餐 Set Menu $ 1,780-2,180

■ 營業時間 **OPENING HOURS**

午膳 Lunch 12:00-13:30
晚膳 Dinner 18:00-20:30

■ 休息日期 **ANNUAL AND WEEKLY CLOSING**

除夕至初二及週一休息
Closed CNY eve to second day of CNY and Monday

JE KITCHEN

時尚歐陸菜 · 親切

European Contemporary · Neighbourhood

富現代感的門楣讓餐廳在光復南路上尤其耀眼。水泥地和灰米色的簡約裝潢，與隨性寫意的氣氛搭配得天衣無縫。雖然氣氛輕鬆，食物卻處處顯露出店家的認真嚴謹。套餐融合法國及北歐元素，道道精緻時尚。主廚貫徹北歐菜物盡其用的原則，並每月推出兩至三道新菜色，展示當季食材和其創意。

This cosy restaurant welcomes diners with a modern façade, a bare concrete floor and a cool colour scheme. The prix-fixe menu shows subtle Nordic and French influences. The chef introduces two to three new creations every month to showcase his creativity and seasonal produces. The Nordic philosophy of making use of each ingredient to the fullest is manifest in the burnt lemon/hazelnut/lemon verbena dish. Artful plating and bold flavours add to the experience.

LE BLANC

牛排屋・法式小餐館

Steakhouse • Bistro

菜單再簡單不過——十盎司美國肋眼和或蒸或烤的波士頓龍蝦。廚師的理念是將菜單去蕪存菁,選用最優質的食材並以純熟技巧烹調。牛排或龍蝦套餐均佐以手工約克夏麵包、沙拉或湯,及無限添加的薯條,配菜和主菜味道同樣出色,甜品更值得一試。龍蝦極受歡迎,建議預訂。漢堡每日限量供應,不妨一試。

The concept is simple: you come here for either rib-eye steak or Boston lobster, or both. The idea is to pare down the menu, use the best ingredients and cook them well. The steak and lobster (steamed or grilled) come with fresh popovers, salad or soup, and unlimited fries. Sides and desserts are also as good as the mains. Lobster lovers should call to pre-order as they can run out. Burgers are served in limited supply everyday.

TEL. 02 2700 7770

大安區大安路一段183號

183, Section 1, Da'an Road, Da'an

■ 價錢 **PRICE**

午膳 Lunch
套餐 Set Menu $ 1,000-1,400
點菜 À la carte $ 700-1,700
晚膳 Dinner
套餐 Set Menu $ 1,000-1,400
點菜 À la carte $ 700-1,700

■ 營業時間 **OPENING HOURS**

午膳 Lunch 11:30-14:30
晚膳 Dinner 17:30-21:00

五月雪客家私房珍釀

MAY SNOW HAKKA FOOD

客家菜·友善

Hakkanese • Friendly

TEL. 02 2700 6248

大安區敦化南路一段329巷16號

16, Lane 329, Section 1, Dunhua South Road, Da'an

www.maysnow.com.tw

■ 價錢 **PRICE**

午膳 Lunch
點菜 À la carte $ 300-500
晚膳 Dinner
點菜 À la carte $ 500-700

■ 營業時間 **OPENING HOURS**

午膳 Lunch 11:30-13:50
晚膳 Dinner 17:50-20:45

■ 休息日期 **ANNUAL AND WEEKLY CLOSING**

初一休息
Closed first day of CNY

掌勺二十多年的老闆冀改變大眾對客家菜油膩厚重的印象，親自研發菜色，並融入多種海鮮與創意。香蔥燜嫩排和紅麴軟絲均很受歡迎，前者選用豬腩排以客家油蔥等燉煮四小時而成，建議預訂；後者則採用來自澎湖的現撈軟絲，以陳年紅麴醃製後油炸，口感軟嫩且帶紅糟香氣。不妨也預訂以臺南放山土雞烹調的山野鹽焗雞。

To subvert the stereotype of Hakkanese cooking being quite heavy, the veteran owner designed most of his recipes from scratch to put a new spin on the cuisine. Tender, savoury red yeast cuttlefish is marinated in red koji sauce before deep-frying while braised pork belly ribs with scallions are slow-cooked with Hakkanese condiments for four hours; the salt-baked free-range Tainan chicken is also excellent. Pre-order the last two items to avoid missing out.

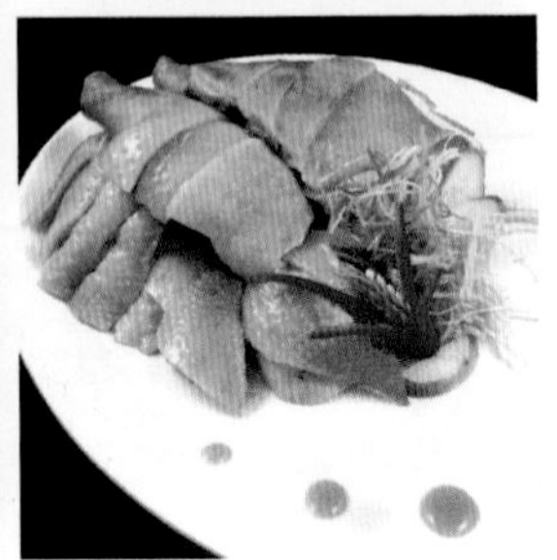

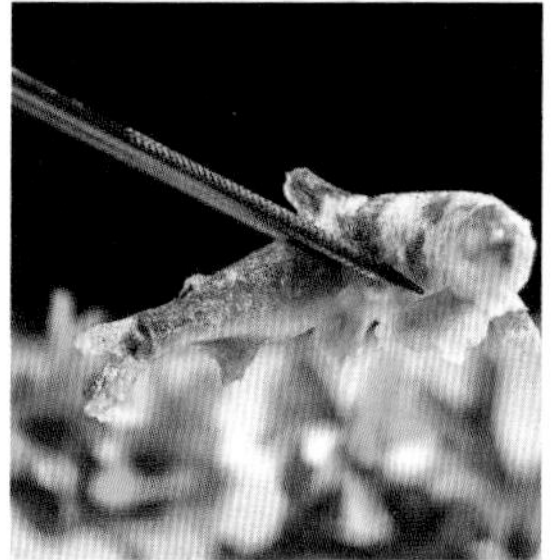

牡丹
MUDAN

天婦羅 · 簡約

Tempura • Minimalist

要品嚐傳統口味的天婦羅，牡丹是個不錯的選擇。料理長曾到日本拜師，更採用來自日本的炸油、麵粉及海鮮，以特殊配方混合炸油和天婦羅粉料，達到外皮清爽薄脆的效果。甜點蕨餅每天現做，軟嫩可口，令人加倍滿足。店家僅接受中午12:30及晚上6:30的訂位，顧客須準時抵達，廚師才會開始料理食材。

This tempura restaurant shows a deep reverence for tradition and the head chef travelled to Japan to learn every skill and trick, which he now follows to the letter. Meat, seafood and vegetables are coated in an ethereal batter made with Japanese flour and water before being fried in a secret blend of four oils sourced from Japan. Reservations are mandatory, with only two slots at 12:30 and 18:30. Food is prepared only after the whole party arrives.

TEL. 02 2706 8699

大安區四維路52巷17號

17, Lane 52, Siwei Road, Da'an

mudantempura.com

■ 價錢 **PRICE**

午膳 Lunch
套餐 Set Menu $ 3,500-6,500
晚膳 Dinner
套餐 Set Menu $ 6,500

■ 營業時間 **OPENING HOURS**

午膳 Lunch 12:30-15:00
晚膳 Dinner 18:30-22:00

■ 休息日期 **ANNUAL AND WEEKLY CLOSING**

元旦、除夕至初五及週一休息
Closed New Year's Day, CNY eve to fifth day of CNY and Monday

TEL. 02 2701 8025

大安區仁愛路四段300巷26弄13號

13, Alley 26, Lane 300, Section 4, Ren'ai Road, Da'an

■ 價錢 **PRICE**

午膳 Lunch
套餐 Set Menu $ 1,500
晚膳 Dinner
套餐 Set Menu $ 2,500

■ 營業時間 **OPENING HOURS**

午膳 Lunch 12:00-13:30
晚膳 Dinner 18:00-20:30

■ 休息日期 **ANNUAL AND WEEKLY CLOSING**

除夕至初二及週日休息
Closed CNY eve to second day of CNY and Sunday

NKU̲

創新菜・型格

Innovative • Design

綠色大門上的標誌隱秘內斂，同色系的內部裝潢令餐廳帶著靜謐典雅的氛圍，滿櫃的木材彷彿在說明柴火於此的重要性。餐廳名在北歐文中有柴火之意，廚師盼以最原始的烹調方式還原食物的天然味道，食材經荔枝木或龍眼木燻製或燒烤，散發炭火的餘香，細膩的味道和精緻的擺盤叫人躍躍欲試。不妨一嚐手工酸種麵包及招牌菜亞洲「馬鈴薯」與「魚子醬」。

The logo on the muted green, birch and glass shop front is quite cryptic. The interior, with its understated elegance, follows the same colour scheme. The menu prominently features Nordic cooking reinvented with wood fire – either smoked with lychee wood or grilled over longan charcoal – but creatively done with intricate skills, a careful balance of flavours and artsy presentations. Try the homemade 'SLOW' bread and the signature An Asian potato & 'caviar'.

橘色涮涮屋 (大安)
ORANGE SHABU (DA'AN)

涮涮鍋・親密

Shabu-shabu • Intimate

此乃全臺首間高檔涮涮鍋專門店，提供美國頂級牛肉、日本帝王蟹及活毛蟹、手切小羔羊等。湯底以新鮮水果、昆布和老母雞熬煮三小時，滋味豐富；推薦手工鮮蝦丸及軟絲丸。店家會為點選海鮮套餐或手切小羔羊的顧客建議一食材多吃，如龍蝦可涮煮及清蒸，如此即能嚐到單一食材的不同風味。最後別要錯過每天現磨製作的杏仁豆腐。

One of the first swanky hotpot places in town serves gourmet ingredients from around the world – premium sirloin from the U. S. , Wagyu from Japan and Australia, king crab from Hokkaido – all blanched in a rich chicken stock. Lamb and seafood can be prepared in two or three ways, such as frying or grilling. Shrimp balls and live lobster also stand out. Make sure you save room for the made-from-scratch almond tofu dessert.

TEL. 02 2776 1658

大安區大安路一段135號B1

B1, 135, Section 1, Da'an Road, Da'an

www.orangeshabu.com.tw

■ 價錢 **PRICE**

套餐 Set Menu $ 780-4,200
點菜 À la carte $ 1,300-1,600

■ 營業時間 **OPENING HOURS**

11:30-01:00

蘭
ORCHID

時尚法國菜 · 時髦

French Contemporary · Fashionable

TEL. 02 2378 3333

大安區安和路二段83號

83, Section 2, Anhe Road, Da'an

www.orchid-restaurant.com.tw

■ 價錢 **PRICE**

午膳 Lunch
套餐 Set Menu $ 1,880-2,880
晚膳 Dinner
套餐 Set Menu $ 2,680-3,880

■ 營業時間 **OPENING HOURS**

午膳 Lunch 11:30-13:30
晚膳 Dinner 18:00-20:30

■ 休息日期 **ANNUAL AND WEEKLY CLOSING**

除夕至初三及週一休息
Closed CNY eve to third day of CNY and Monday

與Monsieur L系出同門，黑金的顏色搭配和耀眼的天花裝飾，格調高雅。混血新主廚於2019年上任，曾旅居紐澳兩地，也活躍於臺灣西餐業界，擅長將臺灣菜的細緻風味融入歐陸料理中。菜色烏魚子、甘藷與牛骨髓，以三種迥異的食材，碰撞出令人意想不到的好滋味。即便甜點也帶有臺灣特色。

A trendy sister to the classic Monsieur L, Orchid wows with its black-and-gold interior and striking ceiling art. The Taiwanese-Japanese chef has worked in some prestigious kitchens in Taipei, Australia and New Zealand, and brings his eclectic culinary experience to the table. The bottarga, sweet potato and bone marrow dish is a combination that works very well. The dessert inspired by Hakkanese lei cha tea is a nod to Taiwanese food culture.

真的好海鮮
REALLY GOOD SEAFOOD

海鮮 · 舒適

Seafood • Cosy

餐廳歷史悠久，採用大量在地海鮮，新鮮度及品質皆有保證。行政總廚會在魚缸附近，為客人介紹各款海鮮的最佳烹調方法。招牌菜包括過橋活鮑魚、鹽焗肥膏蟳和龍江脆皮雞。另外亦提供季節性菜餚。為了方便人數較少的客人，備有多款單人套餐，可以按需要組合不同菜色。店家更販售花枝丸、烏魚子等產品。

As its name suggests, local seafood is big on the menu – and it's good! Diners can pick from the live fish tanks and the executive chef is more than happy to recommend ways to cook them. Needless to say, the seafood is of top quality and freshness given the hefty volume sold daily. Abalone 'crossing the bridge' style and salt-baked mud crab stand out; as does the crispy fried chicken. Small parties can order set menus for one to sample more dishes.

TEL. 02 2771 3000

大安區復興南路一段222號

222, Section 1, Fuxing South Road, Da'an

■ 價錢 PRICE

午膳 Lunch
套餐 Set Menu $ 880-1,500
點菜 À la carte $ 2,000-3,000
晚膳 Dinner
套餐 Set Menu $ 1,800-2,380
點菜 À la carte $ 2,000-3,000

■ 營業時間 OPENING HOURS

午膳 Lunch 11:30-13:45
晚膳 Dinner 17:30-20:30

■ 休息日期 ANNUAL AND WEEKLY CLOSING

農曆新年休息5天
Closed 5 days CNY

TEL. 02 7711 2080

大安區敦化南路二段201號6樓
(香格里拉遠東國際大飯店)

6F, Shangri-La's Far Eastern Plaza Hotel, 201, Section 2, Dunhua South Road, Da'an

www.shangri-la.com/taipei

■ 價錢 **PRICE**

午膳 Lunch
套餐 Set Menu $ 1,280-6,000
點菜 À la carte $ 2,400-4,800
晚膳 Dinner
套餐 Set Menu $ 1,280-6,000
點菜 À la carte $ 2,400-4,800

■ 營業時間 **OPENING HOURS**

午膳 Lunch 11:30-14:00
晚膳 Dinner 18:00-21:00

香宮

SHANG PALACE

粵菜 · 經典

Cantonese · Classic Décor

走進餐廳，立即會被色調沉穩的灰色長廊吸引目光，大紅燈籠與中式花結點綴其上，在迎賓入口還擺放了中西佳釀，感覺高雅舒適。食物方面，新任主廚提供了多元的粵菜選擇，盡顯嫻熟的烹調技巧。午餐提供的傳統點心及多款個人套餐，更適合商務宴請及聚會。建議預訂窗邊座位，透過落地玻璃遠眺敦化南路的景色。

The corridor leading to this elegant dining room features a cool grey hue, dotted with red lanterns and decorative string knots, while the Chinese and Western liquors at the glitzy reception make an oenophilic tapestry. Ask for a table by the windows for the sweeping views of Dunhua South Road. The Cantonese chef skilfully prepares the quintessential classics, including the crispy and juicy roast duck – the must-try item on the menu.

申浦尚宴

SHEN PU SHANG YEN

滬菜·舒適

Shanghainese • Cosy

「申」是上海別稱，而「浦」是宋朝時上海的舊稱，寓意老菜新滋味，既能吃到傳統菜餚，也配合健康趨勢，採用少油少鹽的烹調方式。其廚房由江浙團隊組成，具有多年經驗，拿手菜包括酒釀油爆蝦、甜筒鍋巴蝦仁、古法馬頭魚與螃蟹料理。若喜歡傳統口味，可預訂選用新鮮豬內臟與香糟一同燒製的砂鍋香糟缽斗。

The owner-chef recruited the whole kitchen team from Jiangsu and Zhejiang. He's been in business for 50 years and takes care of every detail in the restaurant, from furnishings to shopping for ingredients. The menu shows his ambition – to put a light, healthy spin on the classics, such as the popular dish fried prawns in puffed rice cone. The pork offal casserole in distillers grains sauce needs pre-ordering. Tilefish and crab also shine.

TEL. 02 2755 3999

大安區信義路四段152號

152, Section 4, Xinyi Road, Da'an

■ 價錢 PRICE

午膳 Lunch
點菜 À la carte $ 800-900
晚膳 Dinner
點菜 À la carte $ 800-900

■ 營業時間 OPENING HOURS

午膳 Lunch 11:00-14:00
晚膳 Dinner 17:00-21:00

■ 休息日期 ANNUAL AND WEEKLY CLOSING

初一休息
Closed first day of CNY

壽司芳 Ⓝ
SUSHIYOSHI

日本菜・簡約

Japanese • Minimalist

壽司芳的第三間海外分店，由大阪主廚設計菜單，並交由來臺多年的日籍主廚管理。其無菜單料理結合日式壽司傳統與西式烹調風格，並多用在地鮮魚。建議點選價格較高的套餐，體驗更多創意菜色，例如牡丹蝦義式薄切，以日本牡丹蝦搭配用蝦膏、蝦頭製作的冰淇淋與魚子醬刨片，滋味鮮甜清爽，僅於大阪本店及臺北店供應。

This is the third overseas outpost of the famous Osaka-based sushiya. Instead of making conventional Edomae sushi, the Japanese chef strikes a fine balance between tradition and the use of creative Western touches, in signatures such as botan ebi carpaccio topped with shrimp tomalley ice cream and shaved black bottarga. Two omakase menus are available for lunch and dinner; the higher priced one lets diners experience the chef's vision to the fullest.

TEL. 02 2721 5560

大安區忠孝東路四段216巷19弄12號

12, Alley 19, Lane 216, Section 4, Zhongxiao East Road, Da'an

■ 價錢 PRICE

午膳 Lunch
套餐 Set Menu $ 3,500-5,500
晚膳 Dinner
套餐 Set Menu $ 6,800-8,500

■ 營業時間 OPENING HOURS

午膳 Lunch 12:00-13:30
晚膳 Dinner 18:00-20:00

上林鐵板燒
THE SUNLIT TEPPANYAKI

鐵板燒・典雅

Teppanyaki • Elegant

一絲不苟是這家鐵板燒與別不同之處：在這兒，鐵板上多餘的油脂會被即時抹去，以免食物沾上了不該有的味道；店家堅持僅用海釣魚；細緻處如酒杯，也會根據酒品而提供專業的搭配。對細節的執著讓老闆堅拒擴店，專心將這餐廳經營至盡善盡美。餐廳劃分為數區，除用餐區外，陽臺和咖啡區亦舒適愜意。

Most teppanyaki chefs can put on a spectacular show and cook the food well. But it's the details that set apart certain establishments from others. Here, any splattered oil is wiped off at once to retain the distinct flavour of every ingredient on the hot plate. Special crystal glasses are available for Bordeaux and Burgundy red wines. A private room with connecting balcony and an area for coffee after dinner also add to the experience.

TEL. 02 2752 8569

大安區敦化南路一段247巷10號2樓

2F, 10, Lane 247, Section 1, Dunhua South Road, Da'an

www.thesunlit.com.tw

■ 價錢 **PRICE**

午膳 Lunch
套餐 Set Menu $ 920-3,680
點菜 À la carte $ 1,000-4,200
晚膳 Dinner
套餐 Set Menu $ 920-5,480
點菜 À la carte $ 1,000-4,200

■ 營業時間 **OPENING HOURS**

午膳 Lunch 11:30-14:30
晚膳 Dinner 17:30-22:30

■ 休息日期 **ANNUAL AND WEEKLY CLOSING**

初一休息
Closed first day of CNY

TEL. 02 2779 0688

大安區仁愛路四段27巷25號12樓
(金普頓大安酒店)

12F, Kimpton Da An Hotel, 25, Lane 27, Section 4, Ren'ai Road, Da'an

www.thetavernist.com

■ 價錢 **PRICE**

午膳 Lunch
點菜 À la carte $ 1,000-2,500
晚膳 Dinner
點菜 À la carte $ 1,000-2,500

■ 營業時間 **OPENING HOURS**

午膳 Lunch 11:30-14:00
晚膳 Dinner 18:00-21:30

THE TAVERNIST

時尚歐陸菜 · 新潮

European Contemporary · Chic

烹飪靈感來自跨越全球的旅遊經驗，主廚以美食作為相冊，具創意地呈現各國佳餚。主要選用本地食材，菜單也會根據季節變更。其中，豬五花豬里肌焦糖鳳梨醬汁香氣四溢，是店裡的招牌菜色。裝潢同樣吸引，牆壁鋪滿竹子，木拱門和珍珠項鍊般的燈飾令餐廳更添韻味。提供多種調酒，餐前可於酒吧輕鬆一下。

The bamboo-clad dining room, with globe pendant light fixtures that connect like an oversized pearl bracelet, evokes old-time charm to go with the fun feel. The food is like a photo album of where the chef has travelled, both in Taiwan and around the world, and is executed using meticulous European techniques. The pork belly and tenderloin-pineapple-sugarcane dish comes with a tiny, smoking stove. The cocktail list is worth exploring.

桌藏
TOH-A'

創新菜 · 型格

Innovative · Design

入口處流水潺潺，小徑上鋪滿古董瓦片，進入這所有八十年歷史的日式建築，木製橫樑和懸垂燈飾營造出新舊對比強烈的特別氛圍。廚師以大量在地食材將臺式元素糅合法式料理中，拼湊出味道、口感皆非比尋常的菜色。午餐和晚餐分別提供五或七道菜的套餐，服務團隊默契十足。

This restored 80-year-old Japanese home houses a rustic and atmospheric dining room. To enter, diners walk through a small courtyard covered in antique tiles with water pooling over them. Only prix-fixe menus are offered; ingredients are mostly from Taiwan, prepared using classical French techniques, with an element of surprise in the tastes, textures and even temperatures of the food.

TEL. 02 2377 0952

大安區和平東路二段76巷23弄9號

9, Alley 23, Lane 76, Section 2, Heping East Road, Da'an

■ 價錢 **PRICE**

午膳 Lunch
套餐 Set Menu $ 1,500-1,980
晚膳 Dinner
套餐 Set Menu $ 2,980

■ 營業時間 **OPENING HOURS**

午膳 Lunch 12:00-13:30
晚膳 Dinner 18:00-20:30

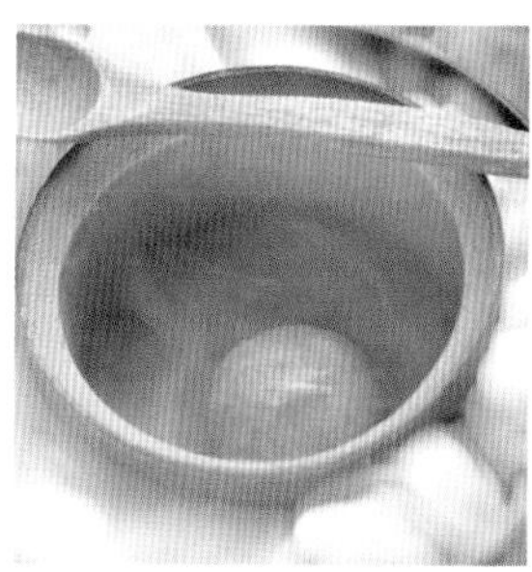

ULV Ⓝ

時尚歐陸菜・時髦

European Contemporary • Fashionable

TEL. 02 8771 0828

大安區敦化南路一段160巷18號

18, Lane 160, Section 1, Dunhua South Road, Da'an

■ 價錢 PRICE

午膳 Lunch
套餐 Set Menu $ 650-880
點菜 À la carte $ 1,300-4,000
晚膳 Dinner
套餐 Set Menu $ 2,480-3,180
點菜 À la carte $ 1,300-4,000

■ 營業時間 OPENING HOURS

午膳 Lunch 12:00-14:00
晚膳 Dinner 18:00-21:15

■ 休息日期 ANNUAL AND WEEKLY CLOSING

除夕至初二休息
Closed CNY eve to second day of CNY

店名發音與臺語的「人」接近，寓意以人為本，提供輕鬆舒適的用餐體驗。主廚深受北歐料理啟發，運用直火、發酵與熟成技法，使用在地食材，呈現各種歐陸美食。和牛塔塔、炭燒小捲為熱門菜色，肥美的炭烤白鰻，以及發酵馬鈴薯餅也值得一嚐。不妨搭配調酒，而康普茶費茲系列的紅茶品項則適合餐前享用。

Ulv translates as 'wolf' but also rhymes with the Taiwanese word for 'people'. The young chef here uses Nordic cooking techniques, such as wood-firing, smoking and fermentation to layer complex flavours. Start your meal with kombucha fizz that cleanses the palate and boasts a subtle aroma. Grilled eel is wonderfully smoky, while the pillowy fermented potato bread comes with sour cream and trout roe for a briny tartness. The hygge décor is also a plus.

梵燒肉 N

VANNE YAKINIKU

燒烤・新潮

Barbecue • Chic

日本Yoroniku的姐妹店，環境典雅，設吧檯、四人方桌及包廂，建議選擇吧檯，方便向服務人員了解肉品知識。店內提供多款日本和牛部位，全由廚師團隊自行切割。推薦夏多布里昂、牛三筋，以及搭配宜蘭生雞蛋的月見涮涮，滋味令人難以忘懷。備有炸牛排三明治和其他隱藏菜單，可於訂位時詢問及預訂。

This elegant interior is the brainchild of a team of Japanese designers and floral artists. A sister restaurant of Yoroniku in Japan, it specializes in rare and premium cuts of Wagyu beef. Besides the signature chateaubriand and misuji, tsukimi sukiyaki is flat iron grilled and dipped into raw egg from Yilan County for a velvety texture. The deep-fried beef sandwich is a favourite not on the menu – it's worth pre-ordering to avoid missing out.

TEL. 02 2771 0597

大安區敦化南路一段235號2樓

2F, 235, Section 1, Dunhua South Road, Da'an

yakiniku-restaurant-2414.business.site

■ 價錢 **PRICE**

晚膳 Dinner
套餐 Set Menu $ 2,580-3,280
點菜 À la carte $ 2,500-4,500

■ 營業時間 **OPENING HOURS**

晚膳 Dinner 17:00-22:30

■ 休息日期 **ANNUAL AND WEEKLY CLOSING**

除夕至初三及週一休息
Closed CNY eve to third day of CNY and Monday

TEL. 02 2711 2080

大安區忠孝東路四段216巷33弄15號

15, Alley 33, Lane 216, Section 4, Zhongxiao East Road, Da'an

■ 價錢 **PRICE**

午膳 Lunch
套餐 Set Menu $ 3,800-4,800
晚膳 Dinner
套餐 Set Menu $ 5,800-6,800

■ 營業時間 **OPENING HOURS**

午膳 Lunch 12:00-13:00
晚膳 Dinner 18:30-19:30

■ 休息日期 **ANNUAL AND WEEKLY CLOSING**

週日休息
Closed Sunday

YUU

日本菜·友善

Japanese • Friendly

主廚烹調日本料理逾二十年，他一改割烹料理以海鮮為主的慣例，採用來自日本的A5級近江牛作主食材，套餐包括了不同部位的牛肉與烹調方式，其中炸菲力和牛三明治的吐司帶著炭火香氣，和牛炸得外酥內嫩，令人印象難忘；店家自製的蕨餅更帶來完美句點。若希望提高套餐中海鮮的比例，可於訂位時提出。

The owner-chef, who has over 20 years of kitchen experience, opened this serene spot serving Wagyu beef-based prix-fixe menus in 2018 to challenge your preconceptions. Counter seats let diners watch him prepare various cuts of A5 grade Omi beef in the most meticulous ways. Stand-outs include deep-fried fillet with a juicy centre and a Wagyu sandwich with a unique smokiness. Homemade warabi mochi proves the perfect end to the meal.

UNCOLOUREDWORLD/iStock

大安區 DA'AN

夜市 NIGHT MARKETS

臨江街夜市 Linjiang Street

舊稱通化夜市，因位處通化街和基隆路之間的臨江街，2000年政府正式將其命名為臨江街夜市，但舊稱更為人所知。

Formerly known as Tonghua night market, it is located on Linjiang Street between Tonghua Street and Keelung Road. In 2000, the government officially named it Linjiang Street night market, but it's still better known under its old name.

梁記滷味
LIANG CHI LU WEI

位於夜市中段，小小長方櫃內滿載豆乾、雞內臟、海帶、鴨翅等廿多款滷味，門庭若市。

This busy stall boasts 20+ types of marinated food such as dried tofu, chicken offal, kelp and duck wings.

大安區通化街39巷50弄
Alley 50, Lane 39, Tonghua Street, Da'an
價錢 **PRICE:** $ 150-500
營業時間 **OPENING HOURS:** 17:50-01:30

駱記小炒
LO CHI HSIAO CHAO

位置隱蔽但值得造訪。品項不多，炒羊肉或牛肉火候掌控絕佳，炒蚋仔鮮味十足。

Tucked away but worth seeking out. The menu is small, with fried lamb, beef or clams the highlights.

大安區通化街39巷50弄27號
27, Alley 50, Lane 39, Tonghua Street, Da'an
價錢 **PRICE:** $ 100-300
營業時間 **OPENING HOURS:** 17:00-00:00

臨江街夜市
Linjiang Street

御品元冰火湯圓
YU PIN YUAN ICED AND HOT TANGYUAN

雪白剉冰上放芝麻或花生口味熱湯圓，再淋上桂花蜜，冷熱交融加上淡淡甜味，口感極佳。

Hot sesame or peanut dumplings on shaved ice drizzled with osmanthus syrup create interesting contrasts.

大安區通化街39巷50弄31號

31, Alley 50, Lane 39, Tonghua Street, Da'an

價錢 **PRICE:** $ 70-100

營業時間 **OPENING HOURS:** 18:00-00:00

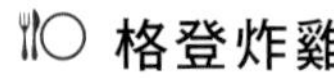

格登炸雞
GOLDEN FRIED CHICKEN

必點招牌炸雞和甜不辣外脆內軟，老闆堅持現點現炸，故製作需時，建議趁熱食用。

Both chicken and tempura are fried-to-order, but the piping hot and perfectly fried items are worth the wait.

大安區通化街39巷50弄35號

35, Alley 50, Lane 39, Tonghua Street, Da'an

價錢 **PRICE:** $ 30-150

營業時間 **OPENING HOURS:** 17:30-00:00

Julien Viry/iStock

酒店
HOTELS

香格里拉遠東國際
SHANGRI-LA FAR EASTERN PLAZA

奢華・典雅

Grand Luxury • Elegant

作為全市最高的酒店，這雙塔般的建築已成為地標。經過近年的大型修繕，酒店房間裝潢中西合璧，既古雅又時尚，窗外則可俯瞰極致城市景色。附設的餐廳提供多元化用餐選擇，日、滬、粵、義式菜餚皆備。想飄然於臺北市全景之上？那在頂樓游泳池暢泳便是不容錯過的體驗。四十樓設有芳療室及理髮理甲服務。

The city's tallest hotel and an iconic landmark was overhauled to encompass luxuriously appointed rooms with superb city views and an Asian-influenced modern interior. A myriad of dining options are available, namely Japanese, Shanghainese, Cantonese and Italian. The rooftop lounge affords a spectacular panorama of the Taipei skyline and the spa is well worth checking out.

TEL. 02 2378 8888
www.shangri-la.com/taipei

大安區敦化南路二段201號
201, Section 2, Dunhua South Road, Da'an

383 客房/**Rooms** $ 9,300-20,100
37 套房/**Suites** $ 15,000-25,800

餐廳推薦/**Recommended restaurants:**
香宮 Shang Palace

TEL. 02 7726 6699
www.madisontaipei.com

大安區敦化南路一段331號
331, Section 1, Dunhua South Road, Da'an

119 客房/Rooms $ 5,000-16,800
5 套房/Suites $ 19,500-60,000

慕軒
MADISON

商務・時尚
Business • Contemporary

林蔭大道簇擁著的是這所提供五種級別房型的時尚酒店。踏進寬敞舒適的地面樓層，已有威士忌或雞尾酒準備好為旅客紓壓；也不妨更上一層，於酒館再酌數杯，佐以各款小點，細味異國風情。各類房型均極富空間感，硬木地板、落地窗，附以藍芽揚聲器等設備，在外也可營造專屬的私人空間，享受豪華住宿體驗。

This modern design-led hotel on a tree-lined boulevard offers 5 different grades of rooms. All come with hard wood floors, king-size beds, floor-to-ceiling windows, Bluetooth speakers and rain showers. The spacious Madison rooms are worth checking out. Take a sip of your favourite whisky or cocktail in the comfy lounge on the ground floor, or dine at their trattoria on the first floor.

金普頓大安 Ⓝ

KIMPTON DA AN

假日酒店・簡約

Holiday hotel • Minimalist

作為亞洲第一間金普頓酒店，建築物大量使用了臺灣的白色手工瓷磚，設計簡約但充滿格調和在地特色。服務周到，大堂設有飲料區，提供咖啡、豆漿、葡萄酒及零點。房內則備有瑜伽墊和二十四小時瑜伽頻道，適合注重健康的房客。另有特別樓層，可攜同寵物入住。部分客房面向臺北101大樓，放煙花時盡享璀璨景致。

This chain's first property in Asia embraces the concept of a home away from home. Check-in is done in the minimalistic but warm 'living room' featuring a vaulted ceiling, Taiwanese white tiles and a pond with flowing water. Pet parents will be thrilled by the amenities and snacks for their furry companion and yogis can leave their mats at home. Some rooms have views of Taipei 101.

TEL. 02 2173 7999
www.kimptonhotels.com/taipei

大安區仁愛路四段27巷25號
25, Lane 27, Section 4, Renai Road, Da'an

129 客房/**Rooms** $ 6,500-16,000

餐廳推薦/**Recommended restaurants:**
The Tavernist

DA'AN 大安區

atosan/iStock

文山區
信義區

WENSHAN & XINYI

文山區 WENSHAN
信義區 XINYI

餐廳
RESTAURANTS

侯布雄
L'ATELIER DE JOËL ROBUCHON

時尚法國菜・時髦

French Contemporary • Fashionable

貫徹了其他分店的設計風格，以紅黑色調，搭配富情調的燈光和開放式廚房，充滿個性。餐廳在2019年迎來新任法籍主廚，是集團於亞洲地區的第一位女主廚。除了以上乘的用料和純熟的技巧，延續經典菜餚，更在口味上增添了細膩風格。菜單品項豐富，既有單點或小份量菜色，當然也不乏套餐選擇。

The moody interior uses the iconic black and red colour scheme as the other members of the group - sit at the counter to appreciate the atmosphere to the fullest. French classics are re-invented with skill, care and a great deal of aplomb; service is engaging, confident and thoughtful. Since 2019, the kitchen has been helmed by the first female head chef in the group's Asian bases; she adds an ethereal touch to the distinctive cooking.

TEL. 02 8729 2628

信義區松仁路28號5樓（寶麗廣場）

5F, Bellavita, 28 Songren Road, Xinyi

www.robuchon.com.tw

■ 價錢 **PRICE**

午膳 Lunch
套餐 Set Menu $ 1,580-6,880
點菜 À la carte $ 3,000-6,500
晚膳 Dinner
套餐 Set Menu $ 2,380-6,880
點菜 À la carte $ 3,000-6,500

■ 營業時間 **OPENING HOURS**

午膳 Lunch 11:30-14:00
晚膳 Dinner 18:00-21:30

■ 休息日期 **ANNUAL AND WEEKLY CLOSING**

農曆除夕休息
Closed CNY eve

TEL. 02 2720 6417

信義區仁愛路四段506號

506, Section 4, Ren'ai Road, Xinyi

■ 價錢 **PRICE**

午膳 Lunch
點菜 À la carte $ 400-500
晚膳 Dinner
點菜 À la carte $ 400-500

■ 營業時間 **OPENING HOURS**

午膳 Lunch 11:00-13:45
晚膳 Dinner 17:00-20:45

都一處 (信義)

DO IT TRUE (XINYI)

京菜・溫馨

Beijing Cuisine • Family

承襲自慈禧御廚的精湛廚藝，讓都一處走過超過一甲子歲月，每道菜都是道地北方佳餚。糟溜魚片選用深海石斑，為店家推薦；以溫體豬腿肉做成的炸丸子，外脆內嫩且充滿肉香，也值得一試。餅食均以小炭爐烤製，耗時費工卻反映店家的堅持，其中供十二人用的蔥油餅乾烙四十分鐘而成，每天限量三份，值得呼朋引伴共享。

The menu at this 60-plus-year-old restaurant offers variations of dishes that the owner's great uncle once cooked for Empress Cixi of Qing Dynasty. Crispy and juicy, the deep-fried pork balls made with hind leg cuts are an absolute must-try. Pork and cabbage pickle casserole, grouper fillet in distiller's grain sauce, and giant inch-thick scallion pancakes are also recommended. It's located on a tree-lined boulevard and comes with large windows and walnut wood furniture.

宋廚菜館
SUNG KITCHEN

京菜 · 簡樸

Beijing Cuisine • Simple

宋廚以皮脆肉嫩的炭爐烤鴨廣為人知，採用來自宜蘭養殖場的土番鴨，廚師以京式不開肚方法處理鴨子，且沒有加入辛香料，以帶出鴨肉本身甜味，烤好的鴨由店東端到客人面前親自片皮。除了烤鴨，各式東北菜亦遠近馳名，用酒糟處理的糟溜魚片北方味十足。需預訂菜色頗多，建議訂位時查詢。

Sung Kitchen is best known for chargrilled Muscovy ducks from Yilan County, with crispy skin and succulent flesh. Ducks are gutted via a small hole under the wing to keep them whole. No spices are added to let the natural umami come through. Apart from the famous duck, other north-eastern Chinese specialities, such as yellow croaker fillet in distillers' grain sauce, are also worth a try. Ask about dishes that need pre-ordering when you book your table.

TEL. 02 2764 4788

信義區忠孝東路五段15巷14號

14, Lane 15, Section 5, Zhongxiao East Road, Xinyi

■ 價錢 **PRICE**

午膳 Lunch
點菜 À la carte $ 350-700
晚膳 Dinner
點菜 À la carte $ 350-900

■ 營業時間 **OPENING HOURS**

午膳 Lunch 11:30-13:30
晚膳 Dinner 17:30-20:30

■ 休息日期 **ANNUAL AND WEEKLY CLOSING**

週日休息
Closed Sunday

寶艾
BEL AIR

牛排屋・新潮

Steakhouse • Chic

TEL. 02 2720 1230

信義區松壽路2號2樓（君悅酒店）

2F, Grand Hyatt Hotel, 2 Songshou Road, Xinyi

www.grandhyatttaipei.com

■ 價錢 **PRICE**

午膳 Lunch
套餐 Set Menu $ 1,880-4,980
點菜 À la carte $ 2,500-7,100
晚膳 Dinner
套餐 Set Menu $ 1,880-4,980
點菜 À la carte $ 2,500-7,100

■ 營業時間 **OPENING HOURS**

午膳 Lunch 11:30-13:45
晚膳 Dinner 18:00-20:45

或許這家位處酒店中的寶艾並不如其加州近郊的同名餐廳般舒適，然而卻為那些在商場中透不過氣的人提供了一扇呼吸的窗口，淺色系的地中海式裝潢和大理石水泉居功不少。在這用餐不得不品嚐其招牌美國和澳洲頂級牛排，肋眼品質尤佳。價格不算平易近人但絕對值得。

Amidst stone-clad columns, a marble fountain under a skylight is set nicely against a backdrop of greenery. Tables are bathed in natural daylight in this airy restaurant that reminds one of the Mediterranean, instead of the L. A. suburb after which it's named. The menu features prime steaks of the highest quality, from the U. S. and Australia, all cooked to perfection. Prices aren't particularly wallet-friendly, but the experience is worth it.

CHATEAU ZOE (N)

創新菜・舒適

Innovative • Cosy

結合酒窖與歐洲料理，環境輕鬆，是上班族聚餐的好地方。主廚為歐洲各地菜餚加入創意，每兩個月更換菜單，並不定期推出時令菜色，為客人帶來新鮮感。熱門選擇包括十二小時油封西班牙脆皮乳豬、來自東北角的炙烤野生小卷，以及宜蘭大溪港進貨的海鮮。不妨請熱情的服務人員提供意見和介紹菜色。

You'll find Château Zoe tucked away down an alley. The food shows the chef's creative ability as well as the influences of various European cuisines. The 12-hour Spanish roast suckling pig is an all-time favourite among diners, while fresh seafood shipped daily from Yilan County, such as grilled wild-caught pencil squids, is also a must-try. Look for the catch of the day on the chalkboard and ask the servers for their recommendations.

TEL. 02 8786 9663

信義區逸仙路32巷7號

7, Lane 32, Yixian Road, Xinyi

■ 價錢 **PRICE**

午膳 Lunch
點菜 À la carte $ 1,000-4,000
晚膳 Dinner
點菜 À la carte $ 1,000-4,000

■ 營業時間 **OPENING HOURS**

午膳 Lunch 11:30-13:30
晚膳 Dinner 18:00-21:00

■ 休息日期 **ANNUAL AND WEEKLY CLOSING**

除夕至初九及週日休息
Closed CNY eve to ninth day of CNY and Sunday

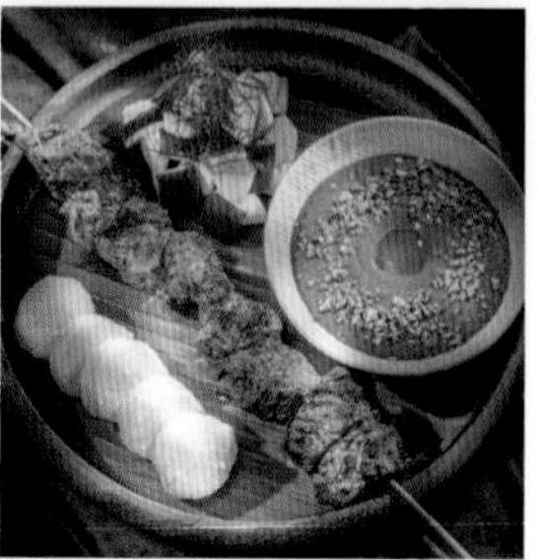

TEL. 02 2723 8118

信義區松高路19號4樓
(新光三越信義新天地A4館)

4F, Shin Kong Mitsukoshi Xinyi Place A4, 19 Songgao Road, Xinyi

■ 價錢 **PRICE**
點菜 À la carte $ 1,300-2,800

■ 營業時間 **OPENING HOURS**
11:30-21:00

CHOPE CHOPE EATERY

東南亞菜 · 新潮

South East Asian · Chic

在新加坡英文中，Chope是指「佔位子」，當地人到小販中心用餐時會把面紙放在座位上，象徵已被佔用。新加坡主廚從餐廳命名已經致力讓客人體會到其家鄉文化。菜單除了有多款新加坡菜，更兼容南洋元素，如蝦醬雞翅、摩卡排骨與自製的印度烙餅。此外，一系列調酒也不容錯過，如擺設有趣、充滿地道風情的小陳涼茶。

While 'chope' means to reserve a seat by putting a tissue pack on it in 'Singlish', you can call to book a table here. The Singaporean chef helming JL Studio in Taichung opened this Kopitiam concept to celebrate casual Singaporean dining. Try har cheong gai (fried wings in fermented shrimp sauce), kopi pai kut (coffee ribs) and house-made murtabak bread. Asian-inspired cocktails such as Tan herbal tea in a plastic bag are both fun and delicious.

老乾杯 (信義)
KANPAI CLASSIC (XINYI)

燒烤・舒適

Barbecue • Cosy

老闆在原有品牌綴上「老」字，冀盼成為專屬成熟大人的聚腳點，可是此店的客人相對年青，許是因它坐落商場之故。菜單與其他分店同出一轍，食客同樣可嚐到由日本直送的穀飼和牛、以北海道七星米所作的釜飯、還有別處嚐不到的滿壽泉清酒。設包廂或吧檯座位，唯後者不設燒烤爐，服務員會將食物烤好後奉上。

This branch of the chain is located in a shopping mall in the city centre and targets a younger crowd. The interior has a neo-Japanese feel to it, with hard wood floors, glass screen doors and moody lighting. The menu is the same as other branches – prime cuts of Japanese wagyu beef, exclusive Ginjo sake rice wine, Nanatsuboshi rice from Hokkaido, Japan, and an impressive wine list. Private rooms and counter seats are also available.

TEL. 02 2725 3311

信義區松壽路9號8樓
(新光三越信義新天地A9館)

8F, Shin Kong Mitsukoshi Xinyi Place A9, 9 Songshou Road, Xinyi

www.kanpaiclassic.com.tw

■ 價錢 **PRICE**

午膳 Lunch
套餐 Set Menu $ 580-980
點菜 À la carte $ 900-1,000
晚膳 Dinner
點菜 À la carte $ 1,500-2,000

■ 營業時間 **OPENING HOURS**

午膳 Lunch 11:30-14:30
晚膳 Dinner 17:00-22:30

MIRAWAN

時尚法國菜・新潮

French Contemporary • Chic

TEL. 02 2345 5222

信義區松智路17號47樓 (微風南山)

47F, Breeze Nan Shan, 17 Songzhi Road, Xinyi

www.mirawan.com.tw

■ 價錢 **PRICE**

午膳 Lunch

套餐 Set Menu $ 1,780-3,660

晚膳 Dinner

套餐 Set Menu $ 2,880-5,240

■ 營業時間 **OPENING HOURS**

午膳 Lunch 11:30-13:00

晚膳 Dinner 18:00-20:00

餐廳名字源於「Miracle of Taiwan」，採用唾手可得的在地食材，呈現法式料理的精神。室內的整面玻璃窗，以及潔白光亮的設計，在日間與晚上產生不同氛圍。只提供套餐，內容隨季節變更，其中的47溫沙拉和彰化熟成鴨是推薦菜色。同時備有佐餐葡萄酒和多款Mocktail，適合不同人士的需要。

A sister establishment of Taïrroir, Mirawan re-interprets French cooking with everyday local ingredients. Before this venture, the chef honed his skills at legendary French restaurant Le Moût in Taichung for a decade. An instant hit among diners since day one, warm salad 47 is like a garden blooming in your mouth. Changhua dry-aged duck with black garlic, angelica and clam is silky and flavourful. Non-drinkers can opt for the mocktail pairings.

穆記牛肉麵

MUJI BEEF NOODLES

麵食・簡樸

Noodles • Simple

店家每天七點就開始熬製湯頭，其秘方除了牛肉、中藥材及每天更換的骨頭等外，還包括了水果，因此特別甜美。牛肉麵採用本地產的牛肉，鮮度十足。斤餅製作從頭到尾由店家一手包辦，與滷味同樣不能錯過。店家待客周到，會細心講解外帶的處理，確保客人吃到應有風味。

The three sisters who run the place are very specific about their cooking. The flavoursome broth is made with beef bones and meat, Chinese herbs, scallion, garlic and a secret fruit that lends a subtle sweetness. The signature beef noodle soup uses only local beef for its unrivalled meaty flavour. Equally addictive is their jinbing – a fluffy pancake made to order with beef or pork wrapped inside. Don't miss their marinated food either.

TEL. 02 2722 2707

信義區吳興街239號

239 Wuxing Street, Xinyi

■ 價錢 **PRICE**

午膳 Lunch
點菜 À la carte $ 100-300
晚膳 Dinner
點菜 À la carte $ 100-300

■ 營業時間 **OPENING HOURS**

午膳 Lunch 11:00-14:55
晚膳 Dinner 17:00-20:55

■ 休息日期 **ANNUAL AND WEEKLY CLOSING**

週三及週四休息
Closed Wednesday and Thursday

TEL. 02 6622 8018

信義區松仁路38號2樓
(寒舍艾美酒店)

2F, Le Méridien Hotel, 38 Songren Road, Xinyi

www.lemeridien-taipei.com

■ 價錢 **PRICE**

午膳 Lunch
套餐 Set Menu $ 1,380-3,980
點菜 À la carte $ 1,500-3,500
晚膳 Dinner
套餐 Set Menu $ 2,580-3,980
點菜 À la carte $ 1,500-3,500

■ 營業時間 **OPENING HOURS**

午膳 Lunch 11:30-14:00
晚膳 Dinner 18:00-21:00

寒舍食譜
MY HUMBLE HOUSE

粵菜 · 型格

Cantonese · Design

低調謙卑的名字，配以紅黑色調的裝潢和水墨畫作，充滿格調和品味。主廚於臺灣土生土長，但烹調粵菜經驗到家，聯同新加入的廚師團隊成員，以優質材料呈現傳統風味。無論點心、燒味或小菜，都令人留下深刻印象。得意之作包括脆皮先知鴨、XO醬乾炒蘿蔔糕，以及採用上肩肉製作、帶焦香的古法叉燒。

Despite its name, the dining room itself is not that humble – red carpet, black furniture and the oversized ink painting speak loudly of style and luxury. The menu is authentically Cantonese, but the quality ingredients are unmistakably Taiwanese. Spice-marinated baby roast duck uses cherry ducks from Yilan city, with juicy tender meat and crisp skin. Dim sum, stir-fries and barbecued meat, such as thick-sliced char siu pork, are also unmissable.

鮨七海

SUSHI NANAMI BY MASA ISHIBASHI

壽司・舒適

Sushi • Cosy

餐廳位於巷弄，店前設日式小庭園，並由身穿和服的服務員引領食客內進。主廚由石橋正和欽點來臺駐店，其壽司飯以赤醋調味，招牌鰻魚棒壽司以其家鄉的八重味噌拌入米飯，配上烤靜岡鰻魚，滋味無窮。最後登場的玉子燒混合了山藥泥和蜂蜜，口感如同濕潤的蜂蜜蛋糕，味甜綿密，韻味悠長。

This really does feel like a tucked away Japanese residence – the kimono-clad hostess walks you through the garden into the dining room with only 12 seats at a cypress counter. The Japanese chef makes Edomae sushi with rice dressed in red vinegar. His signature unagi maki is rice seasoned with tangy miso topped with grilled eel from Shizuoka. Don't miss the tamagoyaki served at the end – it's more like a moist sponge cake than an omelette.

TEL. 02 2758 0266

信義區仁愛路四段452巷6號

6, Lane 452, Section 4, Ren'ai Road, Xinyi

■ 價錢 PRICE

午膳 Lunch
套餐 Set Menu $ 3,800
晚膳 Dinner
套餐 Set Menu $ 5,800

■ 營業時間 OPENING HOURS

午膳 Lunch 12:00-15:00
晚膳 Dinner 18:00-22:00

■ 休息日期 ANNUAL AND WEEKLY CLOSING

元旦、除夕至初四；週二、週五、週日午膳及週一休息

Closed New Year's Day, CNY eve to fourth day of CNY; Tuesday lunch, Friday lunch, Sunday lunch and Monday

THE UKAI

鐵板燒・時尚

Teppanyaki • Contemporary Décor

TEL. 02 7730 1166

信義區松仁路100號46樓（微風南山）

46F, Breeze Nan Shan, 100 Songren Road, Xinyi

www.ukai-tpe.com.tw

■ 價錢 **PRICE**

午膳 Lunch
套餐 Set Menu $ 2,500-3,500
晚膳 Dinner
套餐 Set Menu $ 6,000-7,500

■ 營業時間 **OPENING HOURS**

午膳 Lunch 12:00-14:00
晚膳 Dinner 18:00-21:00

■ 休息日期 **ANNUAL AND WEEKLY CLOSING**

農曆除夕休息
Closed CNY eve

日本Ukai集團在臺灣的第二家餐廳，環境優雅有格調，座位都依著落地窗，可遠眺山景與城內景色。集團分店的菜單均由各自的日籍料理長擬定，唯一不變的是其西式風格。提供兩種無菜單套餐，建議選擇晚間七道菜的六千元套餐，除了和牛主菜，也包含鮑魚岩鹽蒸、蒜香炒飯等經典菜式。用餐後不妨到休息區享用蓬鬆的戚風蛋糕。

This is the second Taiwanese outpost of its namesake in Japan, famous for its Western chef table experience delivered with teppanyaki techniques. There is no à la carte and the two prix-fixe menus change according to the seasons and availability. Signatures include steamed abalone with rock salt, garlic fried rice, and Wagyu beef exclusively from Tamura farm. Round it all off with moist chiffon cake in the comfy lounge with its expansive views.

鳥喜
TORIKI

日本菜・簡約

Japanese • Minimalist

來自東京的餐廳主打日式串燒，所用雞肉為臺灣頂級品種桂丁雞，由日本總廚坂井康人挑選。廚師串肉的方法承襲日本，醬料和調味料亦由日本空運而來；特別推薦手羽燒。三位主廚交替到東京學習，坂井也會定期來台監督運作，務求餐廳水準媲美本店。

An outpost of the celebrated yakitori restaurant in Tokyo, this branch is keen to re-create the authentic experience on this side of the South China Sea. The barbecue sauce and salad dressing are flown in from Japan and even the meat is skewered the same way as the flagship shop. The top-grade Taiwanese Gui Ding chicken is chosen especially for this branch and regular checks are made to ensure its quality is consistent.

TEL. 02 2723 2288

信義區松壽路26號

26 Songshou Road, Xinyi

■ 價錢 PRICE

午膳 Lunch
套餐 Set Menu $ 260-320
點菜 À la carte $ 800-1,500
晚膳 Dinner
套餐 Set Menu $ 800-1,000
點菜 À la carte $ 1,000-2,000

■ 營業時間 OPENING HOURS

午膳 Lunch 12:00-13:30
晚膳 Dinner 18:00-22:30

■ 休息日期 ANNUAL AND WEEKLY CLOSING

除夕至初一休息
Closed CNY eve to first day of CNY

TEL. 02 2722 8886

信義區松壽路9號4樓
(新光三越信義新天地A9館)

4F, Shin Kong Mitsukoshi Xinyi Place A9, 9 Songshou Road, Xinyi

www.wildwood.com.tw

■ 價錢 PRICE

午膳 Lunch
套餐 Set Menu $ 780-2,180
點菜 À la carte $ 1,300-4,800
晚膳 Dinner
點菜 À la carte $ 1,300-4,800

■ 營業時間 OPENING HOURS

午膳 Lunch 11:30-14:30
晚膳 Dinner 17:30-21:00

WILDWOOD

燒烤 · 前衛

Barbecue · Trendy

主廚透過柴燒方式將料理回歸至最原始狀態，每道炭烤菜色都用採自臺南的龍眼木燒烤而成，從主菜美國乾式熟成帶骨紐約客或紅屋牛排，以至配菜炙烤綠蘆筍，皆展現廚師對於火候的精準掌握。餐廳精心調配多款特色醬汁，例如帶東南亞風味的是拉差金桔醬，味道酸甜，與海鮮是絕配。用餐前可於露臺淺酌一杯，近距離欣賞臺北101美景。

A dining concept from owner-chef Lam of Longtail fame, this spot champions a primitive way of cooking – adding smokiness to everything over a longan-wood charcoal grill. Highlights include the 28-day dry-aged bone-in striploin and porterhouse steaks. The chef also makes an array of exotic sauces to go with your food, such as Sriracha kumquat sauce. Before dinner, enjoy a cocktail during happy hour and behold Taipei 101 up close from the patio.

義興樓

YI HSING PAVILION

臺灣菜・簡樸

Taiwanese • Simple

創於1938年，至今已傳至第四代，一直為食客帶來經濟實惠的古早臺灣料理。招牌菜金錢蝦以豬後腿的豬油剖成袋狀包覆內餡，並炸成金黃的小圓餅，一口咬下鮮美肉汁如爆漿般溢出，叫人讚嘆；另一推介為炒豬頭骨肉，口感帶嚼勁。環境雖古樸簡單，一道道菜色卻令人憶起農村時期令人回味無窮的老好滋味。

Founded in 1938, this family business is now run by the fourth generation who still insists on serving good quality, traditional farmhouse cooking at wallet-friendly prices. The interior isn't that lavish, but the food will leave a lasting impression. The signature dish of shrimp-filled 'gold coins' are pork fat medallions stuffed and fried till crisp and golden – flavoursome juices squirt with every bite. Stir-fried pork head is springy and tasty.

TEL. 02 2931 3966
文山區景文街121號
121 Jingwen Street, Wenshan

■ 價錢 PRICE
午膳 Lunch
點菜 À la carte $ 250-500
晚膳 Dinner
點菜 À la carte $ 300-600

■ 營業時間 OPENING HOURS
午膳 Lunch 11:30-13:30
晚膳 Dinner 17:30-20:30

■ 休息日期 ANNUAL AND WEEKLY CLOSING
除夕至初五休息
Closed CNY eve to fifth day of CNY

文山區 **WENSHAN**
信義區 **XINYI**

夜市
NIGHT MARKETS

景美夜市
Jingmei

位置交通便利，販售典型傳統小吃，深受學生及上班族喜愛，光顧用餐的人群絡繹不絕，吸引了不少電視節目採訪。

Focusing on traditional snacks, this night market is popular among students and white-collar workers thanks to its convenient location. It has also featured in many TV programs.

景美鵝媽媽
JINGMEI GOOSE MAMA

招牌鵝肉肉質柔嫩，白切的清甜，煙燻的香氣濃郁。另有鴨肉與鴨肉麵類可供選擇。

Boiled or smoked, the goose is always juicy and velvety. The offal and duck noodles also stand out.

文山區景美街37之3號

37-3 Jingmei Street, Wenshan

價錢 **PRICE:** $ 80-300

營業時間 **OPENING HOURS:** 14:00-22:30

週一休息 **Closed Monday**

景美米粉湯
JINGMEI THICK RICE NOODLES

粗米粉吸盡大骨精華，滑嫩而不軟爛。炸三鮮外酥內嫩，搭配脆口的醃黃瓜，不容錯過。

Noodles soak up the flavourful pork bone soup; deep-fried seafood trio with cucumber is another must-try.

文山區景美街119號

119 Jingmei Street, Wenshan

價錢 **PRICE:** $ 40-195

營業時間 **OPENING HOURS:** 16:00-00:00

文山區 **WENSHAN**
信義區 **XINYI**

酒店
HOTELS

君悅
GRAND HYATT

商務・現代

Business • Modern

處於市內心臟地帶，毗鄰臺北101大樓，單是位置已襯托出酒店的氣派，大堂內鋪設的大理石地板以及中央噴泉，更突顯其富麗堂皇。兩層閣樓包羅各種類的餐廳予客人多樣化選擇。酒店內具備優秀的配套設施，露天游泳池恍如坐落綠洲中，讓人能在鬧市包圍下一洗煩囂。唯標準套房內並未設有浴缸，欲浸浴便要預訂豪華客房。

Located right next to Taipei 101 and World Trade Centre Complex at the CBD, this property from a prestigious global chain comes with a fountain in its marble-floored lobby, a two-tiered mezzanine of restaurants offering various dining options, a spa with an open-air pool and a myriad of meeting and function spaces. Rooms are modern and sleek, but standard rooms have no bathtubs.

TEL. 02 2720 1234
www.grandhyatttaipei.com

信義區松壽路2號
2 Songshou Road, Xinyi

850 客房/**Rooms** $ 6,000-18,600
94 套房/**Suites** $ 6,000-180,000

餐廳推薦/**Recommended restaurants:**
寶艾 **Bel Air**

TEL. 02 7703 8888
www.wtaipei.com

信義區忠孝東路五段10號
10, Section 5, Zhongxiao East Road, Xinyi

357 客房/**Rooms** $ 12,000-30,000
48 套房/**Suites** $ 17,000-50,000

W

商務·前衛
Business • Trendy

矗立於商業區心臟地帶，包羅購物中心於低層，W飯店以設計營造新潮時尚格調。房間設計風格明亮而色彩對比強，能一睹臺北101風光更令其值得選擇。The Kitchen Table全日提供賞心悅目的餐點，頂樓則有提供粵菜的紫豔中餐廳及時尚精緻的紫豔酒吧。酒店另設有健身中心與游泳池。

This towering hotel in the CBD, with a shopping mall on its lower floors, prides itself on its style. Rooms are design-led and come furnished with sleek finishes and colours, but those with the views of Taipei 101 are worth paying extra for. The Kitchen Table for all-day dining is cheerful and bright, while Yen on the top floor houses a Cantonese restaurant with a funky bar.

寒舍艾麗
HUMBLE HOUSE

精品酒店・型格

Boutique Hotel • Design

由一樓的迎賓大廳到六樓的大堂，此精品酒店處處盡現其時尚別緻的設計風格。在酒店內隨行隨走，各類藝術品就躍然於眼前。設施如天臺花園、露天游泳池以及藝廊，處處均流露出輕快活力。房間設計精緻舒適，其中有三分一可觀賞到臺北101大樓，訂房時宜特別挑選；另首席客房具備更寬敞的浸浴空間，物有所值。

This boutique hotel in Taipei's shopping hub appeals to the hip and fashionable with chic designs, bright airy rooms, artsy roof gardens, a funky outdoor pool and impressive eco-credentials. One-third of the rooms have views of Taipei 101 so be sure to ask for one. Superior rooms come with small square tubs that many may find inadequate, so a Premier room is worth paying extra for.

TEL. 02 6631 8000
www.humblehousehotels.com

信義區松高路18號
18 Songgao Road, Xinyi

225 客房/**Rooms** $ 8,000-38,000
10 套房/**Suites** $ 18,000-240,000

臺中

TAICHUNG

天生一對
文思泉湧

N
臺灣大道四段
Sec. 4 Taiwan Boulevard
路思義教堂
The Luce Chapel
西屯區
XITUN
黎明路三段
Sec. 3 Liming Road
中清路二段
Sec. 2 Zhongqing Road
中山高速公路
Sun Yat-sen Freeway
安和路
Anhe Road
臺灣大道三段
Sec.3 Taiwan Boulevard
秋紅谷廣場
Maple Garden
環中路三段
Sec. 3 Huanzhong Road
黎明路二段
Sec.2 Liming Road
臺灣大道二段
Sec. 2 Taiwan Boulevard
五權西路三段
Sec.3 Wuquan West Road
向上路五段
Sec. 5 Xiangshang Road
草悟道
Calligraphy Greenway
五權西路二段
Sec. 2 Wuquan West Road
向上路二段
Sec. 2 Xiangshang Road
審計新村
Shen Ji New Village
南屯區
NANTUN
西區
WEST
環中路四段
Sec. 4 Huanzhong Road
彩虹眷村
Rainbow Village
嶺東南路
Lingdong South Road
南屯路一段
Sec. 1 Nantun Road
建國北路二段
Sec. 2 Jianguo North Road
東西向快速公路 快官霧峰線
Provincial Highway 74
黎明路一段
Sec. 1 Liming Road
環中路五段
Sec. 5 Huanzhong Road
建國路
Jianguo Road
復興路一段
Sec.1 Fuxing Road
中山高速公路
Sun Yat-sen Freeway
中山路三段
Sec. 3 Zhongshan Road
中山路一段
Sec. 1 Zhongshan Road
烏日區
WURI
五光路
Wuguang Road

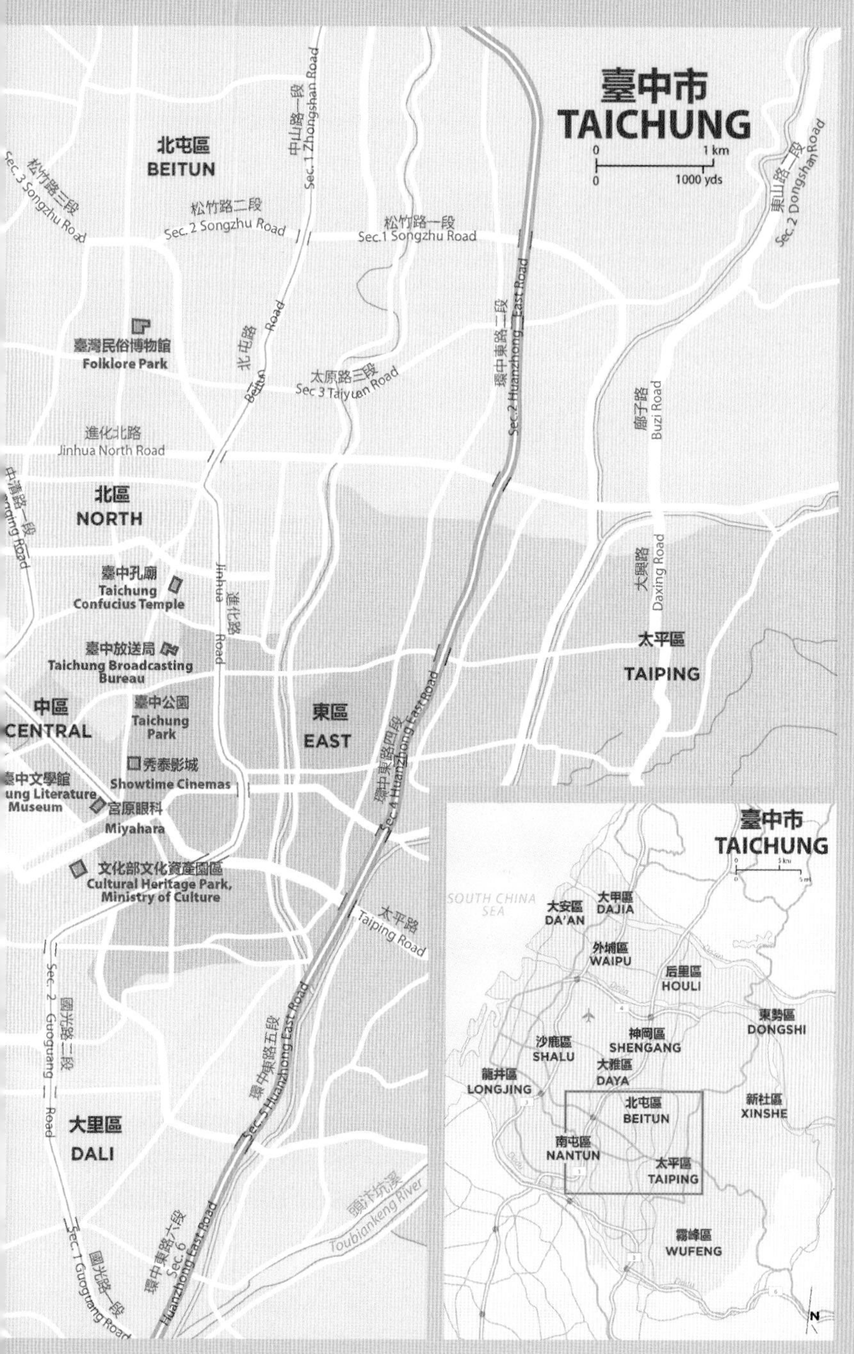

臺中市
TAICHUNG
0
1 km
0
1000 yds
北屯區
BEITUN
北區
NORTH
中區
CENTRAL
東區
EAST
太平區
TAIPING
大里區
DALI
中山路一段
Sec.1 Zhongshan Road
松竹路三段
Sec.3 Songzhu Road
松竹路二段
Sec.2 Songzhu Road
松竹路一段
Sec.1 Songzhu Road
東山路二段
Sec.2 Dongshan Road
北屯路
Beitun Road
太原路三段
Sec 3 Taiyuan Road
環中東路二段
Sec.2 Huanzhong East Road
廍子路
Buzi Road
進化北路
Jinhua North Road
中清路一段
Zhongqing Road
進化路
Jinhua Road
大興路
Daxing Road
環中東路四段
Sec.4 Huanzhong East Road
太平路
Taiping Road
環中東路五段
Sec.5 Huanzhong East Road
環中東路六段
Sec.6
Huanzhong East Road
國光路二段
Sec. 2 Guoguang Road
國光路一段
Sec.1 Guoguang Road
頭汴坑溪
Toubiankeng River
臺灣民俗博物館
Folklore Park
臺中孔廟
Taichung Confucius Temple
臺中放送局
Taichung Broadcasting Bureau
臺中公園
Taichung Park
秀泰影城
Showtime Cinemas
臺中文學館
ung Literature Museum
宮原眼科
Miyahara
文化部文化資產園區
Cultural Heritage Park, Ministry of Culture
臺中市
TAICHUNG
SOUTH CHINA SEA
大安區
DA'AN
大甲區
DAJIA
外埔區
WAIPU
后里區
HOULI
東勢區
DONGSHI
沙鹿區
SHALU
神岡區
SHENGANG
大雅區
DAYA
龍井區
LONGJING
北屯區
BEITUN
新社區
XINSHE
南屯區
NANTUN
太平區
TAIPING
霧峰區
WUFENG
N

Jui-Chi Chan/iStock

中區

CENTRAL

餐廳
RESTAURANTS

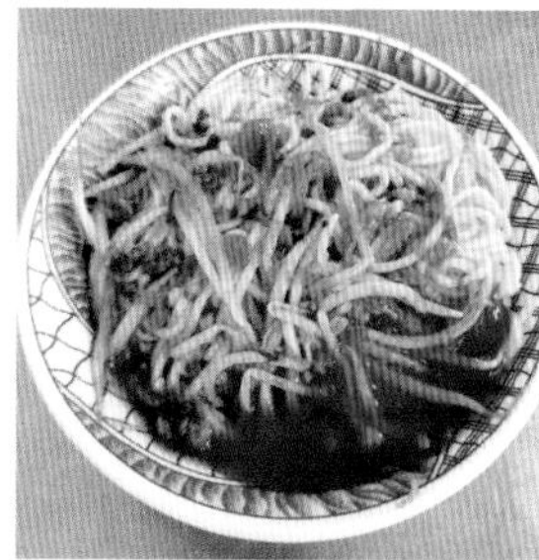

阿坤麵 Ⓝ

A KUN MIAN

麵食·簡樸

Noodles · Simple

顧名思義，麵店由阿坤創辦，目前已經超過五十年歷史，傳至第三代掌舵。小店幾乎沒有裝潢，客人要先在門口點選食物，然後尋找座位。每天早上至中午提供古早味乾麵，搭配特製甜辣醬，十分滋味。湯則可選擇不同配料，包括最受歡迎的水晶餃、油豆腐，還有貢丸、豬血和福州丸等。亦可選綜合湯。

Most Taichungians will be familiar with this shop as it's been around for more than five decades – it's now run by the third generation of the family. Open only till noon, it serves blanched noodles tossed in braised ground pork sauce and fried scallion – and a dab of the sweet chilli sauce is mandatory. Soups with glass dumplings, fried tofu, pork balls or blood pudding are also popular; try them all by ordering an assortment.

TEL. 0955 923 877

中區平等街142號

142 Pingdeng Street, Central

https://restaurant-48129.business.site

■ 價錢 **PRICE**

點菜 À la carte $ 50-80

■ 營業時間 **OPENING HOURS**

06:00-13:00

■ 休息日期 **ANNUAL AND WEEKLY CLOSING**

農曆新年休息5天
Closed 5 days CNY

TEL. 04 2220 7388

中區成功路170號

170 Chenggong Road, Central

■ 價錢 **PRICE**

點菜 À la carte $ 130-300

■ 營業時間 **OPENING HOURS**

10:30-19:30

■ 休息日期 **ANNUAL AND WEEKLY CLOSING**

除夕至初五及週四休息

Closed CNY eve to fifth day of CNY and Thursday

范記金之園 N

CHIN CHIH YUAN

臺灣菜 · 簡樸

Taiwanese • Simple

創立自1978年，現已傳至第二代，其傳統滋味廣受好評，招牌菜為排骨草袋飯。早期的草袋飯是在手工編製的藺草草袋中烹煮而成，藺草混合米香，風味獨特。雖然草袋技術已凋零，店家仍然選用霧峰臺梗九號米，口感飽滿，配合特製的雪裡紅乾，鹹香滋味。另推薦秘製的排骨和沙茶炒牛肉。所有餐點均現點製作，須耐心等待。

Founded in 1978, this shop made its name with its rice – steamed in a soft rush-woven pouch that imparts unique aromas. Though no longer cooked that way, quality local rice is now topped with a dab of house-made pickled potherb mustard for savoury sweetness. Deep-fried pork ribs, and beef in sacha sauce are the hottest choices to go with the rice. The food may take time to arrive as everything is prepared to order. Expect to queue at lunch.

富鼎旺 (中區)
FU DIN WANG (CENTRAL)

臺灣菜 · 簡樸

Taiwanese • Simple

採用特別的滷製方法，以醬油、紅蔥酥、糖和辣椒等代替中藥材，並以細火燉煮，熬製出滷豬腳、腿扣、腿節等美食。豬腳口感軟滑而且鹹香入味，搭配自家製作的辣椒醬，額外美味。同時提供魯肉飯、潤油豆腐等食品，全都價廉物美。小店為自助式，先於店前點餐，再自行入座，氣氛輕鬆隨意。

Diners come to this self-service shop for its pork trotter, hock and leg that are braised in a marinade of soy, fried shallot, sugar and chilli for up to four hours. The pork is gelatinous, tender and flavourful; it tastes even better with the house-made chilli sauce, but as opposed to the typical marinade with strong herbal undertones, its taste is clean and less complex. Braised diced pork rice and braised fried tofu are also good.

TEL. 04 2225 3188

中區臺灣大道一段560號

560, Section 1, Taiwan Boulevard, Central

www.fudinwang.com

■ 價錢 **PRICE**

午膳 Lunch
點菜 À la carte $ 100-200
晚膳 Dinner
點菜 À la carte $ 100-200

■ 營業時間 **OPENING HOURS**

午膳 Lunch 11:00-15:00
晚膳 Dinner 16:30-20:00

■ 休息日期 **ANNUAL AND WEEKLY CLOSING**

週二休息
Closed Tuesday

富貴亭 N

FU KUEI TING

臺灣菜 · 親切

Taiwanese · Neighbourhood

開業逾六十年的富貴亭，是許多居民的童年回憶，販售筒仔米糕和各種當歸湯品。其中，當歸鴨肉麵線味道濃郁，十分美味。但最受歡迎的，始終是當歸鵝肉麵線和燻鵝肉，前者把鵝湯、鴨湯一起加入當歸湯中，香味四溢，每天開賣半個小時左右便會售罄。小店座位有限，無法訂位，也可能需與人拼桌。

Many Taichungians have fond childhood memories of this shop as it has over 60 years of history. Its signature goose noodle soup and smoked goose tend to sell out within the first 30 minutes every morning. The soup base features the Chinese herb Dang Gui, while the bird boasts springy flesh and robust flavours. If goose runs out, try the equally appealing duck version. Rice cakes in bamboo stem are also well made. Be prepared to share a table.

TEL. 04 2227 3001

中區三民路二段18巷31號

31, Lane 18, Section 2, Sanmin Road, Central

■ 價錢 **PRICE**

點菜 À la carte $ 60-200

■ 營業時間 **OPENING HOURS**

11:00-20:30

■ 休息日期 **ANNUAL AND WEEKLY CLOSING**

週日休息
Closed Sunday

上海未名麵點 N

NO NAME NOODLES

麵食 · 親切

Noodles · Neighbourhood

開業逾七十載，經歷三代的傳承，堅持供應家庭風味的上海麵食。他們甚至與造麵廠合作，根據家傳配方，製作出獨家口味、不含化學添加劑的上海麵。推薦用新鮮豬肉烹調的豬排麵，佐以自由添加的醃蔥段，十分解膩。另有多款涼菜供外帶，如酸豆、黃瓜等。鮮製的烏梅汁帶天然甜酸味，更是不容錯過。

With over 70 years of history, this neighbourhood noodle shop is now run by the third generation of the family. Throughout those decades, regulars have been coming for the preservative-free Shanghainese noodle soup served with pork chop, beef shin or zhajiang sauce. The fried-to-order pork chop goes well with iced sour plum tea and the spicy pickled scallion and garlic. Don't miss other side dishes such as pickled cucumber and string beans.

TEL. 04 2225 0377

中區市府路69號

69 Shifu Road, Central

■ 價錢 **PRICE**

點菜 À la carte $ 110-200

■ 營業時間 **OPENING HOURS**

07:00-13:30

■ 休息日期 **ANNUAL AND WEEKLY CLOSING**

週日休息

Closed Sunday

TEL. 04 2220 0735

中區臺灣大道一段129號

129, Section 1, Taiwan Boulevard, Central

■ 價錢 **PRICE**

午膳 Lunch
點菜 À la carte $ 500-1,000
晚膳 Dinner
點菜 À la carte $ 500-1,000

■ 營業時間 **OPENING HOURS**

午膳 Lunch 11:00-14:00
晚膳 Dinner 17:00-20:30

沁園春 N

QIN YUAN CHUN

江浙菜 · 經典

Jiangzhe · Classic Décor

開業逾七十載，至今已經傳至第四代，深受老顧客支持。內部採用傳統中式餐館設計，備有懷舊的沙發座椅、鏡子牆面和木製匾額。致力提供經典江浙菜和點心，小籠包、肴肉、醉雞、鱔糊等應有盡有，而且每道菜色均列明製作時間。小籠包現點現蒸，皮薄、肉餡飽滿且充滿湯汁，建議提早點菜，以免久候。

Run by fourth-generation owners, this 70-plus-year-old family business is usually full of regulars. The dining room is plainly furnished, but customers don't come for the ambiance, but the authentic Jiangzhe classics such as pork trotter aspic, drunken chicken and stir-fried swamp eel. Steamed-to-order xiao long bao boast thin, translucent skin and soupy pork filling. The take-out counter offers quick service for those on the go.

茂川肉丸 Ⓝ
MAO CHUAN

麵食・親切

Noodles • Neighbourhood

別看這小麵店裝潢簡樸，其實擁有過百年歷史。雖然經歷多次名字更改，始終不變的，是其手工製作的招牌肉丸，原材料包括在來米、太白粉、地瓜粉等，充滿嚼勁，而且毫無油膩感。佐以加入砂糖的白色米醬，與加入辣椒的特製海山醬享用，非常可口。另外提供每天現包的鮮蝦餛飩，皮薄透亮，同樣吸引。

This century-old institution had humble beginnings as a market stall. Though rechristened a few times, its signature ba-wan dumplings with ground pork filling in a translucent, bouncy skin have stayed the same. The fourth generation of the family insist on making the dumplings fresh each day. Drizzle with sweetened rice paste and the mildly spicy chilli rice paste for the ultimate ba-wan experience. They make great shrimp wontons too.

TEL. 04 2227 7477

中區臺灣大道一段401號

401, Section 1, Taiwan Boulevard, Central

■ 價錢 **PRICE**

點菜 À la carte $ 60-200

■ 營業時間 **OPENING HOURS**

11:30-19:00

■ 休息日期 **ANNUAL AND WEEKLY CLOSING**

週一休息

Closed Monday

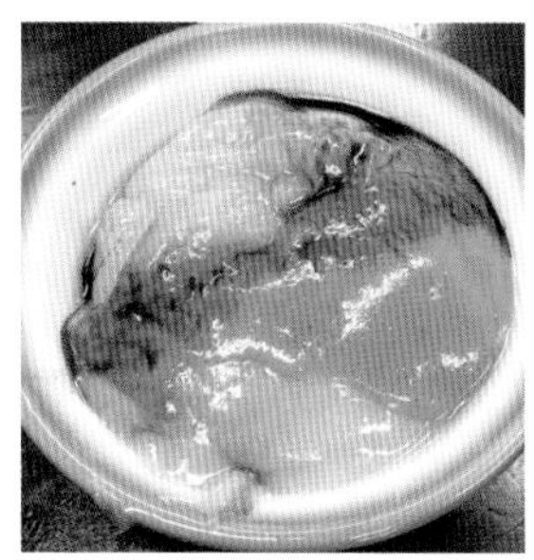

酒店
HOTELS

紅點文旅 N

REDDOT

精品酒店・型格

Boutique Hotel • Design

建築採用紅磚外牆，富有懷舊氛圍，室內設計卻時尚有趣，混合多種藝術元素。最具標誌性的，則是那道貫穿一、二樓的滑梯。房間設備齊全，純白床組佐客家花布作裝飾，簡約並帶臺灣特色。附有酒吧和餐廳，可預約餐廳空間作會議地點。房客可使用特約停車場，或向親切友善的員工租借自行車，遊覽市內景點。

The red-brick architecture exudes the quaint flair of yesteryear. Eclectic design styles such as headboards wrapped in Hakkanese fabric and a metallic serpentine slide connecting the bottom floors are juxtaposed to great effect in this hotel geared towards a hipster crowd. Rooms are well equipped, and come with bathroom amenities organized in a mini suitcase along with a pod coffee machine.

TEL. 04 2229 8333
www.reddot-hotel.com

中區民族路206號
206 Minzu Road, Central

55 客房/**Rooms** $ 2,280-6,880
1 套房/**Suite** $ 3,880-6,200

Jui-Chi Chan/iStock

西區
北區

WEST & NORTH

西區 WEST
北區 NORTH

餐廳
RESTAURANTS

俺達的肉屋 Ⓝ

ORETACHI NO NIKUYA

燒烤 · 友善

Barbecue • Friendly

餐廳名字解作「我們的肉屋」，是一家專賣和牛的燒肉店，提供飛驒牛、橄欖牛、神戶牛等品種。從日本進口原隻和牛之後，會由師傅手工分切，並採取乾式熟成冷藏。特別推薦盛合，即包含五種和牛部位的綜合拼盤，可以按人數調整至合適的份量。服務貼心，不僅有專人代烤，更可請店員介紹肉類特點和隱藏菜單。

With a name meaning 'our meat house' in Japanese, this restaurant specialises in Wagyu barbecue. The menu features Hida beef cuts mainly, but other rare breeds such as Kobe beef from Hyogo and Olive beef from Kagawa are also available at times. The popular assortment of five different cuts is handpicked by the chef each day and servers will grill the meat to perfection at your table. Ask about the secret menu for those in the know...

TEL. 04 2325 0588

西區公益路192之1號

192-1 Gongyi Road, West

■ 價錢 **PRICE**

晚膳 Dinner

點菜 À la carte $ 2,000-3,000

■ 營業時間 **OPENING HOURS**

晚膳 Dinner 17:00-23:00

■ 休息日期 **ANNUAL AND WEEKLY CLOSING**

農曆除夕休息

Closed CNY eve

TEL. 04 2377 0007
西區存中街47號
47 Cunzhong Street, West
www.chilliesine.com.tw

■ 價錢 **PRICE**
午膳 Lunch
套餐 Set Menu $ 388-399
點菜 À la carte $ 500-1,000
晚膳 Dinner
套餐 Set Menu $ 388
點菜 À la carte $ 500-1,000

■ 營業時間 **OPENING HOURS**
午膳 Lunch 11:30-14:30
晚膳 Dinner 17:30-21:00

淇里思 (西區) N
CHILLIESINE (WEST)

印度菜 · 異國風情

Indian · Exotic Décor

開業短短幾年，已經設有分店，證明這家餐廳的吸引力。提供南、北印度美食，由印度籍廚師團隊負責，講究選用當地香料，以確保原汁原味。菜單設計非常貼心，既可選擇辣度，也對素食、適合兒童食用的加上標籤說明。其中，香料塔都雞腿香味十足，鷹嘴豆咖哩也不容錯過。樓高兩層，二樓可包場舉辦聚會。

Now with two branches in Taichung, Chilliesine has been serving authentic food from across India since 2015. The kitchen team hails from both the north and the south and cooks exclusively with spices from home – you can specify your desired spiciness in certain dishes. Tandoori chicken packs a punch with big flavours and aromas; Chanda masala is not to be missed either. The menu also offers vegan options and popular choices for children.

富狀元豬腳 N

FU JUANG YUAN

臺灣菜・簡樸

Taiwanese • Simple

這家知名豬腳餐廳的特色，是不添加中藥材滷包，而將白毛豬隻，搭配特調比例的紅蔥、辣椒、冰糖與醬油，把肉滷至呈琥珀色澤、晶瑩透亮。不論是富含彈性和膠質的豬腳，或半肥半瘦的腿扣，都多汁可口。爽口筍絲等小菜也滋味無窮，再加上一碗白飯加滷汁，風味十足，令人大快朵頤。

One of the most famous places in town for marinated pork trotters, this shop keeps the liquid gold – made with soy, rock sugar, chilli and shallot – on a gentle simmer all day, hence the comforting aroma. While trotters are prized for their gelatinous texture, upper leg cuts strike a balance between fat, skin and meat. Side dishes such as shredded bamboo shoots are also good. Instead of plain steamed rice, try it with a drizzle of marinade.

TEL. 04 2301 3588

西區美村路一段203號

203, Section 1, Meicun Road, West

www.fu-deka.com

■ 價錢 **PRICE**

點菜 À la carte $ 180-250

■ 營業時間 **OPENING HOURS**

11:00-20:00

■ 休息日期 **ANNUAL AND WEEKLY CLOSING**

除夕至初五及週一休息

Closed CNY eve to fifth day of CNY and Monday

GUBAMI Ⓝ

麵食 · 舒適

Noodles • Cosy

名字為臺語牛肉麵的諧音。老闆原為法餐主廚，採用西式烹調技巧與食材，呈現臺灣經典美食。牛肉麵分為清燉與紅燒，兩種湯頭均熬製十小時以上。前者以宮崎和牛搭配特製細麵，後者則選用加拿大帶骨牛小排與特製粗麵，另有黑松露辣醬，十分適合嗜辣者。鵝油燜節瓜、香辣雪耳牛肉等小菜也十分精緻，值得一試。

The chef of a no-longer-open French restaurant opened this beef noodle soup shop in 2018, reinterpreting this classic dish using Western techniques and ingredients. The clear broth version uses Miyazaki Wagyu with fine noodles, whereas the red-braised variety uses Canadian short ribs with chunky noodles and truffle chilli sauce on the side, both slow-cooked for over 10 hours. Noodles are custom-made partly with Italian flour; sides also fare well.

TEL. 04 2376 3801

西區存中街46號

46 Cunzhong Street, West

■ 價錢 **PRICE**

午膳 Lunch
點菜 À la carte $ 450-1,000
晚膳 Dinner
點菜 À la carte $ 450-1,000

■ 營業時間 **OPENING HOURS**

午膳 Lunch 12:00-14:00
晚膳 Dinner 18:00-20:00

■ 休息日期 **ANNUAL AND WEEKLY CLOSING**

週一休息
Closed Monday

陸園 N

LU YUAN

江浙菜 · 友善

Jiangzhe · Friendly

這裡儘管沒有華麗裝飾，卻有美味菜餚和舒適的服務，營造家庭般的溫暖感覺。廚師團隊跟隨創辦人工作三十年餘，經驗豐富，擅於烹調傳統江浙菜色，火候掌握尤其恰到好處。特別推薦蔥燒鯽魚，其飽滿的魚卵，加上酥脆的魚骨，滋味鮮香。另外，寧式鱔糊、干貝絲瓜也是不錯的選擇。大型聚餐不妨考慮包廂座位。

Though founder Chef Lu is no longer at the helm, the kitchen team who worked with him for over 30 years now shoulder the responsibility of realizing his culinary vision – classic Jiangzhe comfort food that emphasizes depth of flavour through the precise use of heat. Braised crucian carp with scallion is filled with plump roe and crispy bones while stir-fried swamp eel strips in Ningbo style, and angled luffa with dried scallops are also good.

TEL. 04 2202 0061

西區民權路248號

248 Minquan Road, West

■ 價錢 **PRICE**

午膳 Lunch
點菜 À la carte $ 300-600
晚膳 Dinner
點菜 À la carte $ 300-600

■ 營業時間 **OPENING HOURS**

午膳 Lunch 11:00-13:30
晚膳 Dinner 17:00-20:30

TEL. 04 2372 5066
西區五權七街57號
57 Wuquan 7th Street, West
www.theme.net.tw

■ 價錢 PRICE

午膳 Lunch
套餐 Set Menu $ 380
點菜 À la carte $ 600-1,000
晚膳 Dinner
套餐 Set Menu $ 380
點菜 À la carte $ 600-1,000

■ 營業時間 OPENING HOURS

午膳 Lunch 11:30-13:45
晚膳 Dinner 17:30-20:45

■ 休息日期 ANNUAL AND WEEKLY CLOSING

週二休息
Closed Tuesday

京華煙雲 N

MOMENT IN BEIJING

京菜・復古

Beijing Cuisine • Vintage

餐廳外觀恍如中國的深宅大院，室內採用雕花窗框與仿古家具，風格典雅。菜單豐富，由單人套餐以至十人宴席，選擇應有盡有。而且不添加味精，吃得健康。招牌菜香酥櫻桃鴨腿採花蓮櫻桃鴨烹製，是道經典的北方菜。東北酸白鍋湯頭鮮甜，相當暖胃。最後來一客甜點驢打滾與養生芝麻糕，為美饌畫上完美句點。

Named after Lin Yutang's novel and styled after grand mansions in northern China with its gable roof and grey tiles, this well-known restaurant has been attracting a loyal following since 2002. Signature crispy duck legs are steamed, deep-fried and served with pancakes, cucumber and sweet-savoury sauce. Pickled cabbage and streaky pork soup is flavoursome, with a hint of tartness. Finish off with sticky rice paste in osmanthus sauce or sesame cake.

新月梧桐 N

1924 SHANGHAI RESTAURANT

江浙菜・復古

Jiangzhe • Vintage

餐廳樓高四層，以上海風情為主題。室內的皮製沙發、古董杯櫃、懷舊吊燈，加上紅色窗簾，彷彿回到三十年代的老上海，充滿懷舊氣氛。週三和週六晚上更設有唱歌表演。食物同樣出色，提供鱔糊、獅子頭、醃篤鮮等傳統江浙菜色以及蘇杭涼菜。為了方便客人，部份菜色更可選擇半份或小份。

This four-storey restaurant has an old Shanghai theme, hence the name. Semi-circular tufted banquettes, pendant faux gas lamps, and ruby velvet curtains are all reminiscent of 1920s glamour. The menu is typical Jiangzhe fare: braised 'lion head' pork balls, stir-fried swamp eel, bamboo shoot and salted pork soup, along with some Suzhou and Hangzhou cold appetizers. Live singing performances on Wednesday and Saturday nights add to the fun.

TEL. 04 2378 3181
西區五權西三街123號
123 Wuquan West 3rd Street, West
www.theme.net.tw

■ 價錢 **PRICE**
午膳 Lunch
點菜 À la carte $ 500-800
晚膳 Dinner
點菜 À la carte $ 500-800

■ 營業時間 **OPENING HOURS**
午膳 Lunch 11:30-13:45
晚膳 Dinner 17:30-20:30

■ 休息日期 **ANNUAL AND WEEKLY CLOSING**
週一休息
Closed Monday

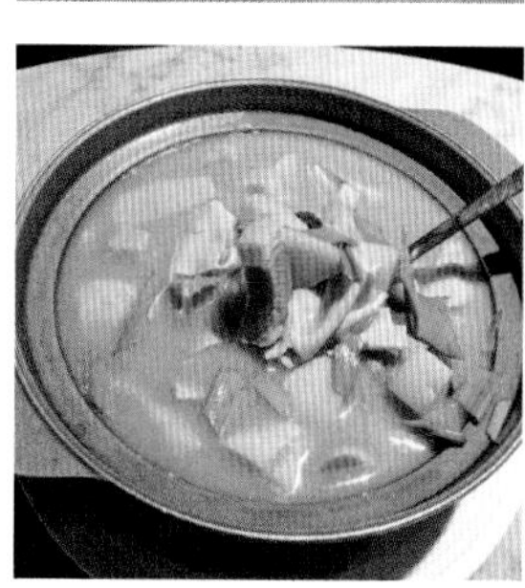

尚牛二館 Ⓝ

SHANG NIU ERH KUAN

火鍋・友善

Hotpot • Friendly

為了讓顧客嚐到最新鮮的溫體牛，老闆每天清晨到牧場挑選優質部位，並堅持現點現切。在多款選擇中，特別推薦油花均勻、肉質軟嫩的超級嫩牛肉盤。火鍋湯底同樣講究，以蔬菜與牛骨熬煮八小時，鮮甜滋味，令人讚嘆不已。別忘了嚐嚐貼於牆上的菜單，如三杯牛筋和熱炒牛肉料理。由於牛肉限量販售，不接受預訂。

The owner travels to a farm in Yunlin every morning for the best beef slaughtered on the spot and then hurries back without chilling the meat – this is called 'wenti' in Taiwan, meaning still at body temperature. Hand-sliced on ordering, the beef is blanched in an ox bone veggie broth for 3 seconds before being eaten – still tender, flavourful and juicy. Besides hot pot, three-cup braised beef tendons and beef stir-fries are also popular.

TEL. 04 2208 0822

北區民權路470號

470 Minquan Road, North

■ 價錢 **PRICE**

晚膳 Dinner

點菜 À la carte $ 500-1,000

■ 營業時間 **OPENING HOURS**

晚膳 Dinner 17:00-23:30

■ 休息日期 **ANNUAL AND WEEKLY CLOSING**

除夕至初五及週一休息

Closed CNY eve to fifth day of CNY and Monday

馨苑 N

SHIN YUAN

臺灣菜 · 舒適

Taiwanese · Cosy

膳馨旗下的品牌，提供份量小巧、減少油鹽的臺灣料理。熱門菜色包括以大甲芋頭與椰奶共同燉煮的芋奶鮮嫩雞骨球，以及適合配飯的菠蘿遇見櫻桃鴨。同時提供多款臺式小吃，如多汁可口、充滿鮮味的花枝楨上雞肉丸，適合搭配佐餐。餐廳著重品茶文化，建議點上一瓶冷泡茶，好好感受用餐環境的寧靜與悠閒。

This spinoff of Shan Shin opened in 2018 and specializes in healthy Taiwanese cooking in small portion sizes – something that will appeal to lone diners. Both chicken lollipops with taro in coconut milk, and Cherry Valley duck with pineapple go well with steamed rice; and do order the springy, juicy cuttlefish chicken balls as a starter. There is an array of quality teas to choose from; the cold-brewed ones are particularly worth trying.

TEL. 04 2302 9989

西區民生北路106號

106 Minsheng North Road, West

■ 價錢 **PRICE**

套餐 Set Menu $ 330-420
點菜 À la carte $ 250-500

■ 營業時間 **OPENING HOURS**

11:30-20:00

■ 休息日期 **ANNUAL AND WEEKLY CLOSING**

除夕至初一休息
Closed CNY eve to first day of CNY

TEL. 04 2371 2525

西區五權六街61巷1號

1, Lane 61, Wuquan 6th Street, West

www.abura.com.tw/abura_yakiniku

■ 價錢 **PRICE**

晚膳 Dinner

點菜 À la carte $ 1,300-2,500

■ 營業時間 **OPENING HOURS**

晚膳 Dinner 17:30-00:00

脂・板前炭火燒肉 N

ABURA YAKINIKU

燒烤・異國風情

Barbecue • Exotic Décor

餐廳裡裡外外都是濃厚的日式風格，庭園鋪上綠油油的草皮，環境優美。採用日本和在地高級食材，包括不同部位的A5級和牛，並由服務員代為炭烤。廚師更以自製海帶取代海鹽調味，層次感更突出。另外提供臺灣生食等級的桂丁雞，以及日本的生食級紋甲烏賊，不要錯過。享用美食之餘，可以請店員搭配清酒。

Various cuts of Japanese A5 Wagyu take centre stage here, but sashimi-grade cuttlefish and local free-range Gui Ding chicken are also unmissable. Instead of salt, meat and seafood are seasoned with ground kombu for extra depth – and servers will happily grill the food for you and pair it with sake from the extensive list. Japanese traditions are honoured in the architecture, the garden and the practice of taking shoes off at the door.

潔 N

ISAGI

日本菜 · 友善

Japanese · Friendly

餐廳建築風雅，一、二樓皆採用落地玻璃，可以看到戶外小庭園。設計師甚至精心計算樹木的位置，令每一桌客人都能欣賞到這片綠蔭。日籍主廚曾於福岡工作，板前料理則由臺灣師傅負責。二人使用日本和在地食材，製作出兩款不同價位的套餐，並根據季節變更菜單。享受美食之餘，也可以選購店內展示的藝術品。

Formerly an art studio for kids, this glass-clad dining room with exposed concrete, solid wood trimmings and furniture still retains traces of its history. Views from every seat were carefully considered to ensure every diner sees at least one tree in the Japanese garden. The Japanese head chef, who once worked in Fukuoka, provides two omakase menus featuring fish and produce from Japan and Taiwan. Certain art pieces on display are for sale.

TEL. 04 2376 1536

西區存中街29號

29 Cunzhong Street, West

■ 價錢 **PRICE**

午膳 Lunch
套餐 Set Menu $ 980
晚膳 Dinner
套餐 Set Menu $ 2,500-3,500

■ 營業時間 **OPENING HOURS**

午膳 Lunch 11:45-13:30
晚膳 Dinner 18:00-20:30

法森小館 Ⓝ
L'AFFECTION

法國菜·法式小餐館

French • Bistro

TEL. 04 2372 1339

西區大忠南街42號

42 Dazhong South Street, West

■ 價錢 **PRICE**

午膳 Lunch
套餐 Set Menu $ 980-2,280
晚膳 Dinner
套餐 Set Menu $ 1,380-2,880

■ 營業時間 **OPENING HOURS**

午膳 Lunch 11:30-14:00
晚膳 Dinner 18:00-20:30

■ 休息日期 **ANNUAL AND WEEKLY CLOSING**

小年夜至初三休息
Closed 2 days before CNY to third day of CNY

餐廳樓高兩層，座位不多但環境舒適。主廚擁有逾三十年經驗，嚴格挑選法國及臺灣食材、有機海鹽等，並堅持不用味精，推廣健康飲食風格。只供應套餐，菜色包括法式洋蔥湯、油封鴨、烤布蕾等經典法國料理，另外可以添加主廚精選菜色。不妨預約面向開放式廚房的位置，欣賞廚師烹調的身姿。

This two-storey bistro has been serving healthy MSG-free French cuisine since 2003. It uses ingredients mostly imported from France, seasoned with artisan snowflake sea salt harvested near Antarctica. The chef has over 30 years of experience and his set menus cover the quintessence of French cooking with several choices for each course – onion soup, duck confit, crème brûlée. Reservations are recommended; ask for counter seats to view the action.

滿堂 N
LE PLEIN

創新菜·簡約

Innovative • Minimalist

餐廳內外的設計都簡潔舒適，建議選擇吧檯座位，近距離欣賞廚師的料理過程。主廚善用在地食材，製作出一道道精緻菜色。不要錯過黑糖糕佐焦糖鳳梨冰，黑糖糕口感彈牙，搭配鳳梨甜香，帶有強烈的臺灣風味。酒單上除了葡萄酒，也提供本地啤酒。平日僅於晚上營業，週末設有午間套餐但須預訂。

Owner-chef Lin cleverly turns local produce and familiar Taiwanese flavours into exquisite dishes with modern twists. Brown sugar cake with caramel pineapple ice cream juxtaposes contrasting textures and temperatures with tropical zest. Ask for the counter seats on the ground floor to watch the chefs at work, or book a room on the upper floor for more privacy. Four-course lunch set menus are only offered at weekends and need to be pre-ordered.

TEL. 0910 833 755

西區五權一街57號

57 Wuquan 1st Street, West

■ 價錢 **PRICE**

午膳 Lunch
套餐 Set Menu $ 1,200-1,350
晚膳 Dinner
點菜 À la carte $ 1,200-2,100

■ 營業時間 **OPENING HOURS**

午膳 Lunch 12:00-12:30
晚膳 Dinner 18:00-20:00

■ 休息日期 **ANNUAL AND WEEKLY CLOSING**

除夕至初三、週三至週五午膳、週一及週二休息
Closed CNY eve to third day of CNY, Wednesday to Friday lunch, Monday and Tuesday

TEL. 04 2329 1239
西區忠誠街26號
26 Zhongcheng Street, West

■ 價錢 **PRICE**
午膳 Lunch
套餐 Set Menu $ 380-1,780
晚膳 Dinner
套餐 Set Menu $ 780-1,780

■ 營業時間 **OPENING HOURS**
午膳 Lunch 11:30-14:00
晚膳 Dinner 17:30-20:00

■ 休息日期 **ANNUAL AND WEEKLY CLOSING**
週一休息
Closed Monday

老吳的西洋料理 Ⓝ
RESTAURANT GO

時尚法國菜・時尚

French Contemporary・Contemporary Décor

老闆兼主廚老吳曾於東京學習法國料理，堅持使用在地蔬果和漁獲，用心製作帶日本元素的法國菜。室內空間簡潔舒適，讓客人在輕鬆的氛圍下享受每道美饌。只供應五道菜套餐，菜單每月更新，務求保持新鮮感。其中的主菜選擇多樣，推薦每天在市場採買的嫩煎鮮魚和櫻桃鴨胸。平日午間造訪，價格更加經濟。

The owner-chef Go-san studied French cooking in Tokyo for four years, before working in hotel kitchens in Taipei and Taichung. In 2009 he opened his low-profile restaurant, which is tucked away in an alley, and has been serving French cuisine with a Japanese twist ever since. The five-course set menu with a number of main dishes to choose from changes each month. Cherry Valley duck breast and pan-seared catch of the day especially stand out.

膳馨 N

SHAN SHIN

臺灣菜·舒適

Taiwanese · Cosy

標榜健康理念的創意臺菜餐廳，不僅減少油鹽烹調，更採用產銷履歷與可溯源的食材，如梨山高麗菜、臺南虱目魚肚等。提供多樣自創菜色，包括配刈包享用的花雕遇見櫻桃鴨。而阿嬤ㄟ芋粿是特定日子限定商品，長條狀芋粿搭配甜鹹醬汁，深受顧客喜愛。在雅致的環境中一邊享受美食，一邊觀賞庭園造景，實在是相得益彰。

Health-conscious diners come here to enjoy the creative Taiwanese cooking made with reduced oil and sodium. Most ingredients have traceable sources and many of the dishes have cheeky names. 'When Huadiao meets Cherry Valley duck' is sliced bird cooked in the famous liquor; 'Grandma's taro cake' with a sweet and salty dip is available on Thursdays only. Full-height glazing separates the well-lit, elegant dining room from the garden.

TEL. 04 2372 1650

西區存中街21號

21 Cunzhong Street, West

www.shan-shin.com

■ 價錢 **PRICE**

午膳 Lunch
點菜 À la carte $ 300-600
晚膳 Dinner
點菜 À la carte $ 300-600

■ 營業時間 **OPENING HOURS**

午膳 Lunch 11:30-14:00
晚膳 Dinner 17:00-21:00

■ 休息日期 **ANNUAL AND WEEKLY CLOSING**

初一休息
Closed first day of CNY

澀 N

SUR

時尚歐陸菜 · 簡約

European Contemporary · Minimalist

TEL. 04 2203 7830

北區育德路201號

201 Yude Road, North

■ 價錢 **PRICE**

午膳 Lunch
套餐 Set Menu $ 900-1,800
晚膳 Dinner
套餐 Set Menu $ 1,800

■ 營業時間 **OPENING HOURS**

午膳 Lunch 12:00-13:00
晚膳 Dinner 18:00-19:30

■ 休息日期 **ANNUAL AND WEEKLY CLOSING**

除夕至初二、週三午膳、週一及週二休息

Closed CNY eve to second day of CNY, Wednesday lunch, Monday and Tuesday

餐廳於2019年遷到現址。年輕老闆兼任主廚，將市場所見的日常食材，用現代烹調方式，重新闡述臺灣料理的細膩滋味。美食以約十三道菜的套餐呈現，依據四季更迭與社會日常來變換菜單。用餐環境同樣經過精心設計，以水泥牆面、細膩花磚及不同的光源，營造沉靜優雅的氛圍，適合約會。唯座位有限，建議預約。

The dining room has a raw edge to it: exposed plaster walls, perforated brickworks, and faux rusty ironworks. The name 'Sur' reflects the young owner-chef's vision to elevate 'above and beyond' everyday Taiwanese ingredients to haute cuisine through the use of modern techniques. It moved to this new location in 2019 and serves a 13-course prix-fixe menu, which changes every season. Reservations are highly recommended as there are only 14 seats.

鮨鈴木幸介 Ⓝ

SUSHI SUZUKI KOSUKE

壽司 · 經典

Sushi • Classic Décor

日籍主廚具有多年經驗，而且說得一口流利國語，樂於介紹食材的來源和特色。壽司飯以長野及臺灣米製作，並混入米醋及熟成六年的紅醋，調校出獨特風味。海產由日本新鮮進口，生魚片切得厚大，口感豐滿。玉子燒可以選擇鹹味的大阪風或是帶甜的東京風，滿足不同喜好。主廚或於一月及四月休假，建議先作查詢。

The sushi chef has over 20 years of experience and communicates with his guests in Chinese. Sushi rice from Nagano is dressed in red vinegar aged for six years for a mellow flavour. Local and Japanese fish is sliced thickly and pressed on a small knob of rice, making it feel quite lavish. Tamagoyaki is made in both Osaka and Tokyo styles – the former salty, the latter sweet. The shop closes in January and April when the chef goes on vacation.

TEL. 04 2320 2155

西區華美街392號

392 Huamei Street, West

8seas.jp

■ 價錢 **PRICE**

午膳 Lunch
套餐 Set Menu $ 2,200-2,700
晚膳 Dinner
套餐 Set Menu $ 3,000-5,000

■ 營業時間 **OPENING HOURS**

午膳 Lunch 12:00-13:00
晚膳 Dinner 18:00-19:30

■ 休息日期 **ANNUAL AND WEEKLY CLOSING**

週一休息
Closed Monday

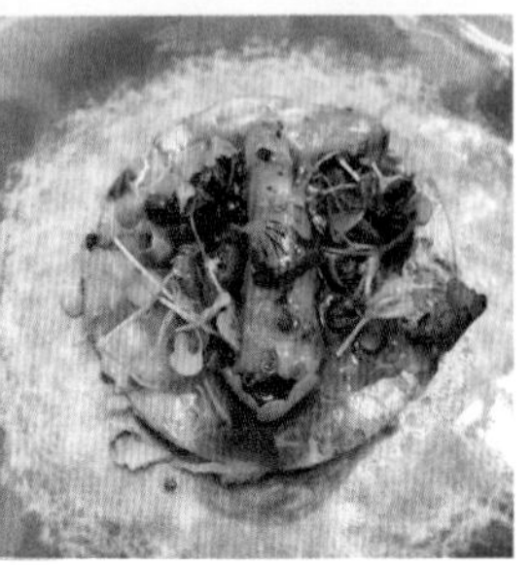

中山招待所 N

YET SEN MANSION

時尚法國菜・典雅

French Contemporary • Elegant

原為美軍留下的老洋房，其後以宋慶齡的上海舊居為藍本，改建成充滿舊上海風情的私人招待所，並於2004年對外開放。外觀低調，大門深鎖，但按下電鈴後，會有親切的門前接待服務。穿過園林，便會抵達雅致的餐室，氣氛非常適合約會。食物以法式料理為主軸，融合臺灣在地元素，並每兩個月更換一次菜色。

Converted from a mansion left by the U. S. army, the house replicates Madame Sun Yat-sen's home in the Shanghai French Concession circa 1920. From the doorbell and tree-lined path to the French doors and warm lighting, it feels more like a home than a restaurant. The menu showcases French cooking melded with local ingredients and changes every two months. The romantic ambiance is matched by detailed service, making it a perfect spot for a date.

TEL. 04 2377 0808

西區五權西六街27號

27 Wuquan West 6th Street, West

www.yet-sen.com.tw

■ 價錢 **PRICE**

午膳 Lunch
套餐 Set Menu $ 1,680
晚膳 Dinner
套餐 Set Menu $ 2,180-2,580

■ 營業時間 **OPENING HOURS**

午膳 Lunch 11:30-13:00
晚膳 Dinner 18:00-19:30

■ 休息日期 **ANNUAL AND WEEKLY CLOSING**

除夕至初一休息
Closed CNY eve to first day of CNY

英才大麵焿 Ⓝ

YING TSAI TA MIEN KENG

麵食 · 簡樸

Noodles · Simple

大麵焿是臺中特有的滋味，然而隨著時代發展，販賣這種古早味麵食的店家已所剩無幾，英才大麵焿是其中一家超過五十年歷史的老店。它不僅保留了原有味道，還添加了紅蔥酥和韭菜，以及獨家秘方的辣椒醬，有助提香和平衡麵條的鹼味。另外也提供燒肉、油豆腐等特色小吃，選擇豐富。

Ta Mien Keng is a noodle soup unique to Taichung. It's one of a group of shops that have been around for half a century, selling the sort of dishes that are hard to come by nowadays. The chunky noodles in a thick broth are garnished with fried shallots and chives for extra aroma. The house-made chilli sauce not only spices up the dish, but also neutralizes the lye in the noodles. Side dishes such as roast pork and fried tofu are also nicely made.

TEL. 04 2201 1718

北區英才路215號

215 Yingcai Road, North

■ 價錢 **PRICE**

點菜 À la carte $ 30-100

■ 營業時間 **OPENING HOURS**

09:00-18:00

Robert CHG/iStock

南屯區

NANTUN

餐廳
RESTAURANTS

JL STUDIO Ⓝ

創新菜 · 親密

Innovative · Intimate

以新加坡主廚的英文名字Jimmy Lim命名，他曾在多家歐陸餐廳工作，但其父親過去在獅城擁有一個供應當地美食的小販攤位，成為他烹飪靈感的來源。品嚐菜單結合了臺灣在地食材、法式料理技巧和東南亞飲食文化，菜色按季更換，以創新面貌呈現海南雞飯、沙爹和辣椒蟹等傳統佳餚。

'JL' is Chef Jimmy Lim who was brought up in Singapore and honed his skills by spending over 10 years working in a number of world-famous restaurants. He excels in re-inventing Singaporean and South East Asian cuisine underpinned with solid French techniques. The tasting menu deconstructs familiar items such as Hainan chicken rice, satay and chilli crab, and re-imagines them in ingenious forms and textures to playfully subvert diners' expectations.

TEL. 04 2380 3570

南屯區益豐路四段689號2樓

2F, 689, Section 4, Yifeng Road, Nantun

jlstudiotw.com

■ 價錢 **PRICE**

午膳 Lunch
套餐 Set Menu $ 2,800
晚膳 Dinner
套餐 Set Menu $ 3,800

■ 營業時間 **OPENING HOURS**

午膳 Lunch 12:00-13:30
晚膳 Dinner 18:00-20:00

■ 休息日期 **ANNUAL AND WEEKLY CLOSING**

除夕至初二、週二至週五午膳及週一休息
Closed CNY eve to second day of CNY, Tuesday to Friday lunch and Monday

TEL. 04 2252 3366

南屯區公益路二段271之1號

271-1, Section 2, Gongyi Road, Nantun

dragon.swmall.com.tw

■ 價錢 **PRICE**

午膳 Lunch
點菜 À la carte $ 300-800
晚膳 Dinner
點菜 À la carte $ 300-800

■ 營業時間 **OPENING HOURS**

午膳 Lunch 11:30-13:30
晚膳 Dinner 17:30-20:30

東方龍 N

ORIENT DRAGON

臺灣菜 · 傳統

Taiwanese • Traditional

餐廳裝潢充滿中式元素，採用紅色燈籠和桌椅，洋溢喜慶氛圍。餐具亦帶有巧思，荷葉邊狀的藍瓷器皿搭配每人一壺的功夫茶具組，令用餐經驗增添意境，適合婚宴或商務聚會。食物方面，以臺灣家常菜為主，佐以少許四川創新菜餚。推薦菜色包括三杯松阪豬、清蒸午仔魚，以及香氣誘人的櫻花蝦炒飯。

The façade may look a bit nondescript, but the interior boasts a red-and-black colour scheme perfect for weddings and power lunches. The blue and white porcelain dinnerware with its ruffled rim complements the teapot sets nicely. The menu focusses on Taiwanese home-style cooking, with a few novelty Sichuanese dishes. Recommendations include three-cup Matsusaka pork, steamed fourfinger threadfin, and the aromatic sakura ebi fried rice.

三喜食堂

SAN HSI SHIH TANG

臺灣菜 · 親切

Taiwanese · Neighbourhood

餐廳隱身於民宅，外觀雖然低調，卻得到街坊和老顧客支持。老闆每天挑選食材、用心烹調，並親自招待客人。不妨留意牆上貼著的當天推薦菜色，海鮮、肉類、各式鍋物、三杯料理等一應俱全。部分手工菜如蒜蒸野泥鰍供應有限，最好於訂位時查詢。用餐環境輕鬆，最適合親朋好友相聚共歡。

Frequented largely by regulars, this small shop is hidden away in a residential area. The owner-chef has years of experience in the business and takes care of every aspect of the operation, from sourcing ingredients to cooking and waiting tables. Look for the poster on the wall for the daily specials, which usually include meat, seafood and three-cup dishes. Some specialities such as steamed wild-caught catfish with garlic need pre-ordering.

TEL. 04 2473 1778

南屯區永春東路140號

140 Yongchun East Road, Nantun

■ 價錢 **PRICE**

午膳 Lunch
點菜 À la carte $ 500-1,000
晚膳 Dinner
點菜 À la carte $ 500-1,000

■ 營業時間 **OPENING HOURS**

午膳 Lunch 11:30-13:30
晚膳 Dinner 17:00-21:00

■ 休息日期 **ANNUAL AND WEEKLY CLOSING**

週二休息
Closed Tuesday

滬舍餘味 Ⓝ
SHANGHAI FOOD

點心 · 友善

Dim Sum • Friendly

老闆來自上海，因為思鄉心切，經過三年的努力，終於研發出記憶中最地道口味的生煎包。此外，小店還提供小籠包、蒸餃和燒賣等上海點心。生煎包有鮮肉和翡翠兩種口味，前者選用肥瘦比例適中的豬絞肉，湯汁豐富；後者的餡料則以青江菜、豆乾和香菇為主，口感脆嫩，味道清新。

A Chinese herbalist by training, the owner hails from Shanghai and was spoilt by his grandpa who made him all sorts of treats. After he moved to Taiwan, he spent three years trying to recreate the most authentic pan-fried buns from memory and opened this shop in 2009. The pork buns boast soupy filling with the perfect ratio of fatty and lean meat. The veggie buns are light and flavourful, filled with bok choy, dried tofu and mushrooms.

TEL. 04 2258 6111

南屯區公益路二段537號

537, Section 2, Gongyi Road, Nantun

shanghaifood.business.site

■ 價錢 **PRICE**

套餐 Set Menu $ 169-289
點菜 À la carte $ 150-300

■ 營業時間 **OPENING HOURS**

11:00-20:00

■ 休息日期 **ANNUAL AND WEEKLY CLOSING**

除夕至初一休息
Closed CNY eve to first day of CNY

台客燒肉粥 N

TAI KE MEAT CONGEE

粥品 · 復古

Congee • Vintage

店長的爺爺於1971年創立忠孝路肉粥，其手藝也一直傳承至今，成為這家新店的重要支柱。如日式屋台的格局配合鏤空木門框、木桌椅，帶懷舊氣氛且風格獨特。採用每天熬煮的大骨、雞骨湯入饌，味道清香。招牌菜秘方燒肉用上逾十種醃料，現點現炸，香酥味美。最後當然要嚐嚐用料新鮮、款式多樣的砂鍋粥。

Tai Ke may have only been here since 2018, but it can be traced back to the owner's grandpa who started a congee stall in Zhongxiao night market almost 50 years ago – the interior is a nod to its heritage. The congee base is braised for hours with pork and chicken bones before ingredients of your choice, such as clams, beef or fish, are added. Deep-fried pork belly is marinated with 10-plus seasonings and is even better with the mildly tart dip.

TEL. 04 2389 0880

南屯區五權西路二段722之1號

722-1, Section 2, Wuquan West Road, Nantun

■ 價錢 PRICE

午膳 Lunch
點菜 À la carte $ 200-500
晚膳 Dinner
點菜 À la carte $ 200-500

■ 營業時間 OPENING HOURS

午膳 Lunch 11:00-14:00
晚膳 Dinner 17:00-01:00

■ 休息日期 ANNUAL AND WEEKLY CLOSING

除夕至初三、週二至週五午膳及週一休息
Closed CNY eve to third day of CNY, Tuesday to Friday lunch and Monday

TEL. 04 2473 2373

南屯區文心南五路一段326之3號

326-3, Section 1, Wenxin South 5th Road, Nantun

■ 價錢 **PRICE**

午膳 Lunch
點菜 À la carte $ 600-1,000
晚膳 Dinner
點菜 À la carte $ 600-1,000

■ 營業時間 **OPENING HOURS**

午膳 Lunch 11:00-14:00
晚膳 Dinner 17:00-21:30

千味海鮮 Ⓝ
CHIEN WEI SEAFOOD

臺灣菜 · 溫馨

Taiwanese • Family

以臺菜為主的餐館，魚缸中不乏時令海鮮，可以配合多種煮法，不妨請店員一一介紹。推薦麻油煮沙母，以乾煸過的薑片和綜合菇菌烹調，味道鮮甜，充滿香氣。多人聚餐的話，點上一份陶板藥膳活鮮蝦與一鍋蒜苗白鯧米粉，一同分享。環境簡潔但服務殷勤，設多個包廂，適合家庭聚會及各類宴請。

A restaurant equally great for family dinners and banquets, Chien Wei Seafood boasts exceptional service and has private rooms in varying sizes. Perfumed by rice wine and ginger, female mud crabs in sesame oil are braised with assorted mushrooms; while live shrimps doubanyaki with Chinese herbs are prepared tableside. If your party is large enough, then order rice vermicelli soup with pomfret and garlic sprouts to share.

金悅軒 Ⓝ
JIN YUE XUAN

粵菜·時尚

Cantonese • Contemporary Décor

位於歐陸風格的獨立建築之中，外觀甚有氣派。門口的大型魚缸滿載各式各樣海鮮：沙公、龍蝦、野生七星斑等應有盡有。廚房各料理區皆由香港人帶領，盡顯傳統粵菜風味。除了一系列港式點心，蜜汁叉燒和避風塘炒龍蝦也是熱門菜色，也可一嚐當季的時令菜，例如秋天的大閘蟹和冬天的羊腩煲。

It's not immediately apparent that this European-style mansion is a Cantonese restaurant. But the chefs from Hong Kong ensure dishes are executed in an authentic Cantonese manner, with char siu pork, and fried lobster in typhoon shelter style being the most popular items. Feel free to pick your seafood, such as crabs, lobsters and groupers, from the live fish tanks. Dim sum is served at lunch and in the morning at weekends.

TEL. 04 2255 7942

南屯區公益路二段213號

213, Section 2, Gongyi Road, Nantun

■ 價錢 **PRICE**

午膳 Lunch
點菜 À la carte $ 600-1,200
晚膳 Dinner
點菜 À la carte $ 800-1,600

■ 營業時間 **OPENING HOURS**

午膳 Lunch 11:30-14:15
晚膳 Dinner 17:30-21:00

湄南河 Ⓝ
MAENAM

泰國菜・田園

Thai • Rural

♿ 🏞 🍽 P

TEL. 04 2386 2678

南屯區龍富十五路36號

36 Longfu 15th Road, Nantun

■ 價錢 **PRICE**

午膳 Lunch
點菜 À la carte $ 500-800
晚膳 Dinner
點菜 À la carte $ 500-800

■ 營業時間 **OPENING HOURS**

午膳 Lunch 11:00-14:00
晚膳 Dinner 17:30-21:00

老闆來自清邁，店內從吊燈、飾品以至餐具都從家鄉運到，充滿泰國風情。他和主廚更會定期到訪清邁，增進料理技巧，加深對當地香料的了解。綠咖哩偏向泰北口味，較為清香，值得一試。另可搭配月亮蝦餅，還有以自製蝦醬烹調的炒菜。戶外用餐區點綴了色彩繽紛的燈籠，洋溢派對氣氛，適合朋友聚會。

The owner hails from Chiang Mai in Thailand and shipped all lampshades, tableware and decorations here from home. He also goes back every few months with the head chef to shop for spices. Colourful lanterns impart a festive mood on the terrace, perfect for parties. The menu focuses more on Northern Thai cooking and the famous green curry made with green chillies and basil is more aromatic than spicy. Fried shrimp cake is also popular with diners.

橡木炙烤牛排館 Ⓝ

MEATGQ

牛排屋・時尚

Steakhouse • Contemporary Décor

由教父牛排的主廚擔任顧問，這家牛排館主要提供不同部位的美國牛排，另有少許澳洲、日本和牛及乾式熟成選項。店員服務親切，會詳盡解釋牛排的種類、來源、口感，亦會建議熟度。選擇餐點後，可以欣賞廚師在開放式廚房裡，以龍眼木烤製肉類，並在香氣氤氳中期待美食上桌。

With Chef Teng of Danny's Steakhouse in Taipei as consultant, the steaks here go beyond mere good quality (abbreviated to GQ). On top of the quality cuts from the U. S. , including USDA prime 'first' steak dry-aged in-house, Australian and Japanese Wagyu options abound. Steaks are grilled to preferred doneness over longan wood: rare for aged steaks, medium for Wagyu, and medium-rare for others, unless specified otherwise.

TEL. 04 2383 0258

南屯區益豐路四段699號

699, Section 4, Yifeng Road, Nantun

www.meatgq.com.tw

■ 價錢 **PRICE**

午膳 Lunch
套餐 Set Menu $ 1,050-3,280
點菜 À la carte $ 1,900-7,200
晚膳 Dinner
套餐 Set Menu $ 1,880-3,680
點菜 À la carte $ 1,900-7,200

■ 營業時間 **OPENING HOURS**

午膳 Lunch 12:00-14:00
晚膳 Dinner 18:00-21:00

■ 休息日期 **ANNUAL AND WEEKLY CLOSING**

農曆除夕休息
Closed CNY eve

TEL. 04 2252 3899

南屯區公益路二段612號

612, Section 2, Gongyi Road, Nantun

■ 價錢 **PRICE**

午膳 Lunch
點菜 À la carte $ 300-1,000
晚膳 Dinner
點菜 À la carte $ 300-1,000

■ 營業時間 **OPENING HOURS**

午膳 Lunch 11:30-14:00
晚膳 Dinner 17:30-20:00

麵廊 Ⓝ

MEE LANG

麵食・舒適

Noodles • Cosy

結合麵食與藝廊，用餐環境優雅，牆上掛滿中式收藏品，令吃麵成為藝術體驗。食品帶點四川風味，但降低了辣度並提供不辣款式。備有湯麵與乾麵兩種選擇，特別推薦湯汁鮮甜的雪藏牛肋麵，搭配店家特製的扁麵條，十分可口。加上東坡炆牛肉、夫妻肺片等小菜，以及黑糖鍋盔餅作為餐後甜點，額外滿足。

Aptly named 'noodle gallery' in Chinese, this dining room boasts high ceilings and Chinese art. Most noodle soups and dressed noodles are based on Sichuanese recipes, but toned down for the Taiwanese palate. Here, beef short rib clear soup noodles come with bone-in beef ribs in a milky ox bone broth. For side dishes, consider Dongpo braised beef cheek, or sliced beef shank tendon, and round off the meal with brown sugar guokui bun.

銘心 Ⓝ
MIN SHIN

壽司 · 舒適

Sushi • Cosy

由日本料理經驗豐富的阿銘師經營，只設十五席，提供無菜單料理。食材均選自日本，並以豐洲市場魚貨為主。首次到訪的顧客，建議先品嚐套餐，由師傅依據當天食材決定餐點內容。若希望品嚐更高檔的食材，也可以請店家調整，服務貼心周到。其中水針魚鳴門捲口感細嫩，十分出色，最後的水果甜點也值得期待。

This low-profile 15-seater may have opened in 2016 but Chef Ming has over 20 years of experience behind a counter. He uses only fish from Japan, mostly from Toyosu Market, to create an omakase menu consisting of sashimi, sushi, cooked courses and dessert. His sayori naruto roll has an exceptionally fine texture and a clean, crisp taste. Besides the standard menu, diners can also pay extra and upgrade to more luxurious items. No children under 12.

TEL. 04 3609 0099

南屯區大觀路66號

66 Daguan Road, Nantun

■ 價錢 **PRICE**

午膳 Lunch
點菜 À la carte $ 3,600
晚膳 Dinner
點菜 À la carte $ 3,600

■ 營業時間 **OPENING HOURS**

午膳 Lunch 11:30-13:00
晚膳 Dinner 17:30-20:00

■ 休息日期 **ANNUAL AND WEEKLY CLOSING**

除夕至初五及週日休息
Closed CNY eve to fifth day of CNY and Sunday

森鐵板燒 Ⓝ
MORI TEPPANYAKI

鐵板燒 · 典雅

Teppanyaki • Elegant

提供全臺首創的無油料理和牛肉分解料理。前者是烹調過程不用油，依靠廚師對火候的控制，做到色香味俱全。後者則根據肉質和油脂比例，配合適當的料理手法，讓食客享受牛肉的多重口感。肉類選項豐富，包括全臺獨家限量供應的日本皇室和牛、澳洲M9和牛、美國金牌極黑和牛，另有龍蝦、伊比利豬等，滿足不同需求。

Mori revamps teppanyaki by not adding oil to the hot plate, thus requiring exceptional skills on the chefs' part. Beef is served deconstructed – divided into parts according to the marbling and texture, each cooked to different doneness with different seasoning. Apart from Japanese Imperial Wagyu – not available elsewhere in Taiwan – choose between U. S. SRF or Aussie M9 Wagyu, Iberico pork, lobster, lamb and non-GMO black tea chicken.

TEL. 04 2382 7779

南屯區益豐路四段502號

502, Section 4, Yifeng Road, Nantun

www.mori-teppanyaki.com

■ 價錢 **PRICE**

午膳 Lunch
套餐 Set Menu $ 980-16,880
點菜 À la carte $ 900-16,300
晚膳 Dinner
套餐 Set Menu $ 1,480-16,880
點菜 À la carte $ 900-16,300

■ 營業時間 **OPENING HOURS**

午膳 Lunch 11:30-13:30
晚膳 Dinner 17:30-21:30

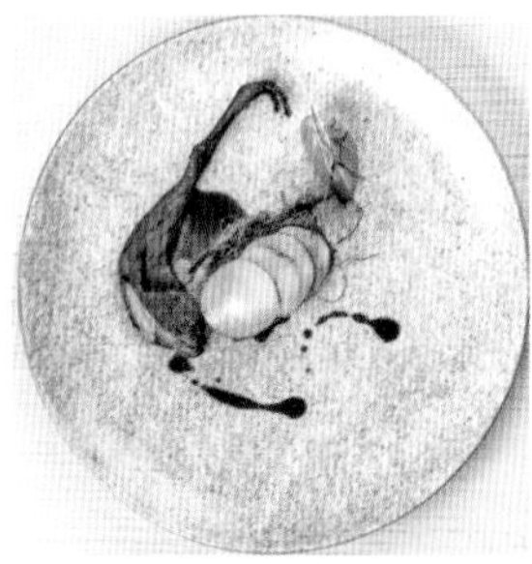

品法 Ⓝ
REVIVRE

時尚法國菜 · 舒適

French Contemporary · Cosy

主廚曾經旅居法國，回臺後開設這家餐廳，希望提供舒適的場所，並運用在地食材，呈現於異地學到的料理手法。為了保持新鮮感，每兩個月更換菜單，特別時節更會推出限定套餐。經典南瓜湯口感絲滑，搭配南瓜薄凍和酥炸菇球，層次豐富。另外，提供逾十種單杯餐酒，進一步還原法國的飲食習慣和餐酒文化。

A relative newcomer to the Taichung food scene, Revivre champions exquisite French cuisine made with local, everyday ingredients. The philosophy is best seen in the silky pumpkin soup complemented by a deep-fried mushroom ball, grilled pumpkin, pumpkin jelly and thyme foam. The by-the-glass wine list features over 10 choices, mostly from the Loire Valley where the chef has travelled extensively. The young team is enthusiastic and friendly.

TEL. 04 2380 0148

南屯區永春東路1320號

1320 Yongchun East Road, Nantun

■ 價錢 **PRICE**

午膳 Lunch
套餐 Set Menu $ 1,280-2,380
晚膳 Dinner
套餐 Set Menu $ 1,280-2,380

■ 營業時間 **OPENING HOURS**

午膳 Lunch 12:00-13:15
晚膳 Dinner 18:00-19:45

■ 休息日期 **ANNUAL AND WEEKLY CLOSING**

除夕至初二、週一及週二休息
Closed CNY eve to second day of CNY, Monday and Tuesday

NANTUN 南屯區

TEL. 04 2252 3519

南屯區惠中路三段30之6號

30-6, Section 3, Huizhong Road, Nantun

■ 價錢 **PRICE**

晚膳 Dinner

點菜 À la carte $ 600-1,200

■ 營業時間 **OPENING HOURS**

晚膳 Dinner 16:00-23:45

■ 休息日期 **ANNUAL AND WEEKLY CLOSING**

農曆新年5天及週一休息

Closed 5 days CNY and Monday

一流海鮮美食館 (惠中路) Ⓝ

YI LIU SEAFOOD (HUIZHONG ROAD)

海鮮 · 友善

Seafood • Friendly

於2012年開業，目前在臺中已經有三間店，而惠中路的這間是本店。儘管面積不大，但設有室內和戶外用餐區，是不少家庭用餐、朋友聚會或下班小酌的好地方。靠近廚房的海鮮冰櫃，供應一系列臺灣海產，可以請親切的店員推薦菜色和建議烹調方法。由於食材新鮮、現點現做，加上價格實惠，因此經常座無虛席。

Yi Liu has three branches in Taichung but this is their original shop, opened in 2012. Seats are limited and divided between indoor and outdoor areas. The décor may be nothing to write home about, but the fresh local seafood cooked to order at appealing prices is the draw that attracts many, making it perfect for casual get-togethers, family dinners or just for after-work. Ask the friendly servers for the recommended ways to cook the seafood.

与玥樓 Ⓝ

YU YUE LOU

粵菜・典雅

Cantonese • Elegant

餐室寬敞遼闊，裝潢以金色和黑色為主，氣派典雅。二樓設有包廂，同時用作大型宴會場地，適合商務宴客或親友聚餐。主廚來自香港，將傳統廣東料理以創新方式展現，午市亦供應多款粵式點心。招牌菜包括用龍眼木烤製的窯烤片皮鴨，建議預訂。此外可以嚐嚐來自澎湖的海鮮，如七星斑和野生七彩龍蝦。

The high-ceilinged dining room imparts an imposing sense of space while the gold-and-black colours and dew-like strings of pendant lamps exude drama. The kitchen team from Hong Kong reinvents Cantonese cooking with creativity. Grouper fillet poached in lobster bisque over crisp rice uses live seafood from Penghu. Cherry Valley duck is roasted in a longan wood oven and needs pre-ordering. Dim sum is served at lunch and private rooms are available.

TEL. 04 2382 9128

南屯區公益路二段783號

783, Section 2, Gongyi Road, Nantun

www.yuyuelou.com.tw

■ 價錢 **PRICE**

午膳 Lunch
點菜 À la carte $ 500-1,500
晚膳 Dinner
點菜 À la carte $ 1,000-2,000

■ 營業時間 **OPENING HOURS**

午膳 Lunch 11:30-14:00
晚膳 Dinner 17:30-21:00

元 N
YUAN

創新菜·友善

Innovative • Friendly

TEL. 0966 667 067

南屯區大墩十七街35號

35 Dadun 17th Street, Nantun

yuanrestaurant.weebly.com

■ 價錢 **PRICE**

午膳 Lunch
套餐 Set Menu $ 320
晚膳 Dinner
套餐 Set Menu $ 2,400-3,680

■ 營業時間 **OPENING HOURS**

午膳 Lunch 12:00-14:00
晚膳 Dinner 18:00-19:30

■ 休息日期 **ANNUAL AND WEEKLY CLOSING**

週二至週四午膳、週一及週日休息
Closed Tuesday to Thursday lunch, Monday and Sunday

採用開放式廚房，讓客人對烹調過程一覽無遺。更有個性的是，只在晚上提供主廚限定套餐，必須訂位並於預約時選擇主菜。約九成食材來自臺灣，糅合歐洲料理技巧，創作出具在地風味的美饌。招牌花園沙拉用了數十種自家栽種的香草花卉作食材，開胃且漂亮。週五、六中午更推出限量的麵食套餐。

The young chef Yuan previously worked in a top restaurant in Japan and opened his own dining concept in 2013. The six-course omakase menu features mostly local ingredients and is underpinned by impressive European techniques. His signature floral garden salad includes up to 40 house-grown herbs and edible flowers, a pleasure as much to the eyes as to the palate. The small service team provide warm and friendly service. Reservations mandatory.

mtcurado/iStock

TPG/Photononstop

西屯區
北屯區
XITUN & BEITUN

西屯區 XITUN
北屯區 BEITUN

餐廳
RESTAURANTS

鹽之華 Ⓝ

FLEUR DE SEL

時尚法國菜・時尚

French Contemporary ·
Contemporary Décor

女主廚擁有三十年西餐與旅外學習經驗，為客人帶來精緻細膩的用餐體驗。七至九道菜的套餐，客人挑選主菜後，便可靜待饗宴啟程，菜色每天更換，令人充滿驚喜。其中果木炭烤乳鴿以自製炭爐，將28至32天的臺灣乳鴿烤製而成，富有風味。建議請侍酒師搭配佳釀。菜單可因應人數作特別安排，亦可預訂Pithivier等傳統法式糕點。

The chef worked in France and Italy for 30 years before opening her restaurant in 2003, which she moved to this contemporary building in 2017. She uses mostly local ingredients to create 7- to 9-course prix fixe menus that change daily and never fail to surprise with their precise execution, whimsical ideas and vivid colours. Chargrilled squab, and fish from Penghu stand out. The wine list is short but offers choices from different regions.

TEL. 04 2372 6526
西屯區市政路581之1號
581-1 Shizheng Road, Xitun
www.fleur-de-sel.com.tw

■ 價錢 **PRICE**
午膳 Lunch
套餐 Set Menu $ 1,580-5,880
晚膳 Dinner
套餐 Set Menu $ 2,880-5,880

■ 營業時間 **OPENING HOURS**
午膳 Lunch 12:00-13:30
晚膳 Dinner 18:00-21:00

■ 休息日期 **ANNUAL AND WEEKLY CLOSING**
週三至週五午膳、週一及週二休息
Closed Wednesday to Friday lunch, Monday and Tuesday

FORCHETTA Ⓝ

時尚歐陸菜 · 舒適

European Contemporary · Cosy

TEL. 04 2255 8111

西屯區惠中七街36號2樓

2F, 36 Huizhong 7th Street, Xitun

www.forchetta.com.tw

■ 價錢 **PRICE**

午膳 Lunch
套餐 Set Menu $ 1,700-3,500
晚膳 Dinner
套餐 Set Menu $ 2,480-4,000

■ 營業時間 **OPENING HOURS**

午膳 Lunch 12:00-13:00
晚膳 Dinner 18:00-20:00

曾於臺北經營十多年，其後遷到臺中，但仍然保留過往的風格。主廚醉心花藝，餐廳採用落地玻璃，透視戶外的盆栽與大樹，一片綠蔭令人心曠神怡。同時尊重時令及在地食材，會根據當天採買到的材料，變化出多款前菜。主菜則提供六種選擇，其中，鴨心與鴨胗佐鴨間稻燉飯糅合了臺灣與西方料理特色，值得一試。

Forchetta is hugely popular with those in the know, but newcomers be warned – the sign is easy to miss. A vet by training, the head chef has a real passion for food and gardening as demonstrated by his east-meets-west creations and his miniature garden. From the set menu, choose your main from the six options available. Duck heart and gizzard risotto uses local rice grown using the aigamo method, cleverly referencing the origins of the ingredients.

東山棧 N

DONG SHAN ZHAN

臺灣菜・舒適

Taiwanese • Cosy

1999年開業，2019年遷至現址，不但座位增加，用餐環境也更加舒適。招牌菜甕缸雞精選2.5至3公斤的黑羽土雞，以龍眼木烤製而成，皮香肉嫩，風味非凡。客人可以選擇原隻上桌，自行扒雞進食，或由店家代為切開，佐雞汁同吃。紹興醉蝦和以雞汁燜煮的菜色亦深受歡迎。

The household name for clay pot-roasted chicken since 1999 moved to this three-storey building in 2019. The larger premises mean more seats, while the exposed brick walls on the lower floors still exude traditional charm. The must-try chicken is grilled over longan wood for an hour for crispy golden skin and juicy silky flesh. You can have it served whole or sliced. Drunken shrimps and veggies braised in chicken juices are also recommended.

TEL. 04 2239 9009

北屯區東山路一段380號

380, Section 1, Dongshan Road, Beitun

0911457718.com.tw

■ 價錢 **PRICE**

點菜 À la carte $ 500-800

■ 營業時間 **OPENING HOURS**

11:00-22:00

溫叨 N

WEN TAO

臺灣菜・傳統

Taiwanese • Traditional

店名「溫叨」是臺語「我家」的諧音，提供古早味臺灣料理。餐廳位於紅磚堆疊的傳統三合院之中，包廂裡有舊日的床組與裝飾，客人也可以在院子享用餐點，氣氛就像辦桌般熱絡。推薦菜色包括三杯料理，以及辛辣鹹香的古法剝椒鱸魚。另一特色菜為柴燒桶仔雞，在院中用柴火燒烤四十分鐘而成，須提前預訂。

Meaning 'my home', this single-storey courtyard house circa 1950s set amid tall residential buildings will instantly teleport guests back to grandma's home in the countryside. The menu is mostly Taiwanese from a bygone era, with occasional Hunan and Xinjiang offerings. Old-time steamed river perch with fermented chillies has complex savoury umami with a mild kick. Barrel chicken is chargrilled in the courtyard and needs pre-ordering.

TEL. 04 2231 1699

北屯區太原路三段191號

191, Section 3, Taiyuan Road, Beitun

■ 價錢 **PRICE**

午膳 Lunch
點菜 À la carte $ 200-600
晚膳 Dinner
點菜 À la carte $ 200-600

■ 營業時間 **OPENING HOURS**

午膳 Lunch 11:00-13:30
晚膳 Dinner 17:00-20:30

■ 休息日期 **ANNUAL AND WEEKLY CLOSING**

初一休息
Closed first day of CNY

游日本料理

ABURA

日本菜・新潮

Japanese • Chic

有別於日本餐廳常見的木材裝潢，此店採純白風格，配合大理石作板前設計，讓環境更加明亮精緻，適合朋友聚餐。料理長希望客人能以實惠的價格品嚐日式料理，故推出兩款入門套餐，但均以熟食為主。若老饕們想一飽口福，品嚐由日本進口的生魚片與壽司的話，不妨提出更高預算，讓店家進行搭配。

The owner-chefs opened Abura in 2019 after working in Taipei for around 10 years. As opposed to a traditional Zen-inspired décor in pale wood, they've opted for an all-white interior – even the cypress counter is replaced with white marble with painterly veining. The two omakase menus feature mainly cooked courses and are priced competitively; those with a larger budget should tell the chef if they'd like a custom-made menu with more raw fish.

TEL. 04 2329 1858

西屯區精誠路50巷12號

12, Lane 50, Jingcheng Road, Xitun

■ 價錢 PRICE

午膳 Lunch
套餐 Set Menu $ 680-1,100
晚膳 Dinner
套餐 Set Menu $ 1,100-3,000

■ 營業時間 OPENING HOURS

午膳 Lunch 11:30-13:00
晚膳 Dinner 18:00-19:30

■ 休息日期 ANNUAL AND WEEKLY CLOSING

初三至初五及週日休息
Closed third to fifth day of CNY and Sunday

TEL. 04 2255 8511

西屯區臺灣大道三段301號4樓
(新光三越)

4F, Shin Kong Mitsukoshi, 301, Section 3, Taiwan Boulevard, Xitun

www.hilai-foods.com

■ 價錢 **PRICE**

午膳 Lunch
套餐 Set Menu $ 1,500
點菜 À la carte $ 400-4,000
晚膳 Dinner
套餐 Set Menu $ 1,500
點菜 À la carte $ 800-4,000

■ 營業時間 **OPENING HOURS**

午膳 Lunch 11:30-13:50
晚膳 Dinner 17:30-20:50

名人坊 Ⓝ

CELEBRITY CUISINE

粵菜 · 時尚

Cantonese · Contemporary Décor

由香港名人坊主廚鄭錦富監督，這裡的粵菜展現出細膩的烹調技藝。菜單約八成與香港本店同步，另外供應一系列為臺灣設計的點心。廚師採用在地食材，包括新鮮海產和來自契作農場的有機蔬果。招牌菜為燕窩釀鳳翼和脆皮炸子雞，後者皮薄肉嫩，但限量供應，建議預訂。用餐環境低調奢華，適合聚餐宴客。

An outpost of its Hong Kong namesake, this restaurant serves almost the same menu but with a few exclusive dim sum. Chef Cheng makes sure his techniques and thoughtful layering of flavours are replicated in this kitchen. The must-try crispy-skin chicken is available in limited quantities and so needs to be pre-ordered; the wafer-thin skin crackles and the meat is juicy and silky. Try also the fried chicken wings stuffed with bird's nest.

富彩軒

FUCHAI

粵菜・經典

Cantonese • Classic Décor

由香港主廚帶領，善用在地新鮮食材，烹調出一系列傳統粵菜，點心、燒味、海鮮、小炒等一應俱全。煲仔菜種類豐富，部分更提供份量選擇，方便不同人數的客人。推薦使用臺灣溫體牛的柱侯牛腩筋煲、賣相精緻的招牌富彩蝦餃，以及需預訂、皮脆肉嫩的金牌吊燒脆皮雞。環境舒適，設有包廂和沙發座，隱密度高。

Chef Yip from Hong Kong uses local ingredients to make traditional Cantonese fare – dim sum, barbecue meat, live seafood, home-style stir-fries... you name it. His signature braised beef brisket and tendons in a claypot made with local beef slaughtered on the day is tender and flavoursome. Crispy skin free-range chicken lives up to its name with crackling skin and juicy flesh. Ask about booth seating and private rooms when booking.

TEL. 04 2259 4188

西屯區市政北二路60號3樓

3F, 60 Shizheng North 2nd Road, Xitun

■ 價錢 **PRICE**

午膳 Lunch
點菜 À la carte $ 1,000-1,800
晚膳 Dinner
點菜 À la carte $ 1,000-1,800

■ 營業時間 **OPENING HOURS**

午膳 Lunch 11:00-14:00
晚膳 Dinner 17:30-20:30

■ 休息日期 **ANNUAL AND WEEKLY CLOSING**

週一休息
Closed Monday

響海鮮 Ⓝ

HIBIKI SEAFOOD

臺灣菜·時尚

Taiwanese • Contemporary Décor

在入口擺放了幾個大型海鮮缸，存放各式各樣的新鮮漁獲，不少由日本或其他國家進口，亦有來自澎湖及宜蘭龜山島海域。客人可自行挑選食材及烹調方式。料理風格以臺菜為主，同時融合了日式技法，令口味更豐富，擺盤也甚為精緻。室內設計時尚，並設獨立包廂，適合宴客聚會，但需要提前預訂。

Judging by the exposed bricks, wood panels and concrete façade, it's hard to tell what cuisine is served here, but the live fish tanks by the entrance give it away. There isn't a menu as guests get to make their own picks from the tank and specify how they want them cooked. Seafood from Yilan, Penghu, Japan and other places are prepared in traditionally Taiwanese ways, but updated with subtle Japanese touches and artful plating.

TEL. 04 2252 2127

西屯區市政北二路356號

356 Shizheng North 2nd Road, Xitun

■ 價錢 **PRICE**

午膳 Lunch
點菜 À la carte $ 800-1,200
晚膳 Dinner
點菜 À la carte $ 1,500-2,200

■ 營業時間 **OPENING HOURS**

午膳 Lunch 11:30-13:45
晚膳 Dinner 17:30-20:45

KR PRIME STEAK Ⓝ

牛排屋・舒適

Steakhouse • Cosy

坐落豪宅地段，樓高兩層，一樓為肉品專營店，二樓則為牛排館，主要提供美國濕式熟成牛排。用餐環境舒適，適合約會或包場舉辦小型聚會。建議點選美國CAB頂級安格斯上蓋老饕，味道可口且充滿肉汁。各款甜點均手工製作，值得一試。特別推薦手工風味奶酪，柔嫩質地搭配時令水果，十分清爽。

This is the place to come for precisely-cooked wet-aged U. S. steaks, especially the Certified Angus Beef USDA Prime ribeye cap, a cut prized for its tenderness, flavour and succulence. Their desserts are also unmissable – silky panna cotta paired with tangy fruits is a great way to end the meal. It's nestled amidst luxurious apartment towers – head to the dining room on the upper floor as the lower floor houses a small shop selling steaks.

TEL. 04 2252 5566

西屯區市政北二路52號

52 Shizheng North 2nd Road, Xitun

■ 價錢 **PRICE**

午膳 Lunch
套餐 Set Menu $ 780
點菜 À la carte $ 1,100-3,000
晚膳 Dinner
套餐 Set Menu $ 1,690-3,500
點菜 À la carte $ 1,100-3,000

■ 營業時間 **OPENING HOURS**

午膳 Lunch 11:30-13:30
晚膳 Dinner 17:30-20:30

■ 休息日期 **ANNUAL AND WEEKLY CLOSING**

除夕至初五休息
Closed CNY eve to fifth day of CNY

TEL. 04 3705 6099

西屯區市政路77號24樓
(日月千禧酒店)

24F, Millennium Hotel, 77 Shizheng Road, Xitun

www.millenniumtaichung.com.tw

■ 價錢 **PRICE**

午膳 Lunch
套餐 Set Menu $ 1,680-3,480
點菜 À la carte $ 1,650-3,500
晚膳 Dinner
套餐 Set Menu $ 1,980-3,780
點菜 À la carte $ 1,650-3,500

■ 營業時間 **OPENING HOURS**

午膳 Lunch 11:30-14:00
晚膳 Dinner 18:00-21:00

極炙牛排館

THE PRIME - GRILL & LOUNGE

牛排屋・舒適

Steakhouse • Cosy

採用優質食材，來源經嚴密管控，如雙重認證的美國牛、澳洲的日本純血種和牛，以及日本和牛，特別推薦以穀物飼養三百天以上的澳洲純血種全和黑毛和牛。鴨肝及牛尾湯只在晚上供應，後者須熬煮十三小時以上，值得一試。預訂窗邊位置可欣賞美麗夜景，逢星期五、六更有現場鋼琴表演，適合約會。

The chef, who has over 20 years of experience, changes the starter menu every three months and injects it with Mediterranean flavours. The signature oxtail soup takes two days to prepare and is only available at dinner. For mains, choose between U.S. prime, Australian and Japanese Wagyu steaks, all grilled to perfection and served with red wine salt, sea salt and black mineral salt on the side. Lovely vistas of the Taichung skyline are also a plus.

THE WANG Ⓝ

牛排屋 · 時尚

Steakhouse • Contemporary Décor

王品集團旗下的新餐廳，提供乾式熟成的頂級牛排，以及多款特色套餐。建議點選二十八日熟成的丁骨牛排，滋味令人一試難忘。兩層樓的空間寬敞舒適，設計糅合了大理石、黑色與金屬元素，展現出優雅而現代的氛圍。客人更可以透過開放式廚房，觀賞燒烤牛排的過程。不過只有一間包廂，必須提早預約。

The contemporary two-storey dining room features a muted palette punctuated by white marble table-tops, champagne gold and black trim. This new brand of a restaurant group specialises in dry-aged prime steaks from the U.S., all grilled in the show kitchen. Among the myriad of prime cuts on offer, the T-bone dry-aged for 28 days is a highlight. Both set and à-la-carte menus are offered, with optional wine pairings available.

TEL. 04 2255 5525

西屯區朝富路137號

137 Chaofu Road, Xitun

■ 價錢 **PRICE**

午膳 Lunch
套餐 Set Menu $ 980-2,380
點菜 À la carte $ 1,600-4,300
晚膳 Dinner
套餐 Set Menu $ 1,780-2,380
點菜 À la carte $ 1,600-4,300

■ 營業時間 **OPENING HOURS**

午膳 Lunch 11:30-14:00
晚膳 Dinner 17:30-21:00

■ 休息日期 **ANNUAL AND WEEKLY CLOSING**

農曆除夕休息
Closed CNY eve

頂園全鴨坊 N
TING YUAN ROAST DUCK

京菜及江浙菜 · 舒適

Beijing Cuisine & Jiangzhe • Cosy

氣氛輕鬆，適合各類社交聚餐。半透明廚房內掛滿三個月大的宜蘭櫻桃鴨，正於恆溫櫃風乾，等待進入果木烤爐。完成烤製後，再在鴨身淋上君度橙酒，營造火焰效果，鴨皮因此帶一層薄薄的糖份，味道可口，肉質軟嫩。配合厚薄適中的自製餅皮，口感一流。烤鴨必須預訂，鴨骨部分可選不同烹調方法，一鴨二食。

The rows of ducks in the show kitchen are quite a spectacle at this popular spot with locals looking for a casual meal. Ting Yuan's signature dish is the three month-old Cherry Valley duck from Yilan County, grilled in a jujube wood-fired oven and basted and flambéed in Cointreau – this gives it mildly sweet, crisp and caramelized skin and juicy, tender flesh. The carcass can be made into an extra dish if you want. Roast ducks are by pre-orders only.

TEL. 04 2259 8957

西屯區市政北二路305號

305 Shizheng North 2nd Road, Xitun

www.ting-yuan.com.tw

■ 價錢 **PRICE**

午膳 Lunch
點菜 À la carte $ 350-800
晚膳 Dinner
點菜 À la carte $ 350-800

■ 營業時間 **OPENING HOURS**

午膳 Lunch 11:00-13:30
晚膳 Dinner 17:00-21:00

MmeEmil/iStock

酒店
HOTELS

萬楓 N
FAIRFIELD BY MARRIOTT

商務・實用

Business • Functional

飯店開業不久，設計時尚而舒適。大堂空間寬敞，提供微波爐及販賣機，供客人選購飲品與點心。客房設大型落地玻璃窗，採光度十足。雖然沒有迷你吧，但附屬餐廳優先招待房客。為方便商務人士，備有一間會議室供小型會議使用，並提供技術支援。健身室全天候開放，讓房客在一天的喧囂後，身心得到舒展。

Hundreds of hanging lamps in sparkling globes add to the charm of the airy, high-ceilinged lobby. Rooms are bright, cosy and simply furnished. With only one all-day dining option and no mini bar, vending machines in the pantry offer fixes for any sudden food cravings. Business travellers will appreciate the meeting room while sports buffs should check out the 24-hour gym.

TEL. 04 3606 5188
www.fairfieldtaichung.com

西屯區環中路二段1155號
1155, Section 2, Huanzhong Road, Xitun

126 客房/**Rooms** $ 2,400-4,900
5 套房/**Suites** $ 5,100-7,000

saml-photography/iStock

太平區
和平區
新社區

TAIPING, HEPING & XINSHE

太平區 TAIPING
和平區 HEPING
新社區 XINSHE

餐廳 RESTAURANTS

彭城堂 Ⓝ

PENG CHENG TANG

臺灣菜 · 復古

Taiwanese • Vintage

門外擺放著臺灣早期客運站牌、郵箱等舊物，餐廳內部的擺設更猶如穿越時空，重返祖父母的年代。除了老闆的珍貴收藏，這裡提供的家常料理同樣充滿親切感。古早味封肉刈包全套滋味鹹香，川七炒牛肉口感細嫩，十分推薦。另有豬油拌飯供自行取用，餐後更提供剉冰，令人有回家吃飯的溫馨感覺。

A Taiwan time capsule circa 1960s, this restaurant amid low-rise residential blocks transports you back in time with its vintage knickknacks. Its home-style food is as warm and familiar as the décor. The gua bao set is hugely popular – steamed buns stuffed with braised pork belly, bamboo shoot, pickles and ground peanuts; while the stir-fried beef with Madeira vine is gingery and flavourful. Help yourself to the steamed rice with lard.

TEL. 04 2351 1122

太平區宜昌路377號

377 Yichang Road, Taiping

■ 價錢 PRICE

午膳 Lunch
點菜 À la carte $ 300-600
晚膳 Dinner
點菜 À la carte $ 300-600

■ 營業時間 OPENING HOURS

午膳 Lunch 11:30-13:30
晚膳 Dinner 17:30-20:30

■ 休息日期 ANNUAL AND WEEKLY CLOSING

除夕至初一休息
Closed CNY eve to first day of CNY

TEL. 04 2582 3568

新社區中興嶺街一段107號

107, Section 1, Zhongxingling Street, Xinshe

■ 價錢 **PRICE**

午膳 Lunch
套餐 Set Menu $ 1,280
晚膳 Dinner
套餐 Set Menu $ 1,280

■ 營業時間 **OPENING HOURS**

午膳 Lunch 11:30-13:50
晚膳 Dinner 17:30-19:50

■ 休息日期 **ANNUAL AND WEEKLY CLOSING**

年廿八至初一休息
Closed three days before CNY to first day of CNY

又見一炊煙 (N)

FOODING SMOKE

創新菜 · 樸實

Innovative · Rustic

坐落於著名花鄉新社，四周綠意盎然，配合日式庭園造景，讓人感到放鬆。其無菜單料理受不同時令啟發，並融入日式與西式烹調元素。在室內用餐區的塌塌米空間完成主餐後，建議移到室外廊道上，一邊享用甜點，一邊感受微風吹拂。也不妨安排一趟綠意之旅，欣賞落羽松或花海。唯不招待十二歲以下孩童。

Its idyllic mountain location makes this restaurant great for a day trip from the city when combined with a visit to the nearby Sea of Flowers Festival or golden pine forest in autumn. The wood-clad dining room with tatami seating exudes serenity, while the omakase menu inspired by the season boasts both Japanese and Western influences. Enjoy dessert in the outdoors to make the most of the pond and garden. No children under 12.

F. Troiani/easyFotostock/age fotostock

太平區 TAIPING
和平區 HEPING
新社區 XINSHE

酒店
HOTELS

虹夕諾雅 谷關 N

HOSHINOYA GUGUAN

渡假勝地・典雅

Resort • Elegant

日本頂級度假村星野集團的首間海外分店。由日籍設計師規劃出五種房型，每間客房都附有半露天溫泉風呂，另外具備戶外的大露天風呂。樓中樓的特殊設計，令屋內擁有無限遼闊的山林視野，讓人遠離煩囂，享受愜意的秘境時光。提供中式、日式、西式三種早餐選擇，建議於訂房時預約，完整地體驗日本溫泉文化。

The first property outside of Japan from this upmarket hotel group seamlessly melds lush nature, Zen-inspired décor and understated luxury. Well-appointed rooms come with private hot spring baths overlooking verdant mountains. Or you can soak in the outdoor public bath to get close to nature. A Chinese, Japanese or Western-style breakfast in the garden makes a great start to the day.

TEL. 04 2595 0008
hoshinoya.com/guguan

和平區東關路一段溫泉巷16號
16, Wenquan Lane, Section 1, Dongguan Road, Heping

48 客房/**Rooms** $ 18,000-40,320
1 套房/**Suite** $ 48,720-65,520

索引

INDEX

餐廳列表
INDEX OF RESTAURANTS

Ⓝ 新增推介 New entry in the guide

N 評級有所晉升的餐廳 Restaurant promoted to a Bib Gourmand or Star

TAIPEI 臺北

TAICHUNG 臺中 N

星級餐廳
STARRED RESTAURANTS

Ⓝ 新增推介 New entry in the guide

N 評級有所晉升的餐廳 Restaurant promoted to a Bib Gourmand or Star

TAIPEI 臺北

TAICHUNG 臺中 Ⓝ

必比登美食推介
BIB GOURMAND LIST

Ⓝ 新增推介 New entry in the guide

N 評級有所晉升的餐廳 Restaurant promoted to a Bib Gourmand or Star

TAIPEI 臺北

TAICHUNG 臺中 N

餐廳 — 以菜色分類
RESTAURANTS BY CUISINE TYPE

TAIPEI 臺北

臺灣菜/TAIWANESE

時尚亞洲菜/ASIAN CONTEMPORARY

燒烤/BARBECUE

京菜/BEIJING CUISINE

粵菜/CANTONESE

點心/DIM SUM

時尚歐陸菜/EUROPEAN CONTEMPORARY

法國菜/FRENCH

時尚法國菜/FRENCH CONTEMPORARY

客家菜/HAKKANESE

杭州菜/HANG ZHOU

火鍋/HOTPOT

淮揚菜及川菜/HUAI YANG & SICHUAN

印度菜/INDIAN

創新菜/INNOVATIVE

國際菜/INTERNATIONAL

義大利菜/ITALIAN

時尚義大利菜/ITALIAN CONTEMPORARY

日本菜/JAPANESE

時尚日本菜/JAPANESE CONTEMPORARY

江浙菜/JIANGZHE

麵食/NOODLES

海鮮/SEAFOOD

涮涮鍋/SHABU-SHABU

滬菜/SHANGHAINESE

川菜/SICHUAN

小吃/SMALL EATS

東南亞菜/SOUTH EAST ASIAN

時尚西班牙菜/SPANISH CONTEMPORARY

牛排屋/STEAKHOUSE

壽司/SUSHI

天婦羅/TEMPURA

鐵板燒/TEPPANYAKI

泰國菜/THAI

素食/VEGETARIAN

滇菜/YUNNANESE

浙江菜/ZHEJIANG

TAICHUNG 臺中 N

臺灣菜/TAIWANESE

燒烤/BARBECUE

日本菜/JAPANESE

江浙菜/JIANGZHE

麵食/NOODLES

海鮮/SEAFOOD

牛排屋/STEAKHOUSE

壽司/SUSHI

鐵板燒/TEPPANYAKI

泰國菜/THAI

夜市街頭小吃列表
INDEX OF STREET FOOD IN NIGHT MARKETS

TAIPEI 臺北

酒店列表
INDEX OF HOTELS

TAIPEI 臺北

TAICHUNG 臺中 (N)

CREDITS:

Page 13: xavierarnau/iStock (top) - Meiyi524/iStock (left) - FotoGraphik/iStock (right) - **Page 14:** Lisovskaya/iStock (top) – plej92/iStock (bottom) - **Page 15:** fazon1/istock (top) - FotoGraphik/iStock (bottom) - **Page 24-25** (from top to bottom and left to right): AzmanL/iStock - K. Cabanis/age footstock - UpPiJ/iStock - stockinasia/iStock - Artit_Wongpradu/iStock - Sean3810/iStock - insjoy/iStock - Chen-Zheng-Feng/iStock

All other photos by Michelin or by the kind permission of the establishments mentioned in this guide.

MICHELIN TRAVEL PARTNER

Société par actions simplifiées au capital de 15 044 940 €
27 Cours de L'Île Seguin - 92100 Boulogne Billancourt (France)
R.C.S. Nanterre 433 677 721

Legal Deposit : 07-2020
Printed in China: 07-2020

Although the information in this guide was believed by the authors and publisher to be accurate and current at the time of publication, they cannot accept responsibility for any inconvenience, loss or injury sustained by any person relying on information or advice contained in this guide. Things change over time and travellers should take steps to verify and confirm information, especially time sensitive information related to prices, hours of operation and availability.